D1739785

The One THOMAS MORE

The One
THOMAS MORE

TRAVIS CURTRIGHT

THE CATHOLIC UNIVERSITY OF AMERICA PRESS

Washington, D.C.

Copyright © 2012
The Catholic University of America Press
All rights reserved

The paper used in this publication meets the minimum
requirements of American National Standards for Information
Science—Permanence of Paper for Printed Library Materials,
ANSI Z39.48-1984.
∞

Library of Congress Cataloging-in-Publication Data
Curtright, Travis.
The one Thomas More / Travis Curtright.
p. cm.
Includes bibliographical references and index.
ISBN 978-0-8132-1995-0 (cloth : alk. paper)
1. More, Thomas, Sir, Saint, 1478–1535—Criticism and
interpretation. 2. More, Thomas, Sir, Saint, 1478–1535—Political
and social views. 3. More, Thomas, Sir, Saint, 1478–1535—
Religion. 4. More, Thomas, Sir, Saint, 1478–1535—Knowledge—
Law. 5. Christian literature, English—History and criticism.
6. Christian literature, Latin (Medieval and modern)—England—
History and criticism. 7. Authors, English—Early modern, 1500–
1700—Biography 8. Statesmen—Great Britain—Biography.
9. Humanists—England—Biography. 10. Christian martyrs—
England—Biography. I. Title.
PR2322.C87 2012
828'.209—dc23   2012003189

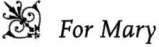 *For Mary*

More: It is in heaven that I am thus and thus,
And that which we profanely term our fortunes
Is the provision of the power above,
Fitted and shaped just to that strength of nature
Which we are born withal.

> Lines attributed to Shakespeare in
> *Sir Thomas More*, ca. 1592, 3.1.1–4

CONTENTS

Acknowledgments   ix

Abbreviations   xi

Introduction: *Non Sum Oedipus, sed Morus*   1

1   Profitable Learning and *Pietas*: *The Life of Pico
    della Mirandola*, ca. 1504–10   15

2   Humanist Realism and *The History of Richard III*,
    ca. 1514–18   42

3   *Si Moro Credimus*: The "Dialogue of Counsel"
    in *Utopia*, ca. 1516   72

4   Humanism, Heresy, and the One Thomas More,
    ca. 1523–33   105

5   Inquisition, Equity, and the "Battle of the
    Books," ca. 1532–33   140

    Conclusion: Iconic Thomas Mores on Trial   174

    Bibliography   201

    Index   217

ACKNOWLEDGMENTS

I am pleased to express my gratitude to those who have made this book possible. *The One Thomas More* benefited from the careful reading and judicious advice of many friends and colleagues, especially Gerard Wegemer, Marc Guerra, Scott Crider, and David Williams. For commenting on chapter 5 with tremendous insight, I thank Henry Ansgar Kelly, Stephen W. Smith, and David Oakley. I am indebted to the Catholic University of America Press for providing generous and expert readers in Anne O'Donnell, Donald Prudlo, and an unnamed reviewer who was particularly helpful. Thanks are due in a special way to the Center for Thomas More Studies for its fruitful conferences and research projects. For invaluable inspiration, I thank many of the Center's advisors and fellows not already listed above: Clarence H. Miller, Elizabeth McCutcheon, Marie-Claire Phelippeau, Seymour House, John Boyle, Louis Karlin, Joseph Koterski, and Jeff Lehman. For financial assistance in completing this work, I am grateful to the Earhart Foundation. I would like also to thank the editors of *Moreana* and *The Ben Jonson Journal* for permission to reprint sections of the chapters on *Utopia* and *The History of Richard III* that previously appeared in these journals. I was fortunate to find a unique combination of discernment and patience at the Catholic University of America Press in Trevor Lipscombe, Theresa Walker, and David McGonagle, as well as in freelance copy editor Carol A. Kennedy. No scholar could ask for better collaborators. Finally, I thank family and friends who provided indispensable support throughout the long process of research and writing that gave rise to this book. My young children, in their own way, were remarkably sympathetic and full of encouragement. My wife, Mary, not only was an excellent reviewer but also provided my bibliography. Without her intelligence and devotion, this book would not have been completed.

ABBREVIATIONS

CCTM   *The Cambridge Companion to Thomas More*

Corr.   *The Correspondence of Sir Thomas More*

CW   *Yale Edition of the Complete Works of St. Thomas More,*
15 vols.

DS   *Doctor and Student*

EA   *Essential Articles for the Study of Thomas More*

LL   *The Last Letters of Thomas More*

SL   *St. Thomas More: Selected Letters*

TMSB   *A Thomas More Source Book*

The One THOMAS MORE

INTRODUCTION

Non Sum Oedipus, Sed Morus

*More believed, as Socrates believed, that "the god had given him a station."
And he strengthened himself, as Socrates had strengthened himself, with
the conviction that no harm can come to a good man after death, and that
the gods do not neglect him or his affairs. In Utopia and on the scaffold we
have those two great articles of More's creed.*

R. W. Chambers, *Thomas More*, 1935

*The Thomas More of the "Tower Works," and of those last letters to Marga-
ret Roper is, on the face of it, a very different person from the persecutor of
protestants, and the hammer of poor Christopher St German—even from
the More who translated Latin with Erasmus and dreamed up the island
of Nowhere.*

G. R. Elton, "Thomas More," 1980

*There is an historical Thomas More, but no one really knows where he can
be found. He is an enigma. He defies objective analysis.*

John Guy, *Thomas More*, 2000

"*Non sum Oedipus, sed Morus,*" More tells his daughter, Margaret,
while in the Tower, "which name of mine what is signifieth in Greek,
I need not tell you." The word *mōrus* means "fool," a joke More made
often, and the lines in Latin allude to a stock character Terence depicts, a servant who cannot understand riddles like Oedipus can, for
he is too simple for that.[1] A simple or foolish man—this is just one

---

1. Quotations from Thomas More's writings are cited internally according to the list of abbreviations. Full bibliographical information is in the Works Cited pages. For the lines above,
see *LL*, 77, and for discussion of the allusion, 168. See, too, *Corr.*, 519.

of the ways More parries his daughter's attempt to convince him to take the Oath of Succession, leave prison, and come home. I mention it here because of its contrast with the quotes above it. More, indeed, might find the subsequent controversies over his life's meaning—from comparisons to Socrates to skepticism about objectivity—an ironic riddle. How did More evolve from Chambers's heroic unity of life to Guy's unknowable "man for all purposes"?[2]

To answer that question requires tracing the progression of particular strands of influential twentieth-century divisions of More's life and thought. In general terms, earlier critics such as Chambers chose to focus upon More's early "humanism" and later "devotional" writings, taking these as paradigmatic for More's intellectual biography. Such divisions of More's writings, in turn, lead to theorizing multiple Mores. Thus, C. S. Lewis announces that by comparing More's humanist and devotional writings, a "third More, out of whom both the scholar and saint have been made" could be discovered. For Lewis, that "third More" is a Londoner, a man whose humor and prose belong to the city.[3] As the critical fortunes of More as Londoner wane, the suggestion of multiple Mores becomes conventional, especially in how scholars evaluate and organize More's writings.[4]

The theory of multiple Mores allows for increased specialization in some one aspect of More's thought. For Paul Kristeller, there is the humanist, what he calls "Thomas More," the statesman, a "Sir Thomas More," and finally, "Saint Thomas More," a martyr. The proposed divisions permit Kristeller to focus upon More as humanist, defining the *studia humanitatis* as a "cycle of studies" that includes grammar, rhetoric, poetry, history, and moral philosophy but not

2. John Guy, *Thomas More* (London: Arnold, 2000), ix, and see ibid., xi: "I no longer believe that a truly historical biography of Thomas More can be written."

3. C. S. Lewis, "Thomas More," in *EA*, 399–400.

4. For a recent biographer who understands London and its importance to More, see Peter Ackroyd, *The Life of Thomas More* (London: Chatto & Windus, 1998). See, too, Caroline M. Barron, "The Making of a London Citizen" in *CCTM*, 3-21.

disciplines such as theology and jurisprudence.[5] Craig R. Thompson, among others, follows Kristeller's approach by naming humanism as first and foremost "an interest in classical texts." To speak of Kristeller's version of "Thomas More," then, means discussing Latinity, rhetoric, style, Greek and Roman influences, translation exercises, all that pertains to "Renaissance humanism in its fundamental signification," which remains "the study of antiquity and the effort to use its legacy to enrich modern life and learning."[6] As a text that illustrates moral and political thought in dialogue with Plato, *Utopia* becomes "the authentic measure of More's humanism," an assessment that privileges a single text against More's entire canon.[7] This version of "humanist More" as best revealed through *Utopia* continues, as we shall see in chapter 3, especially in the criticism of historian Quentin Skinner and in George Logan's analysis of More's political philosophy.

The emphasis upon humanist More, though, would provide an even sharper division. In reply to earlier critics such as Chambers, revisionist scholars focus on More as the author of polemical tracts against Protestantism to "reintroduce a healthy dose of skepticism and irreverence concerning More's conscience and actions."[8] Because of the attention given to *Utopia* and humanism, More as a controversialist seems inexplicable. How could the urbane, witty advocate of social justice from *Utopia* be the same person who burned heretics? In this manner, the "two Mores" theory emerges.[9] In effect, there are two men—one humanist and another cunning councilor and chancellor, a hardened hammer of heretics.

For revisionists, the influential Cambridge historian the late G. R. Elton still provides an important departure point. For Elton, it

---

5. Paul Oskar Kristeller, "Thomas More as a Renaissance Humanist," *Moreana* 65 (1980): 5.

6. Craig R. Thompson, "The Humanism of More Reappraised," *Thought* 52, no. 206 (September 1977): 234, 238.

7. Ibid., 243.

8. William J. Rogers, "Thomas More's Polemical Poetics," *English Literary Renaissance* 38, no. 3 (2008): 387n2.

9. Though the "two Mores" thesis seems present, too, in Thompson, "More Reappraised," 245.

is rash to suppose that More's whole life is preparation for his death. Instead, Elton believes More begins his public service as an ambitious young man and is later frustrated by his lack of influence on policy, but the politics of heresy give More's career some meaning as well as reveal his religious intolerance. More's humanism, then, is "rather adolescent" and "something he grew out of"; it bears "little relevance" to More's "behaviour" or "beliefs" once he enters Henry's service.[10] Elton writes of More: "I think he ceased to be a humanist in any very real sense about 1521, when he started getting worried about the Lutherans."[11] According to Elton, More's public career as a humanist reformer is mythological, and his political influence pales in comparison to that of Thomas Cromwell.

Elton's critique of the traditional portrait of More begins with his essay "Thomas More: Councillor," which claims, perhaps most controversially, that More is a liar, a man who suppresses the truth about his entry into the king's service from Erasmus for at least a year. Elton writes: "More, it would seem, respected Erasmus' known opposition to a scholar's involvement in affairs sufficiently to prevaricate about his own contrary view."[12] To make the case, Elton applies his expertise as an archival historian, examining public records to show that More was a paid councilor of the king as early as the fall of 1517, which was "long before More allowed Erasmus to know as much."[13] Yet, as John Guy shows, the matter of dating More's entry into service as an official councilor to the king remains vexed. Guy notes how More's work as a commercial diplomat or arbitrator appointed by the Crown may be a status distinct from being "formally" in service

10. G. R. Elton, "Thomas More and Thomas Cromwell" in *Studies in Tudor and Stuart Politics and Government*, vol. 4: *Papers and Reviews 1982-1990* (Cambridge: Cambridge University Press, 1992), 149, and see Richard Marius, *Thomas More: A Biography* (New York: Vintage Books, 1985), 189.

11. Elton, "More and Cromwell," 149.

12. Elton, "Thomas More, Councillor," in *St. Thomas More: Action and Contemplation*, ed. with intro. by Richard S. Sylvester (New Haven, Conn.: Yale University Press, 1972), 92. Of Elton's lecture, which Guy first heard as a student of Elton's, Guy claims there was "no doubt" about its iconoclastic "agenda." See Guy, *Thomas More*, 60n40.

13. Elton, "Thomas More, Councillor," 91.

of the king but that commercial envoys could be styled as a "King's councilor" by way of "diplomatic accreditation." So, too, Chancery clerks "were notoriously relaxed about diplomatic status, and no political significance can be attached to discrepancies in style." Finally, grants or annuities could be backdated or recorded in advance of service. Guy concludes that Elton's "seemingly invincible thesis is built on sand."[14] Yet Guy's own words are not published in time to have an impact upon the work of Richard Marius or Stephen Greenblatt. Both of them are influenced by Elton and use his work in developing their own ideas of a "self-fashioning" More.[15] In consequence, Elton's original if uncertain claim contributes to the ongoing accusation of dissimulation against More.

Perhaps inevitably, the question of "two Mores" creates demand for an answer about "the real Thomas More." For Elton, "the real Thomas More" needs to be revealed by historians, which is an especially difficult project because all "modern assessments" render More's life before imprisonment, trial, and death as events that must be shaped toward a hagiographic end.[16] The "real Thomas More" represents an admixture of early ambition and later intolerance, a description that, eventually, causes revisionists to eliminate the appellation of "humanist" altogether. Elton concludes of More: "He was not a liberal humanist; he was not John Paul II. He was a late medieval, very conventional believer in all the essentials."[17] The ostensible contradiction between humanism and religious contro-

---

14. On the refutation of Elton on this point of More's lying to Erasmus, see Guy, *Thomas More*, 50–51.

15. For Elton's influence on Marius, see ibid., 49, "Elton's claim almost certainly paved the way for subsequent assertions by Richard Marius that More 'distorted,' 'twisted' or suppressed evidence at least twice in his career." For Elton's influence on Greenblatt, see Stephen Greenblatt, *Renaissance Self-Fashioning* (Chicago: University of Chicago Press, 1980), 21; 261n18; 267nn90, 91.

16. Elton, "Thomas More," 344–45. See, too, Marius, *Thomas More*, 519–20. Marius writes: "Some will reproach me for not giving in this book a saint from *The Golden Legend*, immaculate and invincible.... But Thomas More belongs to no company of icons to be set glistering in the inaccessible reaches of our imaginations... He was nearer to us, flesh and blood, and in him the good and the bad were always at war" (520).

17. Elton, "More and Cromwell," 150.

versy does not simply emerge from the issue of heresy or the onset of the Protestant reformation. More's adherence to the old religion prevents him from entering any aspect of the "new world" of the Renaissance.[18]

Thus, from two Thomas Mores—humanist and controversialist —emerges one man, the "real Thomas More." Eventually, Alistair Fox writes what Elton deems as a definitive account, *Thomas More: History and Providence* (1985),[19] and Fox finds the "real Thomas More" in a psychological interpretation of irreconcilable tensions between More's religious, scholarly, and political endeavors.[20] So, too, Richard Marius iterates such a portrait by exploring More's personality through analysis of More's own writings.[21] More, in Elton's final analysis, turns from humanist writings to polemical ones against heresy "not from a change of mind but from the same ultimate convictions." Whether writing *Utopia* or against Luther, More rests "all his arguments on an inexorably pessimistic view of fallen man."[22] Or as Fox puts it, "the ultimate purpose of More's doctrinal argument" is to assert "the imperfectible condition of the world."[23]

18. Ibid., 159. So, too, Marius, *Thomas More*, 425, writes of the period of Reformation controversy, "reason seemed to be conquering faith" in a "nightmare that stirred the age." Reformation controversialists, Marius believes, jettison reason and retreat to fideism. Luther makes faith a "surrender" against understanding "anything in religion but the bible"; Tyndale finds "succor" in "powerful emotion" that would assuage doubt by "experience"; More, "as troubled as any of them," rests in adherence to Church teaching. Marius's words comport with the hermeneutic he provides in his acknowledgements, which states that the religious revolutions of the sixteenth century arose "partly out of a profound skepticism about Christianity itself and that many people who battled and burned each other over dogma were fighting away a horrendous doubt that God ruled in His creation" (x); and see 265. Cf. Alistair Fox, *Thomas More: History and Providence* (New Haven: Yale University Press, 1985), 127.

19. Elton, "More and Cromwell," 145.

20. Fox, *History and Providence*, 1: "The two Mores, however, never seem happily to coincide.... Emphasis on the humanist produces an anachronism, and attempts to depict the saint produce only a plaster saint."

21. Marius often conflates More's personality with his theological opinion; for examples see *Thomas More*, 392, 396, 406; on "inner conflicts," see 518.

22. Elton, "Thomas More," 349–51. After More's death, attacking his character for his theological opinions begins with John Foxe's *Acts and Monuments* (1563) but is revisited for modern historians in J. A. Froude's *History of England from the Fall of Wolsey to the Defeat of the Spanish Armada* (1856).

23. Fox, *History and Providence*, 167.

For Elton, there is "surely one characteristic" that enables one to claim decisively the mantle of humanist: "he must think *humaniter* and believe in a human ability to control human fate." Hence, "what no one properly to be a called a humanist could adhere to was an Augustinian belief in the total and helpless depravity of fallen man, or to Lutheran *solifideism,* or to a clericalist view by which the priesthood acted as the sole channel of grace, or to a total denial of free enquiry."[24]

Yet as revisionist scholarship examines the significance of More's faith, traditional admiration of More as a saint of the Catholic Church remains, revealing today's competing discourse communities around a still iconic figure. Accordingly, when John Paul II proclaims Thomas More patron saint of statesmen in 2000, he proposes More as a model of how faith and action should go together. The pope emphasizes the point by quoting *Christifideles laici,* an exhortation on the mission of the lay faithful in the Church and in the world: "The unity of life of the lay faithful is of the greatest importance: indeed they must be sanctified in everyday professional and social life. Therefore, to respond to their vocation, the lay faithful must see their daily activities as an occasion to join themselves to God, fulfill his will, serve other people and lead them to communion with God in Christ."[25] More is heroic not only at his death, but in how he lived, combining contemplation with action.

As if to illustrate the different points of emphasis between religious and revisionist modes of inquiry into More's life and thought, during the same year of the pope's proclamation, Guy describes More as a man of irresolvable contradictions and contrary impulses. One of Elton's best-known students and a noted Tudor historian in

24. G. R. Elton, "Humanism in England," in *Studies in Tudor and Stuart Politics and Government*, vol. 4: *Papers and Reviews, 1982–1990* (Cambridge: Cambridge University Press, 1992), 222.

25. See John Paul II, *Christifideles laici* at http://www.vatican.va/holy_father/john_paul_ii/apost_exhortations/documents/hf_jp-ii_exh_30121988_christifideles-laici_en.html, sec. 17; and see *The Apostolic Letter Issued Motu Proprio Proclaiming Saint Thomas More Patron of Statesmen and Politicians* at http://www.vatican.va/holy_father/john_paul_ii/motu_proprio/documents/hf_jp-ii_motu-proprio_20001031_thomas-more_en.html.

his own right, Guy refutes some of Elton's claims, but retains others, maintaining still, for example, that More is a dissimulator: "The greatest paradox about the political Thomas More will become his ability to dissimulate and speak the truth simultaneously."[26] For Guy, the image of More's integrity is more a reflection of what we want in politicians than an indication of the actual historical record.[27]

So, too, popular and artistic versions of More continue the debate between celebration and skepticism. Most famously, in Robert Bolt's *A Man For All Seasons,* Richard Rich maliciously betrays More. Rich perjures himself in exchange for gaining the position of attorney-general for Wales. More replies: "For Wales? Why, Richard, it profits a man nothing to give his soul for the whole world ... But for Wales!"[28] Despite Bolt's anachronisms, he provides a "Thomas More" from William Roper's account of his father-in-law, a hagiographical depiction.[29] Elton, however, believes Rich spoke the truth about More, and Hilary Mantel's recent and immediately successful *Wolf Hall: A Novel* follows Elton's appraisal.[30] With magnificent contrast to Bolt, in *Wolf Hall,* the jurors simply "want the truth," wishing to know what More, in fact, said to Rich. The jury takes More's "sudden animation" in response to Rich as "shock and guilt" at being "confronted with his own words." As if in reply to Bolt's depiction, Mantel's More, after rebuking Rich, looks "at the jury as if expecting applause," but he finds "faces like stone."[31]

26. Guy, *Thomas More,* 58.

27. Guy writes: "The world will need More as much as ever in the third millennium, but not in an historical guise. We need him as the epitome of the 'man of singular virtue,' 'the King's good servant but God's first.' There is an historical Thomas More, but no one really knows where he can be found" (ibid., 223). Even so, Guy finds Marius "More's most persuasive modern biographer" (31) and his book "the most distinguished modern biography" (15).

28. Robert Bolt, *A Man For All Seasons* (New York: Vintage Books, 1990), 158.

29. Bolt follows William Roper's *Life of Sir Thomas More,* which quotes More's attack upon Rich's character: "In good faith, Master Rich, I am sorrier for your perjury than for my own peril. And you shall understand that neither I, nor no man else to my knowledge, ever took you to be a man of such credit as in any matter of importance [that] I, or any other, would at any time vouchsafe to communicate with you" (Roper, *Life of Sir Thomas More,* in *TMSB,* 58).

30. See G. R. Elton, *Policy and Police: The Enforcement of the Reformation in the Age of Thomas Cromwell* (Cambridge: Cambridge University Press, 1985), 415.

31. Hilary Mantel, *Wolf Hall: A Novel* (New York: Henry Holt, 2009), 525–26.

The contrary depictions of More and Rich show a tremendous change of fortune for the man for all seasons. In answer to the question of whether or not Rich perjures himself, Guy claims "we simply do not know." Yet he acknowledges that Bolt's version runs from Roper through Nicholas Harpsfield and Thomas Stapleton all the way to Chambers, providing the appearance of a "fact" about More's trial, which "everybody knows."[32] Mantel, in contrast, provides a new narrative. Even though More's jury includes the king's courtiers, ranging from Sir Thomas Palmer, Henry's dicing partner, to John Parnell, a Lutheran who filed charges of corruption against More, Mantel characterizes these men as those who "want the truth" that More hides.[33] Winner of the 2009 Man Booker Prize for best novel and widely praised in reviews from the *Guardian* to the *New York Times*, *Wolf Hall* presents More as a self-absorbed villain who plays opposite Cromwell's heroism.[34] As an illustration of how effectively revisionist scholarship continues to undermine a traditional understanding of More, the popularity of Mantel's novel indicates spectacular success.

Revisionists allege confessional bias for More in earlier interpretations of him, but the depiction of More in *Wolf Hall* suggests that it may be time to recognize a prejudice against him.[35] Indeed, the 2011 *Cambridge Companion to Thomas More Studies* attacks the picture of More put forward by Elton, Fox, and Marius. Contributor Eamon Duffy criticizes psychological readings of More's texts,[36]

32. Guy, *Thomas More*, 192–94.

33. On More's jury members, see John Guy, *A Daughter's Love: Thomas More and His Dearest Meg* (London: Fourth Estate, 2008), 259, 323–24.

34. Christopher Tayler, "Henry's Fighting Dog," *Guardian*, Saturday, May 2, 2009, book of the week, http://www.guardian.co.uk/books/2009/may/02/wolf-hall-hilary-mantel; Christopher Benfey, "Renaissance Men," *New York Times*, November 1, 2009, sec. Books / Sunday Book Review, http://www.nytimes.com/2009/11/01/books/review/Benfey-t.html?_r=1&pagewanted=2.

35. On how revisionist readings are now conventional, see Gerard Wegemer, "The Utopia of Thomas More: A Contemporary Battleground," *Modern Age* 37, no. 2 (Winter 1995): 135–41.

36. For example, Eamon Duffy, *CCTM*, 212, writes that "most recent accounts of the *Dialogue* [*Concerning Heresies*] are distorted by a largely baseless psychological reading of More"; he criticizes the readings of Marius, Elton, and Fox in this regard.

and another prominent Reformation historian, Richard Rex, finds an overall coherence in More's defense of the Church. In contrast to revisionist accounts, Rex contends that the evidence does "indeed show us a statesman, not a fanatic: a statesman of conscience, and a statesman of extraordinary insight and foresight."[37] So, too, *Wolf Hall* and other popular historical accounts of More based upon revisionist scholarship are accused of inaccuracies.

The *Companion*, as a whole, shows how More's writings reward fresh analysis. As the pendulum of More studies returns to less eristic analyses of his work, it seems opportune to reinvestigate the theoretical core of More's writings. Instead of seeking contradictions in More, this book will advance the integrity of his Christian humanism. Though the term "humanism" remains vexed, I believe Brendan Bradshaw's definition describes More's view well. More sees the Christian vocation "as a call to perfection in which the classical ideal of *humanitas*" is "subsumed under the Christian ideal of the *imago Dei*." In More's understanding, sanctification through grace remains commensurate with human development achieved through cultivating a life of reason.[38] "The effect of the humanist formula," Bradshaw writes, is "to harmonize the Christian doctrine of salvation by divine grace with the classical conception of human fulfillment as a process of rational development in accordance with the self-perfecting teleology of nature."[39] The differences between Scholasticism and More's Christian humanism, in other words, do not include a dispute over the roles of faith and reason, Christian belief and study of the liberal arts.[40]

37. Richard Rex, "Thomas More and the Heretics: Statesman or Fanatic?" in *CCTM*, 94. Rex, ibid., 114n17, accuses both Elton and Marius of making the charge that More was a liar without evidence.

38. Brendan Bradshaw, "The Controversial Thomas More," *Journal of Ecclesiastical History* 36, no. 4 (1985): 566.

39. Ibid., 567.

40. Ibid., 535–69, addresses revisionists on the matter of More's writings against heresy in light of humanism in this crucial article. For brief introductions to More's humanism, see Richard Sylvester, "Thomas More: Humanist in Action" in *EA*, 462–69; and William Nelson, "Thomas More, Grammarian and Orator" in *EA*, 150–60.

Thompson and Kristeller, in fact, gesture toward this definition of humanism. The dimension of "moral philosophy," for example, strikes Thompson as general enough to include More's texts that are not humanist "in the older stricter, narrower sense as scholarship or literary culture founded on Greek and Latin literature and wisdom." Here humanism addresses "the larger considerations of More's public life and then to his interior, devotional life," enlarging the term "humanism" to include an emphasis upon the *vita activa* and *vita contemplativa* as synonyms for public and private activities."[41] Similarly, Kristeller proposes a combination of "scholarship and religion," which provides a "legitimate core" of "Christian humanism," a distinct if related category to Thompson's more "strict sense." Kristeller argues that Petrarch is an important antecedent, but more immediately, Giovanni Pico della Mirandola provides "More's closest contact with Italian humanism and philosophy," which "also had a strong moral and religious accent."[42] That moral and religious "accent," as some scholars are beginning to emphasize, shows how assumptions about the tension between Christianity and humanism deserve reevaluation.[43]

Kristeller's historical sense seems well placed as a starting point too. The most direct connection between the Northern humanists and the Italian ones in More's own canon is the *Life of Pico.*[44] Of further significance, the *Life* engages Thompson's suggestion that More's humanism focuses upon the topoi of active and contemplative lives. Thompson, however, equates More's devotion with "privacy" and More's politics with "public life," suggesting more contemporary terms of distinction than may be applicable to More's own sense of service. Even so, Thompson identifies a rich area for ex-

---

41. Thompson, "More Reappraised," 246–47.
42. Kristeller, "More as Humanist," 12.
43. See Alasdair A. MacDonald, R. W. M. von Martels Zweder, and Jan R. Veenstra, eds., *Christian Humanism: Essays in Honour of Arjo Vanderjagt* (Leiden: Brill, 2009), 3–102.
44. For a better understanding of Tudor English interest in Pico, see George B. Parks, "Pico Della Mirandola in Tudor Translation," in *Philosophy and Humanism: Essays in Honor of Paul Oskar Kristeller*, ed. Edward P. Mahoney (Leiden: Brill, 1976), 353–56.

ploration because More himself examined the relationship between contemplation and action in his *Life* and then again in *Utopia*'s first book. My first chapter, then, addresses the *Life* by explaining how More's religious commitment, his sense of service, and his scholarly activities constitute a basic coherence. In my reading, More subversively translates the original epideictic account of Pico in order to critique his subject's practice and notion of humanist studies. Rather than a text that calls philosophers to isolation, the *Life* argues for engagement in temporal affairs. Unlike other interpretations of More's humanism, the *Life* rather than *Utopia* will provide my focus. A different view of humanism requires a different textual emphasis.

So, too, my narrative of More's intellectual integrity pursues avenues of continuity between More's classical-Christian approach to humanism, politics, and his polemical theology. The first three chapters chart a trajectory from the spiritual idealism in the *Life of Pico* to the accommodating approach to politics announced by *Morus* in *Utopia*. In this reconstruction, the aspirations for and ideals of virtue present in the *Life* do not indicate More's plans for revolutionary, new forms of governance. As *The History of Richard III* shows, More questions political life as a sphere of human activity best suited for actualizing John Colet's notion of *amor Dei in nobis*. I present More's *History* as a text of political philosophy, which illustrates the limits to humanist aspirations in regimes governed by principles of power and necessity.[45] This reading of the precarious nature of political endeavor serves to moderate the expectations for virtue proposed in the *Life* and provides a crucial context for understanding More's accommodating approach to politics articulated in the first book of *Utopia*. In this way, the *History* carries greater importance than *Utopia* does for understanding More's political thought.

Yet both the *History* and *Utopia*'s "dialogue of counsel" suggest

---

45. Logan, "More on Tyranny: *The History of King Richard the Third*" in *CCTM*, 168, calls the *History* More's "other great political work," a complement to *Utopia*; "both are also supreme achievements of Renaissance humanism."

that reforms within political and public life will concern prudential matters and incremental advances. As I show in chapter 3, the moral imperative of reform and the importance of prudential calculation should be noted especially in the issue of equity, a matter of courts, litigants, and law, but not of revolutionary political ideas of change. If we read book 1 of *Utopia* contextually with the *Life* and the *History*, More's Christian humanism emphasizes engagement in temporal affairs as an attempt to accommodate the social ideals of Christian faith to political limitations.

Of equal importance, within More's earliest humanist writing, I locate an apologia for orthodox doctrine. As More criticizes Pico's liberties in the name of learning, so, too, More rejects the scholarly innovations and interpretations of Reformation theology. The incipient polemical theology in the *Life* anticipates an area in which More would not provide accommodation: his opposition to heretical belief. As More condemns Pico, he will attack Tyndale, illustrating a continuation of More's support of orthodox teaching. The reason for More's earliest and too often ignored defense of orthodoxy becomes most clear in his later arguments against heresy. In his antiheretical tracts, More advances an authoritative discourse community of Christian faith, which I show in chapter 4 to be a matter of humanist semiotics and Catholic doctrine and in chapter 5, a matter of canon law. More's polemical theology proposes "the common corps of Christendom," which I show as a sign system directly related to More's 1515 articulation of humanist *communitas*. Such a connection illustrates a continuation of More's humanist interests in his later polemical theology. Indeed, More's ideas of humanist community parallel his notion of Church as an authoritative discourse community.

In More's view, the Church alone would approve Scripture, teach doctrine, and police for heresy. Hence, More believes he should not apply the accommodating approach he developed in *Utopia* to the religious and political advances of the reformers. Doctrine and ecclesial action are not essentially political endeavors because both are subordinate to More's formulation of the "hole corps of chrys-tendome," an authority that More finds decisive.[46] That distinct sense of authority contextualizes the exchanges between More and Christopher St. German over the freedoms of the *Ecclesia Anglicana*, which I address in chapter 5. Rather than a clash of legal titans or a philosophical debate over the roles of Church and Crown, I show how More and St. German sometimes clumsily joust over the issue of authority, offering, in the process, a new interpretation of how the tone of More's polemical voice should be understood. For revisionist scholars of More, St. German was one of the most important politi-cal philosophers of the period, and More's efforts against him seem lacking in quality by comparison, but in my account these controver-sies represent a historically important yet polemically charged con-text more than a philosophical contest. Rather than an unpersuasive and inadequate reply, More's advocacy for the Church makes a pow-erful if partial case against anticlericalism.

Finally, my conclusion examines More's prison letters with a view toward showing his integrity of thought, an author whose fun-damental principles remain constant. In doing so, I compare More's self-presentation to other recent and more iconic versions in Robert Bolt's *Man for All Seasons* and Hilary Mantel's *Wolf Hall*. These icon-ic Mores enact the debate between traditional and revisionist schol-arship. Yet both portraits, ultimately, capture something important. Elton rightly identifies More's deeper modes of intransigence, which more hagiographical or traditional narratives may not present but Mantel recognizes. Even so, the integrity of More's position re-mains, and Bolt captures something of that quality. In illustrating points of convergence and difference between Bolt and Mantel with the findings from my previous chapters, I present an ironic, defiant, and subversive *ethos* in More's last letters. That *ethos* shows the one Thomas More.

46. More's reference to "the whole corps of Christendom" appears often. For examples, see *CW* 8.1, 343/3–4; *CW* 9, 99/35; *CW* 10, 9/18.

1

PROFITABLE LEARNING AND *PIETAS*
The Life of Pico della Mirandola, ca. 1504–10

More's *Life of Pico* is a Christian guidebook, a translation of the Latin original *Vita Pici*, but how and in what ways More found Pico a Christian paradigm remains contested. For some, Pico represents a personal model to More as a brilliant lay scholar; others read the text for insight into More's own vocational crisis of whether or not to marry in 1504; still others find a statement of the superiority of the contemplative life to action in the world.[1] Such interpretations, though, often pay insufficient attention to the facts that Pico neither marries

---

1. For Pico as paradigm, see R. W. Chambers, *Thomas More* (Ann Arbor: University of Michigan Press, 1958; original ed. 1935), 92. For More's "psychological crisis of 1504," see Stanford E. Lehmberg, "Sir Thomas More's Life of Pico della Mirandola," *Studies in the Renaissance* 3 (1956): 61; Marius, *Thomas More*, 37–38; for the *Life* as an act of "self-definition," see Ackroyd, *The Life of Thomas More*, 103. For refutations or important qualifications of these views, see Peter Iver Kaufman, *Incorrectly Political: Augustine and Thomas More* (Notre Dame: University of Notre Dame Press, 2007), 143–44; *CW*, 1, xxxix; and Eiléan Ní Chuilleanáin, "Motives of Translation: Reading Thomas More's Translation of Pico della Mirandola's Life and Works," in *Italian Culture: Interactions, Transpositions, Translations*, ed. Cormac Ó Cuilleanáin, Corinna Salvadori, and John Scattergood (Portland, Ore.: Four Courts Press, 2006), 114–19. For the *Life* as a contemplative model, see *CW* 1, liii, which states: "Pico's work becomes less a biography and more an appropriate contemplative model for the rejection of the active life of the world." For an influential revisionist account, see Fox, *History and Providence*, 27–35, who rejects Pico as a model for More because the text juxtaposes ambition and spirituality, fleshly rebellion and asceticism, intellectual precocity and humble study.

nor follows a private "inspiration" from God "vnto religion" (*CW* I, 73/24–25) but More lives with the Carthusians before deciding to wed Jane Colt. Pico, in short, represents choices More never makes.

Though More's translation is a gift for "Joyeuce Leigh," or Joyce Lee, of the Poor Clare Convent, his introduction states the *Life* will please all who have "any meane desire & loue to god" (52/12). Such a purpose is obviously *not* the same as the original aim of Gianfrancesco, Pico's nephew, because More's transparent educative purpose differs from Gianfrancesco's epideictic one, even if Gianfrancesco emphasizes he will provide unbiased praise of his uncle.[2] In contrast, More's expanded sense of applicability to all who love God provokes the question of whether the Christian humanist emphasis on piety best explains the sum total of More's changes and additions to the original version. Such an emphasis upon piety, I will argue, runs throughout More's *Life* in a way that privileges learning for what More calls "profit" and elevates the mixed life, a combination of action and contemplation.

To situate More's understanding of profitable learning, this chapter begins with More's letter to Thomas Ruthall and his translation of Lucian's *Cynicus* in hopes of showing the moral nature of learning and the compatibility of pagan authors with Christian revelation. With such a background, More's alterations and additions to the original text of *Vita Pici* indicate much about his own sense of the proper place of liberal arts study. Likewise, the poetry More appends to his version of the *Life* deserves special attention because it is either wholly original or a significant elaboration upon the brief prose apothegms of Pico; there is nothing in the original to compare to the rhyme royal stanzas More writes.[3] As Mary Edith Willow observes, "Thomas More's approach to this work was literary and creative."[4]

More's creative approach I find not in any one particular altera-

2. See *CW* 1, 295.

3. Mary Edith Willow, *An Analysis of the English Poems of St. Thomas More* (Nieuwkoop: Hes & De Graaf, 1974), 232.

4. Ibid., 271.

tion or through the poetry alone, but in his overall theme, which teaches that *virtus*, whether natural or supernatural, cardinal or theological, includes learning or knowledge, what More calls "cunning." Most important, virtue and learning have *pietas* as their end. Righteous conduct, virtuous action, or piety configured as an unfolding of a Christian's love for God mirrors the teaching of John Colet and Erasmus, illustrating how More may have first encountered the notion that *amor Dei in nobis* energizes a life of virtue.[5]

So, too, defining More's early writings on the liberal arts in terms of *pietas* carries ramifications beyond any local reading of one early text. Because More's turn to religious polemics is viewed as an abandonment of humanist principles, a revised understanding of those principles creates the potential for coherence between More's humanist writings and his later polemical tracts against Protestant reform.

LUCIAN

More's translations of Lucian are composed from 1505 to 1506, but in an undated letter to Thomas Ruthall More explains the close relationship between Christian teaching and pagan authors.[6] For

5. Both Colet and Erasmus have been understood as theologians who defend works or righteous behavior or natural piety with a distinctive Christian piety through the practice of charity. For examples, see Manfred Hoffmann, "Faith and Piety in Erasmus's Thought," *Sixteenth Century Journal* 20, no. 2 (1989): 253–58; on Colet's belief of love as intrinsic to piety and the importance of piety with regard to Christian humanism see Peter Iver Kaufman, *Augustinian Piety and Catholic Reform* (Macon, Ga.: Mercer University Press, 1982), 60–68, 111–41; for primary sources that seem particularly appropriate to More's *Life*, see Colet's own interaction with Italian humanism in Sears Reynolds Jayne, *John Colet and Marsilio Ficino* (London: Oxford University Press, 1963), 68–70; see, too, *John Colet's Commentary on First Corinthians*, trans. Bernard O'Kelly and Catherine A. L. Jarrott (Binghamton, N.Y.: Medieval & Renaissance Texts & Studies, 1985), 146–47, 200–203; and Erasmus, "Enchiridion," in *Spiritualia*, ed. John W. O'Malley, vol. 66 of the *Collected Works of Erasmus* (Toronto: University of Toronto Press, 1988), 24–127. O'Malley, xi, ibid., observes: "In his *Enchiridion* Erasmus used the words *pius* or *pietas* over a hundred times, a good indication of the centrality of the idea in his thinking." The *Enchiridion* explores similar themes as the *Life* and was published in 1504. So, too, John Colet is thought to have introduced More to Pico; see CW 1, xli. More, finally, explicitly associates *pietas* with Christian faith, learning, and service to the Church in his *Letter to Oxford*. See CW 15, 146/13–23.

6. On More's decision to translate Lucian and his selection of texts, see CW 3.1, xxiv–xxxix.

More, the value of Lucian may be found in his depiction of the frailties of human nature. Lucian gives the same kind of insights that, if Richard Pace is right, More himself provides by acting as another "Democritus," a laughing philosopher who appreciates human folly.[7] Indeed, More writes to Ruthall that Lucian instructs and delights; everywhere Lucian "reprimands and censures" with honest and entertaining wit. More is especially attracted to Lucian because "no one pricks more deeply," showing "our human frailties," a frailty occasioned by a human tendency to overestimate our importance. Lucian shows "fruitless contentions of philosophers" and, more generally, the "inordinate passion for lying" people seem to possess (*CW* 3.1, 2–5). Contentiousness, lying, bragging, and exaggerating one's importance, all have the same cause: the desire to appear knowledgeable or privileged by the gods.

The didactic purpose of More's letter would seem apparent, even conventional. In fact, David Marsh shows the language of moral wisdom that More employs to be a customary point of emphasis. Humanists of the Quattrocento enjoy not just the rhetoric of Lucian but also, as Marsh's review of manuscript evidence illustrates, Lucian as "a moral philosopher." A codex in Padua containing texts from 1400 to 1440, for example, couples Lucian with St. Basil's *On Reading Pagan Literature,* along with other entries emphasizing liberal education and moral development.[8] Accordingly, the specific historical and thematic connections between More's and Erasmus's translations of Lucian are examined as combining literary and moral concerns.[9] With regard to how More portrays Lucianic cynicism in

---

7. Richard Pace, *De Fructu Qui Ex Doctrina Percipitur,* ed. and trans. Frank Manley and Richard Sylvester (New York: Renaissance Society of America, 1967), 104–5. Pace adds: "More declared all-out war on those who don't tell the truth, or things resembling the truth, but things foreign to their own nature" (ibid., 105). He then recounts More's skepticism about King Arthur making a coat from the beards of giants killed in battle.

8. David Marsh, *Lucian and the Latins: Humor and Humanism in the Early Renaissance* (Ann Arbor: University of Michigan Press, 1999), 2–3.

9. See Robert P. Adams, *The Better Part of Valor: More, Erasmus, Colet, and Vives on Humanism, War, and Peace, 1496–1535* (Seattle: University of Washington Press, 1962), 33–35; and *CW* 3.1, xliii–xlvii.

the *Menippus,* for instance, R. Bracht Branham remarks that More's "serious idealism" and "moral commitment" sometimes appear like a vast divergence from the pagan author More translates.[10]

It is this kind of ostensible contrast between More and Lucian, though, that leads Alistair Fox to claim More's defense of Lucian constitutes a "provocatively disingenuous" presentation.[11] Lucian, at least, is a subtler author than More's defense of him indicates. The letter to Ruthall should be read esoterically as a result. In citing St. John Chrysostom's approval of Lucian, for example, More writes that the *Cynicus* defends a disciplined life and denounces a luxurious one; such lessons edify Christians about leading a life of moderation and frugality (*CW* 3.1, 2–5). For Branham, the actual point of the original *Cynicus* is not directed at *luxuria* but at the "comic inability of either speaker [from the dialogue] to grasp fully the other's point of view." Hence, More bends Lucian's "ironic presentation of Cynic asceticism" into an example of Christian simplicity and moderation.[12] Fox, however, argues this dialogue could be read for moral content only by a "pious Christian-humanist moralist" who seeks "reassurance" in it.[13] Instead, Lucian's dialogues help More forge an idea of truth that is ambiguous and allows for an ironic detachment from "all aspects of human experience."[14] More presents such an outlook to justify his entry into active life because he had just left the Charterhouse monastery, but this mindset supports Fox's overall assessment of the *Life* as oscillating between contrary impulses.

More's point that pagan asceticism offers a corrective model to luxuriant Christians, however, agrees with the teaching of his epigram 260 and with Erasmus's teaching on similar points.[15] In

10. R. Bracht Branham, "Utopian Laughter: Lucian and Thomas More," *Moreana,* no. 86 (July 1985): 30.

11. Fox, *History and Providence,* 36.

12. Branham, "Utopian Laughter," 26–27.

13. Fox, *History and Providence,* 37.

14. Ibid., 35–36.

15. On reading Lucian in light of More's psychological needs, see Fox, 35–38. On the problems with Fox's interpretative methodology, see Bradshaw, "Controversial More," 541,

the dialogue, Cynic tells his interlocutor, Lycinus, that a simple life means associating with those of superior intellect *(scitissimi)*, modesty *(modestissimi)*, and in general with people who desire virtue *(uirtutem cupiunt)* (CW 3.1, 23/22–23). Others, more luxurious, are like those who through greed or incontinence wish to use up everything (15/27–33). More makes the same distinction between those with an appetite for virtue and others who are generally appetitive in his Latin poem, "To a certain fat priest whose habit it was to say 'learning puffs up'" *(scientia inflat)*: "According to you, though others are puffed up with learning, as Paul teaches, you avoid it. How is it then, O substantial father, that you are so swollen? You can hardly manage your bloated belly with its flabby paunch, and your mind is puffed up with empty folly" (CW 3.2, 273).[16] As the lines from the above dialogue address intelligence and moderation against desire, More's poem attacks a cleric for not valuing *scientia* and for living immoderately. So, too, More's verses suggest that Christian virtue and learning are not mutually exclusive of one another but concomitant, mirroring the position More advocates to Ruthall.

Though More's epigram above appears impossible to date with precision, Erasmus writes in 1520 that most of More's epigrams were written twenty years before, and the theme and lines of More above specifically agree with Erasmus's *Antibarbari,* a draft of which John Colet peruses in 1499.[17] Citing the same maxim from Paul, *scientia inflat, charitas aedificat* (1 Cor 8:1), Erasmus claims that "it is ignorance, not knowledge, which puffs *them* up," turning the accu-

---

who states that "the texts are made to say what Fox's hypothesis requires them to say." For problems with Fox's "psychohistorical" approach, see Rainer Pineas, "A Response to Alistair Fox's Treatment of Thomas More as a Religious Polemicist," *Moreana* 21, no. 82 (1984): 119–25.

16. *Quemlibet inflat, ais, uel teste scientia Paulo, / Hanc fugis: unde igitur tu, pater ample, tumes? / Vix gestas crasso turgentem abdomine uentrem / Inflaturque leui mens tibi stulticia* (CW 3.2, 272/1–7).

17. On dating the poems of More and for Erasmus's letter, see CW 3.2,10–11. On dating the *Antibarbari* and its revisions, see Erasmus, *Literary and Educational Writings: 1. Antibarbari / Parabolae*, ed. Craig R. Thompson, in the *Collected Words of Erasmus*, vol. 23 (Toronto: University of Toronto Press, 1978), 3–6; hereafter cited CWE 23. Erasmus placed the *Antibarbari* in dialogue form as early as 1494, though it was not published until 1520.

sation of pride against those who attack learning in the name of piety.[18] For Erasmus, ignorance is the mother of pride, but from learning modesty is born. As erudition grows, the scholar becomes more acutely aware of all that he or she does not know, whereas "the less a person's mind is worth," Erasmus cites here from Quintilian, "the more he tries to aggrandize himself and increase his importance."[19] Returning to Paul's words, Erasmus's Batt observes that Paul says he himself possesses knowledge and studied under Gamaliel. Batt then interprets 1 Corinthians 8:1 in light of Paul's subsequent lines: it does not matter if we eat food sacrificed to idols except when the matter becomes one in which a brother of the faith may be scandalized. "Knowledge puffs up" only where Christians deliberately offend one another over a minor matter.[20] More's poem suggests *virtus* with *scientia;* Erasmus's dialogue illustrates the converse, describing ignorance as the mother of vice. Charity demands concessions in minor matters but candor in defining true *pietas*. With a common understanding, More and Erasmus address a typical humanist theme of learning in regard to Christian wisdom, providing different yet complementary points of emphasis.

In noting that Lucian differs from More's reading of him, though, Fox is correct. More could find a pagan writer imparting Christian teaching only because he ignores contexts such as Lucian's polytheism. More reads Lucian not despite Christian faith but in light of it. In this way, there is no contradiction between Christianity and reading Lucian. As More asks Ruthall: "For what difference does it make to me what a pagan thinks about those articles contained in the principal mysteries of the Christian faith?"[21] Erasmus makes a similar point in his *Antibarbari:* "None of the liberal disciplines is Christian because they neither treat of Christ nor were invented by Christians, but they all concern Christ."[22] On this point, Erasmus

---

18. *CWE* 23, 65/14–15, my emphasis.   19. Ibid., 64/31–32.

20. Ibid., 71/11–72/19.   21. *CW* 3.1, 5/18–20.

22. *CWE* 23, 90/10–12. See, too, Brendan Bradshaw, "The Christian Humanism of Erasmus," *Journal of Theological Studies* 32, no. 2 (1982): 411–47.

and More follow what Augustine recommends in his *On Christian Doctrine:* "Any statements by those who are called philosophers ... which happen to be true and consistent with our faith should not cause alarm, but be claimed for our own use, as it were from owners who have no right to them."[23] More's statement shows exclusion, for Lucian will not be read for theology, and Erasmus's and Augustine's statements indicate inclusion, for any truth of natural or moral philosophy will not contradict Christianity. Yet the principle remains the same: that of reading pagan texts selectively in order to teach lessons appropriate for leading a Christian life. Such a hermeneutic More shares with Erasmus and represents a similar understanding of Augustine or, perhaps, of St. Basil's *Address to Young Men on the Right Use of Greek Literature,* which instructs Christians to use "spiritual perceptions upon profane writings" so that they may grasp the truth through the "shadows and mirrors" of pagan texts.[24] The principle of reading selectively to emphasize Christian *pietas,* however, is best illustrated by the additions and changes More made in his version of the *Life.*

HONOR AND PROFIT

The *Life* begins with More's largest addition to the original text, a section on honor. Rather than a function of heritage, honor properly belongs to virtue, "as a shadow folowith a bodi" (*CW* 1, 53/16–17). That general teaching on the right relationship of honor to virtue, the Yale editors gloss as common or "proverbial,"[25] an interpretation Quentin Skinner explains further, adding that the "appropriate goal for a man of *virtus,* and the fundamental reason for devoting oneself

---

23. Augustine, *On Christian Teaching,* trans. R. P. H. Green (Oxford: Oxford University Press, 1997), 64, sec. 144.

24. St. Basil, *Address to Young Men on the Right Use of Greek Literature,* sec. 2, at http://www.tertullian.org/fathers/basil_litteratureo1.htm. The impact of Basil's booklet on Christian humanism is well documented and its particular influence on More probable. See Germain Marc'hadour, "Basil the Great and Thomas More," *Moreana* 29, nos. 111–12 (92): 47–52, who suggests specific parallels between Basil's and More's letters to Dorp and to Oxford.

25. Commentary on 52/30–53/1 in *CW* 1, 210.

to a life of the highest excellence, is the hope of acquiring the greatest possible amount of honour, glory and worldly fame."[26] Though More inherits the formula—honor as a reward for virtue—from Italian humanists, his use of it, like Petrarch's own later statements, follows a more Augustinian course of thought than More's editors imagine. Whether More writes the *Life* in 1504 or closer to its date of publication in 1510, his early acquaintance with Augustine's *City of God* is certain: More lectures on that text as early as 1501, and its influence, though not specifically named, might be found in the *Life*.[27]

Indeed, More defines noble or excellent or marvelous "cunnyng" as intelligence in pursuit of pious purpose and in contradistinction to pride. He writes that "sume man hath sought connying as well as philosophi as diuinitie for praise and vayneglory and not for any *profet* or encreace of christis church" (62/14–16, my emphasis). Thus, profit for the Church juxtaposes learning as a function of "vayneglory," a term More uses to translate *humanae gloriae* from the original and one that turns the passage into an object lesson against seeking human praise for scholarship (318/29–30). So, too, More's verses clarify "vayneglory" as pride. In the twelve rules of Pico, the devil tempts one to pride by "secretly" proposing laudable deeds:

> Some tyme he secretly castith in thi mynde
> Some lawdable dede to stere the to pride
> As vainglorie makith many a man blynde
> But let humilite be thi sure guide (106/22–25)

In the same sequence, Paul's visions procure him a thorn as protection against "vainglorie," which More defines as "the mother of reprefe" in a rhyme with "the very crop and rote of all mischefe" (109/4–5). "Vainglorie" as the root of mischief here translates *radix omnium malorum superbia est* (376/2), glossing *superbia* as pride.

26. Quentin Skinner, *The Foundations of Modern Political Thought*, vol. 1: *The Renaissance* (Cambridge: Cambridge University Press, 1978), 100.

27. Thomas Stapleton, however, believes More worked on Augustine and Lucian at the same time. See *The Life and Illustrious Martyrdom of Sir Thomas More*, trans. Philip E. Hallett (New York: Benziger Brothers, 1928), 8–9.

Given More's interpolation and verses, Pico's learning may be a "lawdable dede," but without profit for the Church, his scholarship could be a temptation of the devil to inspire feelings of pride, even as Paul's mystical visions require a thorn. Laudable deeds, like the substitution of "vayneglorie" for *humanae gloriae,* invite the Augustinian condemnation against seeking praises, even for praiseworthy action or study. Such a quest for honor remains a "vice" because subordinating virtue to glory undermines the rule of justice, which entails that all glory belongs to God.[28]

Augustine's teaching about honor becomes a clearer context for the *Life* by comparing its account of Pico's fame with More's 1518 letter to Gonell. Rather than recapitulate commonplaces inherited from Italian humanism, More stresses Christian virtue for his children instead of honor, contradicting, in fact, such teachings as those found in Alberti's famous dialogues, *I Libri Della Famiglia* (ca. 1434). In Alberti's text, love of honor is to be encouraged so that young people will practice virtue and, eventually, achieve renown.[29] Alberti writes: "One must surpass entirely that obscure and forgotten crowd behind. One must struggle with all the force and cunning at his disposal for a certain fame and measure of glory." Even choosing an occupation should be made in terms of not just the "reward and profit" that may be gained, but also and especially in how much "honor and fame" may be achieved.[30] Here honor becomes the goal and virtue the means, but More intends the reverse. In the letter to Gonell, More urges virtue in the first place and learning in the second, which is to say, only learning that may be conducive to virtue should be pursued.[31] More's letter also echoes the same metaphor about shadows and a body from the *Life,* but More specifies distinctly

28. Augustine, *City of God,* trans. Henry Bettenson (London: Penguin Books, 1984), 202–4; and see Skinner, *Foundations,* 1:99.

29. Cf. Skinner, *Foundations,* 1:100–101, who views Alberti as manifesting the same Petrarchan emphasis upon fame.

30. Alberti Leon, *I Libri Della Famiglia,* trans. Renee Neu Watkins (Long Grove, Ill.: Waveland Press, 2004), 140.

31. *virtutem primo, literas proximo bonorum loc ducant (Corr.,* 122/55–56).

Christian rewards of wisdom.[32] He characterizes learning in terms of use *(usum)* rather than praise *(non laudem)*, but utility especially with reference to Christian virtues such as piety, charity toward all, modesty, and humility.[33] The "reward of wisdom" depends upon "the inner knowledge of what is right [*recti conscientia*]."[34] After stressing the Christian uses of learning, More adds: "Such has been the teaching of the most learned men, especially of philosophers, who are the guides of human life, although some may have abused learning, like other good things, simply to court empty glory and popular renown."[35] The echo of metaphors and identity of teaching between the letter and the *Life* illustrate an early consistency of thought.

In this context, though, Pico appears like one who abuses learning. More addresses Pico's fame in terms of virtue by substituting "noble cunnyng" and "excellent vertue" in place of the original *gloriosa* and *fama* (59/25–26; cf. 302/34). In that same section, other philosophers visit Pico for "good doctrine"—a motive that is More's reworking of Gianfrancesco's allusion to Cicero and one that More combines with "holesome lessons & instruction of good lyuing" (59/29–60/2). Doctrine and "holesome lessons" become the teachings of philosophy in the *Life*. The original, however, describes Pico as a *mercaturam bonarum artium,* a "marketplace of the arts," *ut inquit Cicero,* alluding to *De Officiis,* where the same *mercaturam bonarum artium* appears as an exhortation to seek honor for oneself and for one's city through study (302/36–37).[36] Gianfrancesco's account privileges learning for fame, but More adjusts that emphasis, presenting, instead, doctrine over art and moral exemplarity over esoteric knowledge.

As More's elevates "good lyuing" in the *Life,* he repeats his mes-

---

32. *quanquam ea quoque virtutem velut vmbra corpus comitabitur* (ibid., 121/19–20).

33. Ibid., 121/30–31 and 122/56–58. For a translation, see *SL*, 104–5.

34. *SL*, 104. *Recti conscientia* is in *Corr.* at 121/22.

35. *SL*, 104.

36. Cf. Cicero, *De Officiis,* trans. Walter Miller (Cambridge, Mass.: Harvard University Press, 1975), III.ii.6.

sage to Gonell that virtue, rather than honor, should take top priority as the fruits of study, though virtue and learning need not and should not oppose each other. More articulates this same ideal in the *Life* as a wedding of "noble connyng" and "excellent vertue" (59/25–26), a refrain often repeated (52/1, 53/20). There is "connyng" for the mind and "vertue" for good living, but by connecting them together, More suggests they should be concomitants, not contraries. Without denying the possibility or justice of fame as a reward for learning, More provides and emphasizes distinctly Christian incentives and purposes, advertising his acquaintance with Augustine.[37] As the letter to Gonell shows, even virtue and study may become splendid vices, if they are not done with humility, and in the *Life*, More stresses pious learning rather than learning for honor or mere learning.

In a way similar to how More alters the importance of honor, he adjusts the praise of Pico from distinctive, individual acumen to learning employed for the sake of the Church. After describing how Pico excelled in all branches of learning, More writes: "And al these thyngis were in him so muche the more meruelouse in y^t he cam therto by him selfe with the strength of his owne witte *for ye loue of god and profit of his chirch* with owt maisters so that we maye sey of him that Epicure the philosophre said of him self that he was his owne maister" (62/22–27, my emphasis). Clare Murphy argues More puns above upon master and *magister*, or teacher, implying that one who is self-taught remains free, an observation that agrees with Eiléan Ní Chuilleanáin's reading of the text as a whole, which privileges the importance of liberty.[38] Yet these observations seem

---

37. Compare More's position in his letter to Gonell to Pope Pius II, *Pius II: Commentaries*, vol. 1, ed. Margaret Meserve and Marcello Simonetta (Cambridge, Mass.: Harvard University Press, 2003), 3, which opens with a consideration of glory, claiming that love of it "sustains the most brilliant intellects" and "encourages and invigorates the human spirit"; this sustaining and encouraging aspect of love of glory "is especially true for the pope of Rome."

38. Clare Murphy, "Humanist Values in Thomas More's Life of Giovanni Pico della Mirandola," in *Acta Conventus Neo-Latini Cantabrigiensis*, ed. Jean-Louis Charlet and Rhoda Schnur (Tempe: Arizona Center for Medieval and Renaissance Studies, 2003), 422; and Chuilleanáin, "Motives," 119.

misleading. More's interpolation (in italics above) shows again how he alters the meaning of the original for his own didactic purpose. Pico's learning comes by "the strength of his owne witte," but More *inserts* immediately afterward "for yͤ loue of god and profit of his chirch." In the original, Pico is praised *only* for a generic love of truth (320/1–4). So, too, "loue of god," in More's addition, again includes "profit," a learning that benefits others. For Stanley Lehmberg, this alteration "illustrates a change of attitude towards the relationship between philosophy and religion," as humanists employ a *theologia rhetorica* in place of Scholastic abstractions in hopes of explaining the divine in a more immediate way.[39] Yet More's change may also be articulated in light of what we have already discovered. Just as More encourages Gonell to instruct his children in useful knowledge, in the *Life* More recommends that "cunnyng" be of service to the Church. The emphasis upon intellectual service, too, agrees with More's defense of Erasmus in the *Letter to a Monk* (1519), which amplifies how Erasmus suffers because he devotes his scholarship totally to the benefit of others, pursuing ideas for public fruits (*CW* 15, 299). Such points may exist as part of an ongoing dispute between humanists and Scholastics, but More seems attuned to correcting Pico's excesses instead of attacking Scholasticism.

Rather than hint at how liberty should include intellectual freedom of thought distinct from authority, More emphasizes the opposite. Intellectual work operates in tandem with and for the benefit of the Church, even as study affirms and aids a general practice of the virtues. And indeed, More's own preface to the *Life* declares the profitability of Pico's writings, informing his addressee that the advantages to reading about Pico may include learning "temperaunce in prosperite" and "purchasing of patience in aduersite" and especially "desiring of heuinly felicite" (*CW* 1, 52/6–9).

39. Lehmberg, "More's Life of Pico," 73.

ORTHODOXY AND THE LIBERAL ARTS

In addition to stressing virtue instead of honor and profitable learning in place of philosophy for its own sake, More indicates how piety should follow orthodox doctrine. As earlier critics of More's translation are quick to point out, More deletes all references to Pico's defense of himself from the charge of heresy as well as the long list of contemplative thinkers whom Pico values but More, apparently, less so. Pico's interests, even in More's redaction, include "the secret misteries of the hebrieus / Caldaies / & Arabies ... and many thingis drawen owt of yᵉ olde obscure philosophie of Pythagoras / trimegistus / and orpheus / & many other thyngis strange" (57/4–7). Later, in a section on Pico's study of Scripture, "newer divines" are considered: "But of all these new doctours he specially commendith saint thomas as him yᵗ enforcith him self in a sure pillar of treuth" (61/1–3). "Of all the names listed by Gianfrancesco," Myron Gilmore rightly observes, More singles out St. Thomas for "particular praise."[40]

Such admiration of Aquinas is not unique in More's writings, though the point is often lost upon those who identify Aquinas too exclusively with a particular methodology or with those later Scholastics who live contemporaneously with More and Erasmus.[41] Writing against Luther, More calls Aquinas *sanctissimus,* a saint whom all Christians venerate and one whose holiness Luther's impiety cannot bear (*CW* 5.1, 354/19–21). Addressing Tyndale, More claims "the most cunnynge men" of the Church call Aquinas "the

40. Myron Gilmore, "More's Translation of Gianfrancesco Pico's Biography," in *L'Opera e il Pensiero di Giovanni Pico della Mirandola nella Storia dell'Umanismo* (Florence: Instituto nazionale di studi sul Rinascimento, 1965), 2:303.

41. See, for example, Thompson, "More Reappraised," 234. Yet Aquinas's *Catena Aurea* represents a commentary on the Gospels rather than the *pro et contra* method employed in the *Summa Theologicia,* and there is evidence that both Erasmus and More admired the text. Erasmus writes that the *Catena Aurea* shows how Aquinas "read both sacred literature and the old authors" in *CWE* 8, trans. A. B. Mynors (Toronto: University of Toronto Press, 1987–88), 238/470. More shows his own acquaintance with the "*Cathena aurea*" in CW 8.2, 685/18-20. On More's later use of the *Catena* in his Tower writings, see M. Thecla, "S. Thomas More and the Catena Aurea," *Modern Language Notes* 61, no. 8 (Dec. 1946): 523–29.

very floure of theology" (*CW* 8.2, 713/20–24).[42] Similarly, Erasmus writes in his *Antibarbari:* "That most noble writer Thomas Aquinas brought out commentaries on the pagan philosopher Aristotle, and even in his theological *Questions*, where he is reflecting about the first principle and about the Trinity, he offers evidence from Cicero and the poets."[43] Erasmus's sincere regard for Aquinas emerges, too, when he specifically praises him to Colet.[44] In the same way, even before More writes his polemical theology, the *Life* elevates Aquinas above Pico's "things strange."

Indeed, in J.M. Rigg's early assessment of Pico's "curious trilogy" of works—*Heptaplus, De Ente et Uno,* and *Canzone dello Amore Celeste e Divino*—Pico is guilty of "insane extravagances" with the "wildest possible jumble of incompatible ideas." Because Pico combines Neoplatonist, Cabalist, and Pythagorean sources with the Bible, Plato, Aristotle, Cicero, and Seneca, Rigg condemns Pico's labors.[45] Perhaps, too, Rigg captures More's own attitude. Pico's trademark syncretism, after all, is present in his condemned theses. "The attempt to reconcile Platonism, Aristotelianism, and Christianity," writes Lehmberg of Pico's disputed propositions, creates "scarcely Christian" results.[46]

At the very least, More emphasizes a "commitment to orthodox Christianity" in these changes by simplifying Pico's "intellectual interests."[47] Gilmore notes that after Pico is accused of heresy,

42. Though a more coherent body of Thomism emerged after More's writings, Aquinas became a point of contestation between More and the reformers. When Tyndale compares the biblical exegesis of Aquinas with the Talmud, he names Aquinas a "dunce" who was used by Catholics to establish "lies" and falsify Scripture (*An Answere unto Sir Thomas Mores Dialoge,* ed. Anne O'Donnell and Jared Wicks [Washington, D.C.: The Catholic University of America Press, 2000], 46/29–47/5). More, in contrast, names Aquinas as a "a man of that true perfect faith and Christian living thereto, that God hath himself testified his holiness by many a great miracle, and made him honored here in his Church in earth, as he that exalted him to great glory in heaven" (*CW* 8.2, 713/25–28).

43. *CWE* 23, 112/4–8.

44. Erasmus's dispute with Colet is cited from *CWE* 8, 238/467–239/483. Though Erasmus diminishes his praise of Aquinas because of Colet, he does not negate it. See, too, ibid., 15/289–301.

45. J.M. Rigg, "Introduction," in *Giovanni Pico della Mirandola: His Life by His Nephew Giovanni Franscesco Pico* (London: D. Nutt, 1890), xiii–xiv.

46. Lehmberg, "More's Life of Pico," 62.

47. Gilmore, "More's Translation," 303.

Gianfrancesco provides a defense for Pico, including Pico's own citation of Augustine, *errare possum, haereticus esse non possum,* all of which More omits, adding, instead, an original commentary.[48] After noting that Pico's theses are forbidden by the Church, More writes: "Lo this ende had Picus of his hye mynde and prowd purpose / y^t where he thought to haue goten perpetuall prayse: there had he much warke to kepe him self vpright: that he ranne not in perpetuall infamye and sclaundre" (*CW* 1, 58/29–32). More's support of orthodox teaching again resonates with the letter to Gonell, which warns how pride obscures learning, altering the object of learning to the goal of praise, and with More's rebuke of Pico for seeking "perpetuall prayse" rather than virtue. In the *Life,* when pride serves as motivation, Pico's heresy results, thereby providing a characterological assessment of heresy that More applies here and, as I will show in chapter 4, More employs against Protestant reformers such as Thomas Bilney.

As More's *Life* contrasts right doctrine with Pico's "prowd purpose," it illustrates how orthodoxy becomes an essential component to More's translation. In this way, More's vision of humanist studies again contrasts with the Italian version of it as presented by Pico, which agrees with though does not prove what Roberto Weiss calls a "compromise and subordination to medieval culture rather than antagonism with it" in forming "the characteristics of the New Learning as practiced by Grocin, Colet, Linacre, and More."[49] To a greater extent, as R. J. Schoeck comments, "there was then a much more pronounced movement towards orthodoxy in More, an awareness of and a sympathy for the sense and consensus of tradition" than may be found in Pico himself.[50]

---

48. Cited from ibid., 302.

49. Roberto Weiss, *Humanism in England during the Fifteenth Century* (Oxford: B. Blackwell, 1943), 183.

50. R. J. Schoeck, "Thomas More and the Italian Heritage of Early Tudor Humanism," in *Arts Liberaux et Philosophie au Moyen Age* (Montreal: Institute d'etudes medievales, 1969), 1196.

ACTION AND CONTEMPLATION

Pico's own letters appended to the biography address the place of philosophy in a less clear way than the import of More's above additions and alterations do, illustrating how More as translator struggles with Gianfrancesco's original presentation on the place of learning. In Pico's letter to Andrea Corneo of Urbino (see *CW* I, 232–33), or Corneus, one from about fifty letters that More selects to include with the *Life*, the role of learning and profit emerge in terms of the active versus contemplative life. Corneus believes Pico excessive in study; learning should be of use, especially to princes. More's own introduction to this section elaborates upon Pico's rebuttal by formulating useful learning in the pejorative terms of "mercennary" philosophy, studying "not for pleasur of hit selfe" or for "instruction of his mynde in morall vertue" but to gain "sum lucre or worldly aduauntage" (85/9–11). Pico himself writes of Corneus's line of reasoning that it renders philosophy into something "eithir seruile or at yᵉ lest wise not princely to make yᵉ study of wisedom other then mercennarye. Who may well here this / who may suffre hyt?" (86/22–24). Hence, Pico will privilege his books, his "little house" and "study," writing to Corneus that such a life compares well to "all your kingis palacis / all your commune busines / all your glory / all the aduauntage that ye hawk aftir / and all the fauoure of court" (87/21–24). The final position of Pico places contemplation over action because philosophy should be valued for its own sake.

Yet Pico's own rejoinder to Corneus invites a dissenting view by proposing a third option between action and contemplation and a distinct sort of profit available to those who study philosophy. Pico himself suggests a middle position: "But here ye will sey to me thus. *I am content ye study / but I wolde haue you outwardli occupied also.* And I desire you not so to embrace martha that ye shulde vttirly forsake Mari. *Loue them & vse them both aswell study as worldly occupation*" (86/5–9, my emphasis). The italics represent More's interpolations, indicating how he amplifies the position that Pico provides as a compromise between himself and Corneus: the mixed life. So, too, Pico redescribes the possibility of philosophy's "profit" from his other statement of mercenary knowledge. He writes:

> *Nor* I loke *not* for this frute of my study y^t I may therby herafter be tossed in the flode and rombeling of your worldly besynesse: but y^t I may ones bring forth the children that I trauaile on: y^t I may giue owt some bokes of myn owne to the commune *proffit* which may sumwhat sauour: if not of cunnyng yet at the lest wyse of wit and diligence. (87/25–88/2, my emphasis)

The double negative indicates that Pico will look to "proffit," a word that More inserts, and where the original employs a pun upon children and books, with the word *liberos,* More provides "books of mine own," thereby capturing metaphorical offspring as the result of learning. Pico wishes to avoid the tumult *in rerum publicarum,* political things or affairs, what More translates as "worldly besynesse," but More augments Pico's sense that learning contributes to the "commune proffit" (see 350/36–352/4).

The letter to Corneus, then, presents two contradictions or disjunctives: first, philosophy for its own sake *or* philosophy for "public" benefits; and second, an active life that may include contemplation *or* an active life that is wholly without merit, that is, an active life that must exclude contemplation. Pico allows for each, though logically he may not do so. If philosophy is pursued for the profit it provides in other spheres of life, it is not sought for its own sake. If an active life may include contemplation, it need not be beset with prideful concern for honors. Though such goods may be compatible, they cannot be so and remain mutually exclusive of one another. More's additions render Pico's own preference for the contemplative life into a contradictory apologia, indicating how More the translator suggests the mixed life as an unarticulated answer to Pico's clashing disjunctives.

More's selection of and additions to the letter to Corneus highlight other contradictions Pico poses in the biography, which show how Pico pursues a leisured life after a disordered manner. In a sec-

tion that addresses the active and contemplative life, More adds a title to reveal his subject's character, "What he hated & what he loued"
(69/12). Similar to the position in the letter to Corneus, Pico hates
politics, lords, and palaces, finding them proud people and places,
deserving a blanket condemnation. But "liberte," More writes of
Pico, "a boue all thing he loued to which both his owne naturall affection & ye study of philosophy enclined him" (69/21–23). Anticipating the tone and argument of Raphael from *Utopia*, Pico views
action in terms of politics, and politics as vice; contemplation means
freedom and freedom means virtue.

So Pico loves philosophy, but fails to discipline that love under
piety. We learn of Pico's desire to preach Christ to others and, in
a clause More adds, of "the especial commaundement of god" by
which Pico is called to enter the Dominican order (70/18–19; cf.
330/13–14). Pico delays answering that call, hoping to follow it "aftir
certaine bokes" of his are finished (70/15). In Gianfrancesco's version, Pico decides upon the Dominican order without special revelation, and, in passage deleted by More, Pico publishes the "certaine
bokes" mentioned above (330/13–15). More's version of events, however, shows Pico as impious: Pico rejects a direct command from
God, and the time spent in delay fails to produce scholarly fruit.

Later, Savonarola reveals Pico's secret: "a priuey inspiration" by
which God invites Pico "vnto religion." Yet Pico "shrank from the labour," neglecting his vocational call (73/24–74/3). For that omission,
Pico must spend time in purgatory, a verdict Savonarola affirms by
his own visions. The fate of Pico illustrates there is no learning exclusively for the sake of learning. In this case, piety demands that
Pico's learning complement the preaching he is called to perform
as a Dominican, turning study into "profit" for the Church, a con-
version of souls. More subordinates learning under *pietas* to such a
degree that Pico's refusal to accept God's call to enter religious life
deserves purgatorial punishment. Pico's deferral of religious life
mirrors his confusion about the profit he owes the Church.

Pico's fate and More's additions to the letter to Corneus show that Pico never considers the mixed life. Rather than contemplation instead of action or vice versa, study and contemplation accompany duties and service in a mixed life. More probably knows the idea of a mixed life from Augustine or even Walter Hilton, a spiritual writer popular among the Carthusians with whom More lived before writing the *Life*. Augustine's own consideration of the best way of life teaches that leisure, action, or any combination of the two may attain everlasting reward. For Augustine, the life of action should be sought not for honor but because the office itself provides the power to achieve what is just and helpful to the common good. Offices are tasks, not honors. Similarly, leisure exists for investigation of truth, not for lazy inaction. Augustine writes of balance: "For no one ought to be so leisured as to take no thought in that leisure for the interest of his neighbor, nor so active as to feel no need for the contemplation of God."[51] Leisure should be sought out of love for truth and righteous engagement by a compulsion of love. In either case, honor never acts as an incentive. If engagement in affairs is imposed, it should be undertaken out of love.

The relationship of engagement and charity is iterated as well by Walter Hilton (d. 1396), whose *Scala perfectionis* More specifically recommends and is a text that in early printed editions includes an *Epistle on the Mixed Life*.[52] Hilton's *Epistle* recommends the mixed life to men "with high temporal rank and large holdings of worldly assets, and a kind of authority too over others to direct and support them"—for individuals, in other words, precisely like Pico.[53] These will pray and contemplate, but not at the expense of neglecting temporal duties. Hilton warns in several passages that such neglect violates the order of charity:

51. Augustine, *City of God*, 880.
52. MS. Lambeth Palace 472, for example, includes *the Mixed Life*. For More's reference, see *CW* 8.1, 37/31; for text's publication history and circulation see: *CW* 8.3 commentary on 37/31 at 1474; James Monti, *The King's Good Servant but God's First: The Life and Writings of Saint Thomas More* (San Francisco: Ignatius Press, 1997), 69; and Walter Hilton, *The Scale of Perfection*, trans. and ed. John P. H. Clark and Rosemary Dorward (New York: Paulist Press, 1991), 33.
53. Walter Hilton, *Mixed Life*, trans. Rosemary Dorward (Oxford: SLG Press, 2001), 8.

For if—considering the responsibilities and duties these men have undertaken—they want altogether to abandon the business of the world which in
reason should be used for the fulfillment of their charge, and give themselves up entirely to contemplative life, they are not doing right, because
they are not keeping the order of charity.[54]

. . .

If you neglect the necessary business of the active life, recklessly taking no
care over the management and use of your property, and if you have no concern for your dependants and your fellow Christians because of your desire
and will to give yourself entirely to spiritual pursuits, which you think will
excuse you: if you behave like this, you are not doing wisely.[55]

For Hilton, charity demands that at one time "you must be busy
with Martha" and at another "with Mary" so that "you will pass from
one to the other with *profit*."[56] Though each must discern his or her
vocational call, "eminent laymen" with responsibilities should take
into account their state in life.[57]

Such warnings from Hilton provide a commentary to More's
portrayal of Pico's own household governance. In the original, Pico's
friends warn him that he should be more attentive to matters of money lest others accuse him of providing opportunities for theft and
charge Pico with creating occasions of sin, but More changes that
account. More adds the clause "that his [Pico's] negligence & setting
nought by money" and inserts it beside "gaue his seruauntes occasion of deceyt & robbry" (68/4–6; cf. 326/20–23). Thus, when Pico's
steward presents him with the finances, More's Pico replies, "I know
wele ye haue mought oftyn tymes and yet may desceyue me & ye list:
werfore the examination of these expensis shal not nede" (68/13–15).
Pico refuses to review the books because his "negligence" invites any
theft that may occur. More's version of events makes the same accusation that the original depicts as a potential slander, a charge that

54. Ibid. 55. Ibid., 11.
56. Ibid., 6, my emphasis.
57. The mixed life was More's own choice. For Nicholas Harpsfield, More's rejection of the
contemplative life did not mean that More's overall way of life was not exemplary. See Harpsfield, *The Life and Death of Sir Thomas Moore, Knight*, ed. E. V. Hitchcock (London: Humphrey
Milford, 1963), 8.

Pico's friends wished to protect him from. Gianfrancesco writes the accusation of providing occasions of sin could be *verum* or *falsum*, but More *makes* the charge *verum*.[58] More's change means that he believes that what appears as liberality in Pico actually is an invitation to robbery. Though Pico himself lives a kind of moderation, his practice is self-regarding rather than for others, a false virtue. He lacks the Augustinian compulsion of love to fulfill the duties incumbent upon his state of life, a mandate Augustine gives whether or not the active life is desired or imposed. Like a Socrates who refuses to attend to his wife and children, Pico ignores household management.

What Pico's purgatorial fate and More's adjustments in the letter to Corneus show is an early attempt to suggest the mixed life. As John Guy writes of the *Life of Pico*, "If, then, the riddle of More's vocation and the extent to which it was determined by his sexuality has fascinated his biographers, it has distracted attention from the humanist emphasis on philosophy" and, in particular, "the proper relationship between philosophy and public life."[59] Guy recognizes in Pico one whose "career" is a "cautionary tale" because Pico gives into the "sin of pride" in refusing God's call, but coincidentally, Guy affirms the *Life* "functioned as a guide" to those in the cloister or on the street by a promotion of "universal Christian virtues." Pico represents an exemplar of virtue, and yet he is proud. Such an opposition Guy may purposefully favor because, like Fox, he believes "there was nothing in which he [More] took greater delight than in an open-ended debate that left competing viewpoints unresolved." As a result, More does not validate "any particular standpoint as to the merits of the 'active' and the 'contemplative' lives.'"[60] Yet Guy does not realize how the argument between active and contemplative ways of life pertains to the practice of virtue; they are not sepa-

---

58. Cf. *Ab amicis quoque saepius admonitum comperimus, ut in totum divitias non contemneret, asseverantibus id sibi probro dari cum vulgatum foret, sive id verum sive falsum, furti dispensatoribus praebuisse occasionem* (CW 1, 326/20–23).

59. Guy, *Thomas More*, 38.

60. Ibid.

rate issues but one. In refusing a vocational call, Pico obviously fails, a sin of pride, but even with regard to the lay state, Pico neglects the duties of the mixed life. In *that* way, Pico represents not a paradigm for imitation but an edifying warning. Guy recognizes the importance of the text for discovering More's humanist principles and rightly concludes the *Life* is a warning but without connecting Pico's faults to the profit or service that *pietas* demands of Pico.

IMAGO DEI AND PIETAS

The appended letters and poetry, like the letter to Gonell and the biography of Pico, emphasize *virtus* with *pietas*. Tantamount to the practice of virtue is the recognition of man as *imago dei,* a point that not only the poetry makes but also More's preface. After the biographical portion, More presents the story of Circe as an introduction to Pico's own use of that character, a witch who proffers drink to turn men into animals. In More's hands, the episode becomes a figure for the moral life. More warns against the wine of sensuality and especially that of the flesh whereby the soul leaves "ye noble vse" of reason, turning the proud man into the lion (76/24–25). So, too, More's preface warns "y^t we be not dronken in ye cuppis of Circes" lest we "deforme ye image of god in oure sowles aftir whose image we be made." Idolaters turn images of animals into gods; men turn themselves, images of god, into animals. The latter is more "odiouse to god" (77/14–20).

In the same way, More's concluding poetry, "The Twelve Weapons of Spiritual Battle," iterates the "nature and dignite of man." More writes:

> Remembre how god hath made the resonable
> Like vnto his Image and figure
> And for the suffred paines intollerable
> That he for angell neuir wolde endure.
> Regarde o man thyne excellent nature.
> Thou that with angell art made to bene egall,
> For very shame be not the deuilles thrall. (111/25–112/5)

In these verses, as Vittorio Gabrieli writes, More's version of *hominis dignitas* significantly slants "in a religious direction with very little humanistic flavor or heightening."[61] That observation corresponds with the biographical section, which strikes what Gianfrancesco narrates about how his uncle may have been considered divine due to learning. Lehmberg justifies More's omission because neither More nor Joyce Lee "would have thought that any man should be called divine."[62] Indeed, More's overall tone is very different from that found in Angelo Poliziano's letters, which offer an array of epithets for Pico, from "paragon of liberal studies" to "Pico the polymath" to a "man of divine intelligence."[63] Likewise, rather than praise man's nature as miraculous for reaching the transcendent through reason, as occurs in Pico's own *Oration on the Dignity of Man*, More refuses all classical contexts of the philosopher as divine, simply emphasizing nature in terms of reason and reason as a weapon of spiritual battle.

Similar to More's verses, Colet's "Ryght fruitfull [ad]monicion" on the "order of a good christen mannes lyfe" maintains that one must know "God of his greatte grace hat[h] made the[e] to his own similitude or ymage." Such self-knowledge, man as *imago dei,* provides a hierarchy for ordering life whereby temporal goods are for the body, the body for the soul, the soul for "reason and grace," and by "reason and grace" to know "thy duetie to God and to thy neighbour."[64] Reason appears here as functional with respect to living well, as in More's poetry. Elsewhere, Colet defines philosophy and the use of reason, after the example of King Solomon, as a distinctly moral knowledge, which provides a way of life that enables

61. Vittorio Gabrieli, "Giovanni Pico and Thomas More," *Moreana*, nos. 15–16 (1967): 50.

62. Lehmberg, "More's Life of Pico," 70.

63. Angelo Poliziano, *Letters*, vol. 1, ed. and trans. Shane Butler (Cambridge, Mass.: Harvard University Press, 2006), 63, 82, 100.

64. John Colet, "A ryght fruitfull monicion concernyge the order of a good christen mannes lyfe, very profitable for all maner of estates, and other, to beholde and loke upon: Made by the famous doctour Colet, sometyme Deane of Paules," in *A Life of John Colet*, trans. and ed. J. H. Lupton (Eugene, Ore.: Wipf & Stock, 2004), 306. I make no claim that Colet's "monicion" influenced More's text, yet the contextualization of charity through action deserves greater attention in More's circle.

good people to use even evils well, following the Pauline precept of overcoming evil with goodness.[65] As in More's letter to Gonell, philosophy provides such living wisdom.[66] So, too, Colet's *viva sapientia* or "living wisdom" defines wisdom in a similar manner to More's "good lyuing" from the *Life*.[67]

More's reevaluation of reason in terms of moral conduct again points to practical, active life as the arena of sanctification he wishes to emphasize, which becomes More's theme by ending the poetry sequence with a series of stanzas on love of God. The context of More's idea of love is important, for A. G. Edwards claims love leads to contemplation, away and out from the world. In the context of Erasmus's and Colet's emphasis upon *viva sapientia* and how that wisdom may be animated by *amor*, however, the final poems may be read as highlighting love as the spiritual means of pursuing piety and justice in any endeavor.[68] As More dedicated his *Life* to all those with a desire and love for God, the concluding poems return to the opening, providing a theme in which virtue, whether contemplative or active, may be seen in terms of piety, but piety as love of God.

From Augustine, Hilton, or Colet, More could find sources in which love is not disengaged from action but implicit in it. In regard to Colet, rather than an endorsement of contemplation alone, the approach and point of More's qualities of a lover form a poetic counterpart to the more Platonic and direct tone of the *Admonition*. For Colet, "as a man loueth, so he is: for the louer is in the thing loued more properly than in hym selfe." We become our loves; as an image of God, we better mirror the divine the more we love him. Colet

---

65. On Solomonic philosophy, see Colet in Jayne, *Colet and Ficinio*, 115–16.

66. William Shaw's assessment, *Introductory Lectures on the Oxford Reformers: Colet, Erasmus, and More* (Philadelphia: American Society for the Extension of University Teaching, 1893), 22, still seems accurate: "The distinguishing mark of the reforming programme of Colet and the Oxford Reformers was that it aimed at changes in life and practice, not in doctrine."

67. Colet writes, "Living wisdom makes man worship God humbly, and live temperately, and lovingly serve his fellow man" (*Joannis Coleti Opuscula quaedam theologica*, trans. and ed. J. H. Lupton [London: George Bell and Sons, 1876], 55). On *viva sapientia*, see Kaufman, *Augustinian Piety*, 60.

68. *CW* 1, lx.

writes: "Wherefore, yf a man loue erthely thynges, he may be called an erthely man. And if he loue principally heuenly thynges or God, he may be called an heuenly or a godly man."[69] Colet, though, writes his "admonition" to people in every state of life, married or religious. Making the same conclusion as More, Colet advises that man love God, a permanent, never diminishing good that transforms lovers by helping them "order" their lives for God no matter what state they occupy. For Colet and More, love of God and learning, more than virtue and honor, are like a shadow and a body.

And indeed the *Life* concludes by exhorting readers to love God by considering the conditions of a lover, as More employs Petrarchan conceits into the qualities of one who loves God above all.[70] As with the rules and weapons poems, there are twelve conditions of a lover, but the eleventh Willow rightly identifies as "an excellent synthesis" of the entire languishing lover conceit.[71] In these stanzas, the lover's heart is "diversely passioned," which ranges from hope to dread and fear to bliss and "sorrow smart." The second stanza makes the application to God:

> Like affectiones felith eke the brest
> Of goddis louer in praier and meditation:
> Whan that his loue liketh in hym rest
> With inward gladnes of pleasaunt contemplation
> Owt breke the teris for Ioy and delectation
> And whan his loue list eft to parte him fro
> Owt breke the teris a gaine for paine & woo. (119/6–12)

Here "inward gladnes" hearkens back to the biography. In that section, More writes of the "in ward affectes of the mynde," which come from cleaving to god "with very feruent loue and deuotion" (70/7–8). In the first letter to Francis, too, Pico himself advises daily prayer

69. Colet, "fruitfull monicion," 309.

70. The twelve conditions or qualities of a lover "are original with the exception of the last two stanzas. These verses are a paraphrase of a short Latin excerpt, which has for its thesis three principal considerations exhorting us to the service of God" (Willow, *English Poems*, 221 and see 242–44).

71. Ibid., 246.

that comes from the "inwardnes of thin hart" (83/23). Though Pico's love isn't great enough to follow God's invitation to join the Dominicans, More appears to be captivated enough by the idea of inner rapture. For "inward gladnes" reflects back upon what More finds in parts from *Vita Pici* and wishes to develop. Rather than stress a binary opposition of body to soul, as Fox alleges More in fact does, More's lines propose a synthesis, where erotic longings and oscillating emotions of bliss and longing exist in meditation.[72] That turn to love and interiority represents the humanist emphasis upon the immediacy of God, but a daily means, too, of undertaking the duties of any state of life where *pietas* becomes a guide.

MORE'S PICO

A review of More's early work as a translator reveals a morally didactic purpose to his art, with both Lucian and Gianfrancesco's texts. Whether reading selectively or translating so, More applies the Erasmian ideal of wedding learning with virtue. Instead of depicting ambiguity or ironic detachment, these early works show a conventional humanist emphasis upon moral wisdom. Where Ciceronian commonplaces exalt honor, More looks for Christian usefulness, following Augustine. Rather than privilege Pico's polymathy and genius, More favors orthodox teaching. If Pico himself exalts in contemplation, More qualifies philosophy, raising questions about "profit" for the Church and attendance to duty in accord with charity. As conventional tropes may immortalize love in verse, More poetizes love as intrinsic to success in the ascetical struggle. Man as *imago dei* indicates piety more than philosophy. Yet the ideals present here, we shall see, More would put to the test in writing the *History of Richard III*.

72. Cf. Fox writes of "More's radical segregation of the physical and spiritual, the material world and the transcendent" in *History and Providence*, 34.

2

HUMANIST REALISM AND *THE HISTORY OF RICHARD III*, CA. 1514–18

A. F. Pollard identifies a significant problem of Thomas More's *The History of Richard III*, which he calls "the motive of its conception," a problem that closely allies with the question of More's intellectual identity.[1] Does More write the *History* to provide a factual account of Richard's rise to power, or to practice his skills of declamation, or to dramatize a moral fable? Is More a Tudor propagandist, an early modern historian, a rhetorician, or a poet? Recent critics argue that More did not intend to write a history, but a work of literature. Some contend the *History* presents a medieval morality play about Richard's usurpation; others find the dramatic elements of the *History* a reflection of More's imitation of Roman historians; still others find evidence in the *History* that the work should be understood in terms of rhetorical practices of the early English Renaissance.[2]

This chapter is an expanded and revised version of my earlier "A 'Pre-Machiavellian Moment': Thomas More's Poetry and the *History of Richard III*," *Ben Jonson Journal* 13 (2006): 63–82.

1. A. F. Pollard, "The Making of Sir Thomas More's *Richard III*," in *EA*, 421–31, points out the historical "errors" and the problems of classification involved in assessing More's work as an actual history.

2. On More as Tudor propagandist, see Walpole's *Historic Doubts on the Life and Reign of King Richard III*, in *Richard III: The Great Debate*, ed. Paul Kendall (London: Folio Society, 1965) and compare with *CW* 2, lxv–lxxx.

On multiple readings of More's purpose, Leanord F. Dean, "Literary Problems in More's

Following last chapter's emphasis upon More's humanism, I will situate the *History* in the context of what George Logan calls the debate about the proper relationship of *honestas* to *utilitas* "both because some Italian humanists had embraced the notion of a political necessity that sometimes demands immoral policies, and because northern humanists, to whom such claims were detestable, were interested in ways of countering them." In particular, Logan sees More "protesting against nonmoral statecraft" in the *History,* a text which shows a "powerful object lesson in the destructive and self-destructive nature of the pursuit of supposedly expedient immoral policies."[3] Logan's political reading of the *History* rightly acknowledges that More's model for Richard was the Emperor Tiberius from Tacitus's *Annals.*[4] Like More's own *History,* Tacitus's rhetorical historiography renders characters such as Tiberius into figures that become vehicles for describing a tyrant's typological traits or overall character.[5] That Tacitus introduces personality into history through his characterization of political figures and that More follows both Tacitus's and Suetonius's models are important if commonplace

---

Richard III," *PMLA* 58, no. 1 (1943): 38, suggests that More's narrative is "part of the movement from allegory to realism." Elizabeth Story Donno, "Thomas More and *Richard III*," *Renaissance Quarterly* 35, no. 3 (1982): 401–47, thinks the *History* exemplifies a denunciation, or *vituperatio,* the opposite of an encomium. For the resemblance to the exemplarity of medieval morality plays, see Arthur Noel Kincaid, "The Dramatic Structure of Sir Thomas More's *History of Richard III,*" *Studies in English Literature* 12, no. 1 (1972): 223–42. For further discussion of typological characters and allegory, see Alistair Fox, "Archetype and Antitype: *The History of King Richard III, The Four Last Things,*" in *History and Providence,* 75–107. For the moral and political context in terms of More's models, see *CW* 2, lxxx–civ.

3. George M. Logan, *The Meaning of More's Utopia* (Princeton, N.J.: Princeton University Press, 1983), 52–53.

4. Logan, "More on Tyranny: *The History of Richard III,*" in *CCTM,* 181, "the characterization of Richard himself—whose ruling traits, according to More, were dissimulation and a ready willingness to use cruelty to advance his ends—is strikingly similar to Tacitus's portrayal of Tiberius."

5. Quintilian, Tacitus's contemporary, writes of this historiography that it has a "certain affinity to poetry and may be regarded as a kind of prose poem." See Quintilian, *Institutio Oratoria,* trans. H. E. Butler, Loeb Classical Library (Cambridge, Mass.: Harvard University Press, 1922, 1968), X.i.31. The close relationship between rhetoric, poetry, and history is proclaimed by Aristides, cited from Cornelius Tacitus, *The Annals,* trans. A. J. Woodman (Indianapolis: Hackett Publishing, 2004), xviii, who places historians "between orators and poets." See, too, Logan, "More on Tyranny," 176–77.

critical observations, which show how the tyrant acts as a deceiver, playing between an invisible interiority of plots and a public display of civic-mindedness.[6]

Yet Logan's general assessment of the *History* as a distinctly political may be confirmed as well by showing how the *History* develops several political themes advanced in More's Latin and early English poetry.[7] The *History* resonates particularly with More's other writings on the transition from paternal models of kingship to ones in which consent of the governed plays an important role and with More's treatment of the political consequences of fortune.[8] This chapter will show how More's political epigrams provide ideals that his *History* enacts and undermines. Such a pattern of dialogue, I will argue, indicates how More wrote the *History* primarily as a vehicle for thinking through the politics of *utilitas*, a point Erasmus pursues at the same time in the *Julius exclusus*. Erasmus composes and revises *Julius* from 1513 to 1517, with a first edition by 1518, but the text circulates before its publication date; More appears to know it.[9] Of note, Thomas Inghirami, papal orator for Julius II and a man known

6. See CW 2.lxxx–civ. As Sylvester writes of More: "how thoroughly he himself read the *Annals*, especially their first six books, is manifested in the pages of the *Richard*" (xci).

7. I compare More's English and Latin poetry to the Rastell version of the *History* for three reasons: first, the Rastell edition is more complete, including the episodes of the princes' murder, Richard's death, and the Morton conspiracy; second, Rastell claimed that he printed from More's autograph; third, the possibility that the Louvain editors were aggressive in changing their edition of the text. For discussion of textual variants of the *History*, see CW 2. xvii–lix. Finally, "the English version of the History is an utterly exhilarating work, and the most accomplished piece of English prose of the earlier sixteenth century" (Logan, "More on Tyranny," 169).

8. I have not found an article or monograph that focuses just on how the English version of the *History* relates to the political themes of More's poetry despite the fact that both appear to have been written during the same period. On the date of composition of the *History*, critics believe it ought to include a range of years, beginning from 1513, but extending to 1519, to 1527, or, in one singular case, to 1532. See John Guy's "Reluctant Courtier?" in *Thomas More*, 49; Fox, "Archetype and Antitype," 75; Allison Hanham, "The Texts of More's *History of King Richard III*," in *Richard III and His Early Historians, 1483–1535* (Oxford: Oxford University Press, 1975), 217–19. This chapter follows Richard Sylvester, CW 2.lxiii–lxv, who argues for 1514–18, which would mean More may have finished the *History* just as his poems were published. Once we consider that the *History* may have been begun as early as 1513, but in progress for years afterward, its connection to the poems becomes clear. At least part of the *History* was composed during the same period in which More was writing his Latin poems, a collection of which Erasmus would publish in 1518.

9. See CW 15, 263, and commentary on 260/21, 585, which states: "it seems certain that More

for his appeals to *necessitas* and *utilitas publica* to justify Julius's wars, serves as a source for Erasmus's parody.[10] Erasmus's satire of Julius illustrates how coercive, deceptive, pragmatic methods of statecraft render questions of justice into the matter of dark comedy. More and Erasmus, in other words, appear to work on the same problem from different vantage points: Erasmus addresses tyranny in Church politics while More does so in Richard's monarchy; both are concerned about the ramifications of appeals to *necessitas* and *utilitas* and, more generally, an overall vision of politics in which pragmatic concerns for the sake of retaining and expanding power predominate.[11]

Most important, within More's overarching condemnation of tyranny, he suggests a means of amelioration, a reconsideration, in effect, of Erasmus's position against expediency. More's presentation of Cardinal Morton indicates where methods of utility may be used, thereby distinguishing More from both Machiavellian and Erasmian positions on expediency.[12] Such a position may surprise because, as

---

himself knew that Erasmus had written the satire; in fact, even as More tries to dismiss the monk's arguments for Erasmian authorship he avoids making any explicit denial."

10. For the context of Inghirami, see Cathy Curtis, "'The Best State of the Commonwealth': Thomas More and Quentin Skinner," in *Rethinking the Foundations of Modern Political Thought*, ed. Annabel Brett and James Tully (Cambridge: Cambridge University Press, 2006), 108–9.

11. For evidence of More's dislike of tyranny summarized in light of his poetry, *History*, and *Utopia*, see Ewe Baumann, "Thomas More and the Classical Tyrant," *Moreana*, no. 86 (1985): 108-27; for a broader though helpful discussion of tyranny, see W. A. Armstrong, "The Elizabethan Conception of the Tyrant," *Review of English Studies* 22, no. 87 (1946): 161–81.

12. Erasmus writes that if the prince "cannot defend ... [the] kingdom without violating justice," then he should "abdicate." He adds: "Stand fast in your resolve and prefer to be a just man rather than an unjust prince. You can see, that even the greatest kings are not without their crosses if they want to follow the right course at all times, as they should" (*The Education of a Christian Prince*, trans. and ed. Lisa Jardine [Cambridge: Cambridge University Press, 2003], 19–20). Contrarily, Machiavelli writes: "For whoever has appeared good for a time and wishes for his purposes to become wicked ought to do it by due degrees and to conduct himself with opportunities, so that before your different nature takes away old favor from you, it has given you so much new that you do not come to diminish your authority ; otherwise, finding yourself uncovered and without friends, you are ruined" (*Discourses on Levy*, trans. Harvey C. Mansfield and Nathan Tarcov [Chicago: University of Chicago Press, 1998], 1.41). See, too, Machiavelli, *The Prince*, chap. 15.

More did not read Machiavelli, but expediency and deception as political principles were pronounced before Machiavelli became famous for such teachings. See Skinner, *Foundations*, 1:248–54; and Paul Strohm, *Politique: Languages of Statecraft between Chaucer and Shakespeare* (Notre Dame: University of Notre Dame Press, 2005), especially 1–86, for his overall argument

Quentin Skinner observes, "between Erasmus and Machiavelli—writing at the same moment from within the same intellectual tradition—lies the greatest of ethical divides."[13] Yet rather than welcome all forms of expediency in the name of *necessitas* or condemn it wherever a deviation from *honestas* occurs, in the figure of Morton, More allows for a kind of expediency, a practice necessary to remove tyrants such as Richard. Tyrannicide, in short, justifies deception, flattery, and destruction of one's enemies, advertising an accepted area of *utilitas*. If Pico, ultimately, fails to live well, Morton's capacity to manipulate others will earn More's praise. In these contexts, then, More emerges as a political philosopher rather than a translator, rhetor or historian, or Tudor partisan.[14] Indeed, the *History* is crucial in illustrating More's intellectual development from the *Life,* and as I show in the next chapter, the *History* indicates how sections of *Utopia* should be understood.

KING EDWARD IV

The first political ideal More addresses is that of fatherly king in the person of King Edward IV. In the image of a fatherly king, More revisits the central theme advanced in the *Life of Pico*. As love was necessary for a life of true virtue in the *Life,* in Edward communal love emerges as a paragon of perfect rule. Early in the *History,* More

---

and examination variety of texts from 1450 to 1485, which show a "broad contemporary confluence of shrewdly informed, unsentimental writings, keenly concerned with political practice in the world." Strohm rightly declares, "Machiavelli, for all his brilliance, looks less like an inaugurator and more like a participant in a general tendency" (1). Strohm does not consider More's *History,* but his comments on *politique* elaborate well what Logan, in Thomas More, *The History of King Richard III: A Reading Edition,* ed. George M. Logan (Bloomington: Indiana University Press, 2005), xxi, calls the "unfettered *realpolitik*" of Richard's tyranny. For an earlier suggestion of Machiavellian content in More's *History,* see Sylvester at *CW* 2, cii–ciii.

13. Skinner, *Foundations,* 1:250.

14. For a contrary view, see Elton, "More and Cromwell," 152: "People seem to think that More owned a great original mind in affairs and in everything. The one original thing he really did was to produce writings in which a kind of poetic originality expressed itself. This is certainly the case with *Utopia,* in which there is nothing really original in substance, but a great deal of poetic originality in composition.... He was not original in his theology.... He was not original in his scholarship.... His was essentially, and I am not saying this as a term of abuse, an unoriginal mind ... a mind content with things as they were."

describes Edward's final days of reign in near utopian terms: "In which tyme of hys latter daies, thys Realm was in quyet and prosperous estate: no feare of outewarde enemyes, no warre in hande, nor none towarde, but such as no manne looked for: the people towarde the Prynce, not in a constrayned feare, but in a wyllynge and louynge obedyence: amonge them selfe, the commons in good peace" (*CW* 2, 4/25–30).[15] Because Edward's treatment of his people is benevolent, they respond by respecting his rule. Edward rules by the natural affection his people feel toward him as he secures a "wyllynge and louynge obedience" from them. More emphasizes this loving obedience by calling Edward's treatment of the people "soo benygne, courteyse and so familyer." This benevolent king invites the mayor and aldermen of London to his estate "for none other eraunde, but too haue them hunte and bee mery with hym"; he treats them with "familier chere"; he sends venison "frelye into the Citye." When Edward dies, he is said to pass away with the "loue of hys people and theyr entiere affeccion" (5/6–24). Political harmony—freedom from wars abroad and from strife at home—coincides with natural affection of the people for their king and of the king for his people.

The early depiction of Edward corresponds with More's epigrams on the good king. Leicester Bradner and Charles A. Lynch observe that More's unique addition to the genre of epigrams was to include a consideration of political rule in them; "in fact," they write, "we know of no other sixteenth-century poet who used this theme for short poems."[16] Though some of the ideas are commonplaces, the innovation of using epigrams to explore them demonstrates their special importance to More.[17] Besides writing on the theme of love, More's verses examine kingship and tyranny, illustrating and debating the differ-

15. For a modernization of the text, see Logan's edition of *History*.

16. *CW* 3.2, 62.

17. The political importance of the poems is also highlighted by the author's tone. Bradner and Lynch, *CW* 3.2, 62, argue that epigram No. 80, which addresses tyrannicide as revenge for sufferings inflicted by the tyrant upon the innocent, expresses "such bitter and sardonic hatred as to leave no doubt that More is here giving vent to his own emotions."

ences between them. In the epigrams, More distinguishes between king and tyrant: "A king who respects the law differs from cruel tyrants thus: a tyrant rules his subjects as slaves; a king thinks of his as his own children" (*CW* 3.2, 163); and he elaborates in a later poem, "What is a good king? He is a watchdog, guardian of the flock, who by barking keeps the wolves from the sheep. What is the bad king? He is the wolf" (165).[18] For More, the first image of a king, that of father, should include the second, that of guardian; together, they form a paragon of good governance.

In the *Life*, More employs the model of kingship as fatherhood to what he understands as God's beneficent governance of the cosmos. In the verses following More's translation, he includes Pico's prayer, petitioning that, at the moment of death, his soul

> may the finde / o well of indulgence /
> In thi lordeship not as a lorde: but rathir
> As a very tendre louing fathir
> Amen. (*CW* 1, 123/9–12)

The paradox of a lordship without a lord indicates a merciful and loving ruler—a model for earthly kings to imitate. As God rules the universe like a "very tendre louing fathir," a king, too, ought to treat the people like children; for, as More puts it, "a devoted king will never lack children [*liberis*]; he is father to the whole kingdom. And so it is that a true king is abundantly blessed in having as many children [*liberis*] as he has subjects" (*CW* 3.2, 163).[19] Here *liberis* is pun, a word that may translate "children" or "free men," and one that Cathy Curtis finds elsewhere in the same series of epigrams, indicating how free men are like children who enjoy the paternal protection of a father king.[20]

---

18. *Legitimus immanissimis / Rex hoc tyrannis interest. / Seruos tyrannus quos regit, / Rex liberos putat suos* (No. 109, *CW* 3.2, 162); *Quid bonus est princeps? Canis est custos gregis inde / Qui fugat ore lupos. Quid malus? ipse lupus* (No. 115, ibid., 164).

19. *Princeps pius nunquam carebit liberis. / Totius est regni pater. / Princeps abundat ergo felicissimus, / Tot liberis, quot ciuibus* (No. 111, *CW* 3.2, 162).

20. See Curtis, "More and Skinner," 103.

The Latin poems continue the model of fatherly rule applied to human affairs, indicating a relationship of mutual service between king and citizen and therein the achievement of political harmony. As the king looks toward his people's advantage like a father after his children, the people exert themselves on their king's behalf. In a poem entitled, "On the Good King and His People," More describes this relationship:

A kingdom in all its parts is like a man; it is held together by natural affection. The king is the head; the people form the other parts. Every citizen the king has he considers a part of his own body (that is why he grieves at the loss of a single one). The people risk themselves to save the king and everyone thinks of him as the head of his own body. (165)[21]

The first line reads, *totum est unus homo regnum, idque cohaeret amore*, and a more literal translation of *amore* would indicate that a kingdom is not drawn together by "natural affection" but by the more potent power of love. As More privileges "love" as an engine of individual righteous conduct in the *Life*, so, too, political association represents a community of *amor*.

That community of love is explained above by a comparison of the king as head with the people as the body's members, all of whom are bound together by love, an analogy that resembles Paul's discussion of the mystical body of Christ, wherein we find an image of the Church. In 1 Corinthians 12, Paul distinguishes the various gifts of different charisms within the Church received by Christians who together make up an entire body, with Christ as its head. Likewise, the people of a kingdom form various parts of a regime, each performing a separate function within it, as the king considers each group a part of his body politic.[22] Paul follows his discussion of the Church

---

21. *Totum est unus homo regnum, idque cohaeret amore. / Rex caput est, populus caetera membra facit. / Rex quot habet ciues (dolet ergo perdere quenquam) / Tot numerat parteis corporis ipse sui. / Exponit populus sese pro rege putatque / Quilibet hunc proprij corporis esse caput* (No. 112, *CW* 3.2, 164).

22. For other literary representations of charismatic leadership, see Raphael Falco, *Charismatic Authority in Early Modern English Tragedy* (Baltimore: Johns Hopkins University Press, 2000), especially his analysis of Paul's delineation of charisms, 3–9.

with his *hymnus caritati,* indicating that the Church is a community of love, and More makes a similar suggestion in his poem about political life. Kingship patterned after Christ's care of the faithful becomes More's most idealistic expression of how a realm ought to be governed, illustrating a harmony between the Church as *corpus mysticum cuius caput Christus* and *corpus reipublicae mysticum,* a mystical body of the commonweal.[23] More like a covenant than a social contract, *amor* will hold the political community together, an ideal to which More will return in his depiction of Edward's plan for succession. In the figures of fatherhood from More's poetry, he presents a benevolent and protective ruler as the ideal of divine and human governance, which corresponds to the beginning of the *History,* portraying a king after the paternal manner.

Yet as Fox points out, Edward's virtues and the affection he enjoys are transitory.[24] Both before his final days and after his decease, the kingdom is in turmoil. More writes of Edward that "hee was of youthe greatelye geuen to fleshlye wantonnesse," but this "faute not greatlye gryeued the people" because it did not directly affect them; besides, it lessened and "wel lefte" as Edward aged (*CW* 2, 4/19–25). After defending Edward's faults as peccadilloes, More exaggerates them. The harmless picture of Edward's "fleshlye wontonnesse" is undermined by both the *History*'s flashbacks and Buckingham's oration at the Guildhall, wherein we discover that Edward's appetite respected neither the vows of marriage nor the political alliances marriage might represent.[25] In Buckingham's allegations, More shows that Edward's principle of marriage—that no man should be wed against his appetite (63/20–21)—causes civil war, resulting in Edward's temporary

---

23. On these orders, see Ernst Hartwig Kantorowicz, *The King's Two Bodies* (Princeton, N.J.: Princeton University Press, 1997), 207–32.

24. Fox, "Archetype and Antitype," 78–81, points out Edward's lust, ambition, gluttony, responsibility for Clarence's death, and marriage to Elizabeth Grey, noting how More "subjected the didactic simplifications of the humanist view to ironic scrutiny" in undermining Edward as an ideal prince.

25. See *CW* 2.61ff. and 2.72ff. for the episode of King Edward and Dame Grey and Buckingham's speech to the Guildhall.

loss of the throne; even after Edward successfully regains power, Buckingham reminds his audience of the number of women Edward seduced and the resentments such affairs may have incurred. More includes kings who "violate marriages" as a sign of tyrannical character in his *Tyrannicida,* and the abandon with which Edward pursued women may have reminded More of Plato's account of a tyrant, as one whose lustful dreams become realities once power is acquired.[26] The later reports of the effects of Edward's sensuality render the earlier, paternal picture of Edward dubious, and as the question of Edward's sensuality is raised, More presents Edward with a more obvious fault, that of failing to provide for peaceful succession.

In More's account, such a failure creates an opportunity for Richard's future machinations, implying, in the process, that Edward's sensuality is less egregious than his imprudence. More writes that under Edward's rule there exists a "long continued grudge and hearte brennynge betwene the Quenes kinred and the kinges blood" and that Edward worries these two factions will battle for power after his death (9/26–29). Even so, Edward takes few precautionary measures to ensure that a conflict will be avoided after his death. More writes: "Kynge Edwarde in his life, albeit that this discencion beetwene hys frendes sommewhat yrked him: yet in his good health he sommewhat the lesse regarded it, because hee thought whatsoeuer busines shoulde falle betwene them, hymselfe should alwaye bee able to rule bothe the partyes" (10/10–14). At the end of his life, when Edward considers the future of his children, and suspects the political turmoil to which they would be subjected, he calls together those nobles who were "at variaunce" in order to give them words of final instruction (10/26). Rather than offering plans for his son's coronation, or even commanding its completion before his death, Edward's last speech is a homily against "a pestilente serpente" known as "ambicion and desyre of vaineglorye." In addition

26. See More's *Tyrannicida* in *CW* 3.1 at 103 and *The Republic of Plato,* trans. Allan Bloom (New York: Basic Books, 1968), 574d–575b.

to speaking against the evils of desire, Edward recounts other moral commonplaces in highly artistic language, covering generic themes such as how small disputes can grow great through misunderstanding. Edward tells the allies of his wife and those of Richard, "ye neuer had so great cause of hatred, as ye haue of loue" (12/4–25). Edward's explanation of the great cause of love becomes his prominent appeal. In the name of that love "our lorde beareth to vs all," and the love Edward feels for all members of his royal family, he petitions his audience, "from this time forwarde, all grieues forgotten, eche of you loue [the] other" (13/19–21).

Surprisingly, this discourse represents his entire attempt to thwart the future civil strife he foresees. Edward's plan for peaceful succession, like that of Shakespeare's King Lear, is a test of love. In providing Edward with a plan for succession that is based upon charity and forgiveness, More dramatizes the question raised by his poetry. The issue of succession becomes the question of the possibility of fatherly rule. As the question is raised, More provides an answer in describing the response to Edward's speech: "But ye lordes recomforting him with as good wordes as they could, and answering for the time as thei thought to stand with his pleasure, there in his presence (as by their wordes appered) ech forgaue [the] other, & ioyned their hands together, when (as it after appeared by their dedes) their herts, wer far a sonder" (13/26–31). In the character of Edward, and in how the aristocracy responds to him, More indicates that God's ways of governance are not those of men. Even if kings treat the people with the love fathers should feel toward children, the threat of conspiracy remains. As Arthur F. Marotti notes with regard to the later Elizabethan sonnet cycles, the language of "love" often serves as a metaphor for harsher political realities, with terms such as "jealousy" and "hope" indicating political rivals and ambition.[27] As in the poems on fatherhood, the *History* opens with Edward in possession of

27. Arthur F. Marotti, "'Love Is Not Love': Elizabethan Sonnet Sequences and the Social Order," *ELH* 49 (1989): 396–428.

his people's love, but as the narrative progresses, that love becomes a euphemism for managing power. The "love" addressed in More's *Life* and politicized in the Latin poems become an irrelevant standard.

More's poetry again includes the change of theme found in the *History*. More writes of a king's safety: "The stern bodyguard, hired for a pittance, offers no protection, for the guard will serve a new master as he served the old. He will be safe who so rules his people that they judge none other would promote their interests better" (*CW* 3.2, 169).[28] And at Edward's death, More shows how the king failed to reconcile the factions within the aristocracy that only his rule managed to hold together for a time. Edward's lack of prudence provides Richard with the opportunity to divide the aristocracy and, eventually, to use that mistrust and dissent in order to rise in power. More writes of Richard, "hee well wiste and holpe to mayntayn, a long continued grudge and hearte brennynge betwene the Quenes kinred and the kinges blood" (*CW* 2, 9/27–29). Richard thought this division "a fortherlye begynnyng to the pursuite of his intente, and a sure ground for the foundacion of al his building" (10/1–3); that "intente," of course, is to be king, and "his building" represents a plot of usurpation.

If the early portrait of Edward corresponds to More's fatherly ideal of kingship, we should conclude that More takes great care to undermine it, suggesting how Edward's reign contributed to Richard's rise. In More's depiction, either Edward is a good and fatherly king for part of his reign, but that behavior does not suffice for dealing with ambitious subjects like Richard, or when the sentimental glow of his dying days is removed, Edward is never a good king at all; he is indulgent in his sensuality during the early part of reign and naïve at its end. No sooner than Edward dies, Richard and the queen compete to place their allies in positions of influence around the young prince, hoping to use him against their enemies.

28. *Non rigidus uili mercabilis aere satelles / Qui sic alterius fiet ut huius erat. / Tutus erit, populum qui sic regit, utiliorem / Vt populus nullum censeat esse sibi* (No. 120, *CW* 3.2, 168/5–8).

The notion of fatherly rule, then, emerges as an unmet standard. If More's Latin poems propose the ideal, they also contradict it, as More writes, "among many kings there will be scarcely one, if there is really one, who is satisfied to have one kingdom. And yet among many kings there will be scarcely one, if there is really one, who rules a single kingdom well." Significantly, the title of this poem is "On the Lust for Power" (*CW* 3.2, 257).[29] As a transition from the *Life* to the *History*, More indicates how *virtus* and *pietas* cannot coexist with "the lust for power." Erasmus would make a similar point with regard to the papacy. In punning over the title "Pontifex Maximus" Peter calls Julius a "Pestis Maxima" before declaring that if Julius wants to be "Optimus" he must be "holy."[30] Holiness for Erasmus parallels More's *virtus* and *pietas* as aspirations lost in the midst of power struggles, whether in the order of *pontifex maximus* or of *summus imperator*. Like an Erasmian observer of the action, then, More constructs the early narrative of his *History* to reveal the appetites of those in power, independent of how they portray themselves to the people or to fellow aristocrats.

LAW AS SANCTUARY

After Edward's death, Richard exploits the divide within the aristocracy. By instigating quarrels with the Lord Rivers (the brother of Edward's queen, Elizabeth Woodville) and the Lord Marquis (her son), Richard eventually takes possession of England's heir apparent, claiming that the queen's family meant to rule the realm by influencing the prince. Elizabeth responds by seeking sanctuary in the abbot's palace at Westminster, taking her younger son with her. In the meanwhile, through a pretense of responsible concern, Richard convinces the council to name him "protector" of the elder

---

29. *De Cvpiditate Regnandi*, no. 243, *CW* 3.2, 256: *Regibus e multis regnum cui sufficit unum, / Vix Rex unus erit, sit tamen unus erit. / Regibus e multis regnum bene qui regat unum, / Vix tamen unus erit, si tamen unus erit.*

30. "Julius Excluded From Heaven: A Dialogue," in *Collected Works of Erasmus*, vol. 27, trans. Michael J. Heath (Toronto: University of Toronto Press, 1986), 169.

prince. Yet both of Edward's sons, the elder one in Richard's care, and the younger in sanctuary, need to be eliminated for Richard to rise. The problem is that sanctuary allowed fugitives to find safety in any of the chartered churches, which prominently included Westminster Abbey, where Elizabeth fled. Richard's dilemma involves overcoming the laws that privilege sanctuary in order to retrieve the younger prince from his mother, and he will use the accomplished speaker, Buckingham, to achieve his goal.

More's narrative of the sanctuary debate is the longest in the *History* and one of the least understood. John G. Peters rightly observes that most commentators view the breaking of sanctuary as More's attempt to discredit Richard, but the arguments why Richard deserves this judgment often fail to emphasize the history of abuses against sanctuary.[31] Isobel D. Thornley provides the most convincing account in showing that the abuses of sanctuary—such as the protection of criminals, thereby granting them opportunity to commit fresh crimes, sanctuary as a holding place of stolen goods, for forgery of documents and false craftsmen's work, and its protection from taxation—were bitterly resented by laymen of London.[32] Thornley writes that the speeches of Buckingham in the *History* against sanctuary "represent fairly the opinion of all sensible laymen regarding the privilege and its abuse," and the acts of Parliament she cites—from 1377 to 1512—substantiate her view that the privilege of sanctuary was resented.[33] Indeed, the historical evidence of sanctuary's abuse is such that Peter Iver Kaufman declares that More made Buckingham—Richard's unscrupulous advocate— "a man of gentle but telling reason" in arguing that one may without sin take persons from sanctuary.[34] Finally, Thornley and Kaufman's

31. John G. Peters, "Sanctuary in More's *The History of Richard III*," *Moreana* 34, nos. 131–32 (1997): 26.

32. Isobel Thornley, "The Destruction of Sanctuary," in *Tudor Studies*, ed. R. W. Seton-Watson (Freeport, N.Y.: Books For Libraries Press, 1969).

33. Ibid., 186–200. For Henry's opposition to sanctuary abuse in 1519, the year after More entered the king's service, see 201.

34. Peter Iver Kaufman, "Henry VII and Sanctuary," *Church History* 53, no. 4 (1984): 471.

assessment concurs with the position of Pope Innocent VIII's attempts to reduce the abuses of sanctuary, though not to abrogate the privilege, a program of curtailment that Cardinal Morton appears to have pursued in England.[35]

As an undersheriff of London and close associate of Morton, More probably thought the privilege of sanctuary in need of vast reform, and if so, the reason why the sanctuary episode discredits Richard may be found in the overall legal dilemma of who should have custody of the prince and in how More depicts the rise of the tyrant as concomitant with overcoming the laws of the realm. In the debate over sanctuary, More indicates how English common law, natural law, and the prerogatives of the Church should serve as a defense from aspiring despots. So, too, Buckingham's jurisprudential chicanery mirrors Machiavellian ideas of prudence defined as calculation. Buckingham plays the fox more than the lion, providing an example of tyranny that More defined in his poetry as a failure to respect the law.[36]

Buckingham's speech emphasizes three points. First, sanctuary laws are meant to protect the innocent from a viable threat; second, in the absence of that kind of threat, remaining in sanctuary represents an abuse; throughout his oration, Buckingham benefits from a third point, that the council is aware of the political ramifications involved in allowing the younger prince to remain separated from his brother and his brother's protector, Richard. The consequence of the one prince remaining in sanctuary, after all, is that Richard—and his council—appear somehow inadequate for, or even threatening to, the preservation of rightful succession. On each point, Buckingham's speech diverts attention from the pertinent question of Richard's legal claim to be guardian of both princes, providing

35. See Rev. Claude Jenkins, "Cardinal Morton's Register" in *Tudor Studies*, ed. R.W. Seton-Watson (Freeport, N.Y.: Books For Libraries Press, 1969), 40–42, and C.S.L.Davies, "Bishop John Morton, the Holy See, and the Accession of Henry VII," *English Historical Review* 102, no. 402 (1987): 2–30, and 16–19 especially.

36. See No. 109, *CW* 3.2, 162–63.

an example of what Renaissance legal theory condemns as "cavilla-tion" or *cavillatio*, which is "connected with avoidance or attempted avoidance of the law by categories not specifically named in the law." More broadly, however, cavillation "resides in a misuse of language and logic" and results from obvious motives such as serving a cli-ent's interest by misconstruing law.[37]

Thus, for Buckingham, the innocent find sanctuary everywhere. On the question of whether sanctuary laws were designed to pro-tect those who are not in danger, Buckingham says: "For agaynste vnlawful harmes, neuer Pope nor Kynge entended to priueledge anye one place. For that priueledge hath euery place. Knoweth anye manne anye place wherein it is lawefull [for] one manne to dooe an-other wrong? That no manne vnlawfully take hurt, that libertie, the Kynge, the lawe, and verye nature forbiddeth in euery place, and ma-keth to that regarde for euerye manne euerye place a Saintuarye" (*CW* 2, 31/30–32/6). For the innocent, the natural and common law provide protection throughout the realm. The question before the council is whether sanctuary is necessary to protect the innocent from "vnlawful harms." Because the prince is not guilty of any of-fense, so Buckingham reasons, he may enjoy liberty and protection wherever he goes. There can be no sanctuary for those "whose lyfe or libertye can by no lawfull processe stand in ieopardie" (33/13–14). As Richard Sylvester notes, Buckingham here paraphrases an ar-gument that More probably found in Tacitus, where Gaius Cestius claims that although princes are equivalent to deities, the gods lis-ten only to just suppliants.[38] Reworking Cestius's words, Bucking-ham argues that if the prince is just, his cause for sanctuary is not.

If the prince does not need sanctuary, why would Elizabeth wish him to remain there? Buckingham declares the answer less a mat-ter of "womannishe feare" than of "womannishe frowardenesse"

---

37. Ian Maclean's *Interpretation and Meaning in the Renaissance: The Case of Law* (Cam-bridge: Cambridge University Press, 1992), 136–37; see, too, 181–86.

38. See *CW* 2, xcvn4.

(28/19–20). Since there is no threat to the prince, the queen must be using the special prerogative of sanctuary for the purpose of stirring slander against Richard and his council. If the younger brother keeps sanctuary, after all, he must do so out of fear—fear that either Richard or the elder prince wishes him dead. By allowing Elizabeth to keep the younger prince in sanctuary, the council lets her insinuate Richard's corruption. As a result, if she will not hand him over, the child should be removed from sanctuary by force. Buckingham's speech ignores the actual malice of Richard and falsely imputes malice to the queen, thereby presenting Richard's case from fictional premises. Here the false premise of Richard's innocent intentions leads to the conclusion that there is no threat to the prince and that, as a result, there is no need for sanctuary. In More's presentation, then, Buckingham's sophistry becomes inseparable from fraud and eventual murderous usurpation.

The queen's speech in defense of sanctuary rights emerges as a foil to Buckingham. Elizabeth argues that since she is legal guardian, she may place her son in sanctuary, even if he does not desire it. No matter what are her intentions for placing her son in sanctuary, the law gives her the right to do it. Elizabeth says of her son: "he is also my warde, for as my lerned counsell showeth mee, syth he hath nothing by discent holden by knightes seruice, the law maketh, his mother his gardaine" (38/28–30). In making this argument, Elizabeth illustrates two aspects of deliberation wholly absent from the council's decision. First, she references her "lerned counsell," making the decision one of legal right, rather than political intrigue; second, the common law says that since the prince owns no land, the queen is his guardian, and as guardian, she has the right to place her son where she will. Like other possessions lawfully held, she may take her son into sanctuary, or anywhere else. In following the particular law of guardianship, Elizabeth presents a contrary model of law to that of Buckingham. She summarizes that model thus:

Wherfore here intend I to kepe him sins mans law serueth yᵉ gardain to kepe the infant. The law of nature wyll the mother kepe her childe. Gods law pryuelegeth the sanctuary, & the sanctuary my sonne, sith I fere to put hym in the protectours handes that hath hys brother already, and were if bothe fayled, inheritour to the crowne. The cause of my fere hath no man to doe to examine. And yet fere I no ferther than yᵉ law fereth which as lerned men tell me forbiddeth euery man the custody of them, by whose death he may inherite lesse lande then a kingdome. (39/25–33)

Whereas Buckingham articulated platitudes about the natural and common law in claiming that liberty is protected throughout the realm, Elizabeth develops a more sophisticated understanding in which the natural law specifically indicates that the infant should remain with his mother and the common law holds the guardian ought to decide where his or her child should live. It turns out that Buckingham's idea of liberty requires forcibly separating mother from son, legal guardian from child.

Neither may Buckingham justly accuse Elizabeth of abusing the privilege of sanctuary, for she fears for her son's life on the basis of law, not personal grudge. The law in question here "forbiddeth euery man the custody of them, by whose death he may inherite lesse lande then a kingdome." As Sylvester observes, the use of the word "lesse" implies "that the law would forbid such a thing still more stringently where a kingdom would be the inheritance."[39] Because Richard stands to gain so much from the deaths of those who are under his care, he should be disqualified as protector. There is an enormous conflict of interest for Richard. Rather than woman-ish fear or forwardness, More shows that the Queen fears "no fer-ther than yᵉ law fereth." In Elizabeth's speech, More indicates how the question of sanctuary privileges should be decided by lawyers considering the questions of guardianship, the prerogatives of the Church, and the laws regarding Richard's protectorate with respect to his status as third in line to the throne. Though sanctuary abuses

39. See "Commentary" on 39/33 in *CW* 2, 206.

may have been egregious, More's presentation illustrates that Elizabeth's case is not such an abuse.

Yet the debate over sanctuary does not simply indicate More's ideal of how law should be practiced through the position of the Queen. Instead of using the entirety of the sanctuary episode to display a prescriptive teaching enacted by paradigmatic rulers, More offers a negative exemplum in Buckingham, whose actions embody the Machiavellian dictum that princes should assume the nature of a "fox" and "be a great hypocrite and deceiver," illustrating a realism detached from moral consideration.[40] In More's presentation of the sanctuary debate, the council members agree with Buckingham not out of fear for their own safety, but because they personally believe that the prince will be safe outside of sanctuary; in effect, they substitute their own judgment for that of the law. More writes of the impact of Buckingham's words that "the temporall menne whole, and a good part of the spirituall also, thinking none hurt erthly ment towarde the younge babe, condescended in effecte, that if he were not deliuered, he should be fetched" (33/20–23). More's presentation of the "temporall" and "spirtuall" men again resonates with Machiavelli, who observes, "men are so simple, and so obedient to present necessity, that he who deceives will always find one who will let himself be deceived";[41] thus, a crafty prince, or an aspiring protector, may dupe men in order to acquire power. In this way, Buckingham's success here—similar to his later performance at the Guildhall—enacts a Machiavellian understanding of a prince's ability to deceive his followers. Where Erasmus focuses on the "evil genius" of Julius, More attends to the immoral possibilities of calculation and persuasion.

Again, More's poetry provides a helpful point of contrasting context. In epigram 121, the consent of the people *(populus consen-*

---

40. Niccolo Machiavelli, *The Prince*, trans. Leo Paul de Alvarez (Long Grove, Ill.: Waveland Press, 1980), 108. More's Buckingham here represents a continuation of what Paul Strohm refers to as a pre-Machiavellian moment, which redefines *politique* behavior from prudent concern for the common good to "those who employ lies, deceptions, and even falsely sworn oaths as possible elements of good political practice" (*Politique*, 5).

41. *Prince*, 108.

tiens) gives sovereignty *(regnum)* and may take it away; hence kings or princes are fundamentally powerless *(impotentes principes)* and should not be proud because they rule "merely on sufferance" (*CW* 3.2, 169).[42] In epigram 198, More elaborates by asking which is the better form of government, a monarchy or a senate. Here More observes that the people, as a result of *consilium* or reasonable consent, elect a senator, as opposed to the blind chance that puts a king on the throne through birthright (229–31).[43] In epigram 121, the people's consent may serve as a check to the pride of kings, and in 198 More privileges *consilium.* The poems' emphasis on reasonable agreement and accountability to the populace indicate checks against a ruler's ambition in favor of communal deliberation.[44] As Gerard Wegemer argues, More associated especially law with public deliberations about the pursuit of justice.[45] Yet the sanctuary debate shows how assemblies or councils may not reveal a plethora of reasonable options for a virtuous ruler to consider but, instead, provide opportunities for sophists, a point similar to the one Hythloday makes with regard to the problem of counsel in More's concurrent project of *Utopia*'s first book.[46] In making such an acknowledgement, More presents a low estimation of the capacity of clergy and aristocrats to discern a prudent political course of action. On the basis of persuasion, the council charts a new trajectory of power that the rest of the narrative reveals as tragic. After Buckingham gains the princes,

42. *Quicunque multis uir uiris unus praeest, / Hoc debet his quibus praeest. / Praeesse debet neutiquam diutius / Hi quam uolent quibus praeest. / Quid impotentes principes superbiunt? / Quod imperant precario?*(No. 121, *CW* 3.2, 168). The title is *Popvlvs Consentiens Regnvm Dat Et Avfert.*

43. *Alter ut eligitur populo, sic nascitur alter. / Sors hic caeca regit, certum ibi consilium* (No. 198, *CW* 3.2, 228/12–13).

44. In More's own public career, he might have hoped that public deliberations would replace monarchical absolutism; his own efforts as speaker of the House of Commons were to procure free speech for parliament. See Gerard B. Wegemer, *Thomas More on Statesmanship* (Washington, D.C.: The Catholic University of America Press, 1996), 65–67, who discusses how More viewed free speech as intrinsic for providing "right substantial counsel" to kings and senates alike.

45. See Gerard Wegemer, "The Civic Humanism of Thomas More: Why Law Has Prominence over Rhetoric," *Ben Jonson Journal* 7 (2000): 186–98.

46. For discussion of Hythloday on counsel, see chapter 3 of this volume.

More shows that Richard "opened himself more boldly" in his plans to usurp the throne, making the sanctuary episode one that occurs before Richard's more audacious ploys and the turning point in his rise to power and (42/25–26).

MORTON AND FORTUNE

More's depiction of Buckingham may be viewed as an elaboration of Richard's general style of leadership, but both Richard's and Buckingham's cunning mirrors More's presentation of Cardinal Morton. Unlike More's continual denunciations of Richard's ploys, the presentation of Morton includes praise, though the difference between Richard's and Morton's political maneuvering remains ambiguous.

More, after all, ascribes the demise and eventual death of Richard III to the actions of Morton, his own teacher, rather than to fortune or providence, advertising a political realm of human rather than divine agency. Morton encourages Buckingham to rebel against Richard and, though Buckingham fails, Morton later allies with Henry Tudor to succeed.[47] More's *History* does not show Henry Tudor's ascent; instead, it remains unfinished, concluding with Morton's manipulation of Buckingham.

Morton, then, may represent another version of More's crafty politician, a statesman who recognizes the importance of expediency but employs it within certain confines.[48] More writes that Morton "hadde gotten by greate experience ye verye mother & maistres of wisdom, a depe insighte in politike worldli driftes" (*CW* 2, 91/19–21). That "greate experience" makes Morton an apt manipulator; he was, More tells us, "lacking no wise waies to win fauor" (90/23). As

---

47. Charles Ross, *Richard III* (Berkeley: University of California Press, 1981), 113, writes of the intrigues between Buckingham, the queen-dowager, Henry Tudor, and Margaret Beaufort, "the master-mind behind the entire plan may well have been the wily John Morton, bishop of Ely."

48. Wegemer, *Thomas More on Statesmanship*, 7, 70–71, argues that evidence for a negative assessment of such methods may be found in More's statement on Morton's final days. Morton's "godly" death is stated as a change from how he had lived. Here Morton may represent to the *History* what Pico did in the *Life*, a representation of goodness that includes serious flaws.

Morton perceives that his captor, Buckingham, is proud and envious of Richard's power, Morton "craftelye sought yᵉ waies to pricke him forwarde taking alwaies thoccasion of his coming & so keping himself close wᵗin his bondes, that he rather semed him to follow hym then to lead him" (91/25–93/2). Buckingham, who manipulates the sanctuary debate, is now manipulated himself.

Morton does reference the "secret judgments" of God's providence, whereby Edward is replaced by Richard, but rather than abide by them, Morton tempts Buckingham to defy them. Morton says: "Howebeit if yᵉ secrete iudgement of god haue otherwise prouided: I purpose not to spurne againste a prick, nor labor to set vp that god pulleth down. And as for the late proctector & now kyng" (92/12–14). Morton continues no further, but the suggestion takes effect, as More records, "Then longed the duke sore to here what he would haue sayd, because he ended with yᵉ king & there so sodeinly stopped …" (92/17–18). That sudden stop represents feigning an unfinished thought, what Thomas Wilson calls "A Stop, or Half Telling of a Tale." It happens "when we break off our tale before we have told it."[49] Such a "half telling" George Puttenham calls *aposiopesis,* or an "auricular figure of defect"; it occurs when "we begin to speak a thing and break off in the middle way, as if either it needed no further to be spoken of, or that we were ashamed or afraid to speak it out."[50] Morton, in other words, employs the manipulative speech of a courtier.[51]

After these suggestive stops, Buckingham petitions Morton to give him "faithful secret aduise and counsayle," as More juxtaposes the secret judgments of God's providence to the secret counsel Morton will offer Buckingham by way of conspiracy (92/22). Morton then shares his mind with Buckingham, telling him that "it might yet haue pleased Godde for the better store, to haue geuen

49. Thomas Wilson, *The Art of Rhetoric* (1560), ed. Peter E. Medine (University Park: Pennsylvania State University Press, 1994), 205.

50. George Puttenham, *The Art of English Poesy: A Critical Edition*, ed. Frank Whigham and Wayne A. Rebhorn (Ithaca, N.Y.: Cornell University Press, 2007), 250.

51. On the courtier's art, see ibid., 378–86.

him [Richard] some of suche other excellente virtues mete for the rule of a realm, as our lorde hath planted in the parsone of youre grace" (93/22–25). By directing Buckingham's thoughts toward usurpation, More writes that Morton's "wisedom abused his [Buckingham's] pride to his [Morton's] own deliueraunce & the dukes destruccion" (90/21–22).

"Abusive wisdom" poses a paradox. Morton acts in an ostensibly virtuous way in opposing Richard, yet he employs methods similar to those of the tyrant he seeks to remove. More, however, maintains an ethical difference between the two, suggesting a distinction he may have discovered in reading Cicero. The Ciceronian context is an important one because, as Jennifer Richards reminds us, the meaning of the word "honest" is complicated in the period by attempts to translate and understand Cicero's *honestas*. Following *De Officiis*, "honesty" includes moderation, decency, and decorum (*Oxford English Dictionary*, meaning 2). Such an understanding differs from "straightforward speaking," a notion already emerging in the sixteenth century (*Oxford English Dictionary*, meaning 3d).[52] For Cicero, *honestas* in regard to speech is part of a moral virtue in which moderation and an economy of truth are directed toward justice; to be honest here means to be prudent, knowing how to speak, when to do so, what to address, and what to withhold, given audiences and the speaker's objectives.[53] Erasmus concurs, writing of St. Paul in *De libero arbitrio* that the apostle "knew the difference between what things are lawful and what are expedient. It is lawful to speak the truth; it is not expedient to speak the truth to everybody at the same time and in every way."[54]

52. Jennifer Richards, *Rhetoric and Courtliness in Early Modern Literature*, (Cambridge: Cambridge University Press, 2003), 27–28. See 21–64 for an introduction to "honesty" in the period.

53. Cicero, *De Officiis*, trans. Walter Miller (Cambridge, Mass.: Harvard University Press, 1975), I.xxvii.93–xxviii.99. Hereafter abbreviated as *De Off.*

54. *De libero arbitrio* in *Luther and Erasmus: Free Will and Salvation*, ed. and trans. E. Gordon Rupp with A. N. Marlow, Library of Christian Classics 17 (London: SCM Press, Ltd., 1969), 40–41.

Morton, however, goes beyond mere withholding or an economics of truth; he directs others through misdirection. Erasmus would not have approved with what More calls an appeal to Buckingham's pride, in effect, a form of flattery. Morton's suggestive "stops" constitute the mark of what Erasmus calls "the most pernicious flatterers of all," who are "those who operate with apparent frankness but in some remarkable way contrive to urge you on while seeming to restrain you."[55] Cicero uses similar language of condemnation, writing that of all forms of injustice "none is more flagrant than that of the hypocrite who, at the very moment when he is most false, makes it his business to appear virtuous."[56]

Yet Cicero's condemnation of dissimulation is not all encompassing, and his distinctions between noble and expedient actions are less than perfectly clear.[57] In *De Oratore*, Cicero suggests that prudence must navigate between courses of *honestas* and *utilitas:* "it is disputed whether the chief consideration should be integrity [*honestati*] or expediency [*utilitati*].... But in both departments it is of the greatest importance to inquire what is possible and what is impossible of achievement, and also what is inevitable [*necesse*] or the reverse."[58] Those words compare well to Machiavelli's advice that the prince "have a mind so disposed that he can turn as the winds of fortune and the variations of things command him; and, as has been said above, not to depart from the good, if he is able, but to know how to enter the bad, when necessitated to do so." The difference is that Cicero redescribes "the bad" as "inevitable" in the case of tyrannicide and therefore in accordance with *honestas;* Machia-

55. Erasmus, *Education of a Christian Prince,* 57.

56. *De Off.,* I.xiii.41.

57. On dissimulation in service of the republic, see the example of Solon in *De Off.,* I.xxx.108. On Socratic jesting or irony, see Cicero, *De Oratore,* trans. E. W. Sutton and H. Rackham (Cambridge, Mass.: Harvard University Press), II.lxvii.269–270.

58. *De Oratore,* II.lxxxii.335–337. Compare the passage quoted above to Machiavelli, *Prince,* 109: "It is needful that he [the prince] have a mind so disposed that he can turn as the winds of fortune and the variations of things command him; and, as has been said above, not to depart from the good, if he is able, but to know how to enter the bad, when necessitated to do so."

velli employs a more comprehensive formulation. Dissimulation applied to an unjust end, then, better qualifies Cicero's condemnation of "flagrant hypocrisy" because deception practiced for the sake of a tyrannicide would be licit.

Indeed, in *De Officiis* Cicero defines tyrannicide as just because "we have no ties of fellowship with a tyrant .... as certain members are amputated, if they show signs themselves of being bloodless and virtually lifeless and thus jeopardize the health of the other parts of the body, so those fierce and savage monsters in human form should be cut off from what may be called the body of humanity."[59] That deception would be necessary for a successful conspiracy against a tyrant seems tautological. Dissimulation belongs to the nature of conspiracy, and conspiracy remains an essential part of tyrannicide. Hence, deception would not triumph over moral rectitude because in the case of tyrannicide "moral rectitude has gone hand in hand with expediency" [*honestas utilitatem secuta est*].[60] And for Cicero, the nobility of tyrannicide is architectonic: "what more atrocious crime can there be than to kill a fellow-man, and especially an intimate friend? But if anyone kills a tyrant—be he never so intimate a friend—he has not laden his soul with guilt, has he? The Roman People, at all events, are not of that opinion; for of all glorious deeds they hold such an one to be the most noble [*pulcherrimum*]."[61]

Morton's "abusive wisdom," then, constitutes a deceptive rhetoric aimed at a good end of tyrannicide, which thereby reconfigures conventional expectations about *honestas*. In all problems where duty and expediency ostensibly clash, recommends Cicero, "we have to determine what moral duty is, as it varies with varying circumstances."[62] The question—what arises if the moral duty of tyrannicide requires unseemly means?—cannot be answered in *De Officiis* because questionable means cease to be so in the particular end of tyrannicide, a teaching that now appears similar to Machiavellian at-

---

59. *De Off.*, III.vi.32
61. Ibid., III.iv.19.

60. Ibid., III.iv.19; cf. I.xliv.159–160.
62. Ibid., III.vi.32.

tention to "ends" instead of "means."[63] Some ends, at least, require extraordinary means. Like Cicero might have done, More favors Morton's dissimulation and "abuse" of Buckingham unto "destruction" and yet condemns Richard's deceit and murders; that is because in the removal of tyrants the way of the fox constitutes dutiful behavior. Morton may possess Ciceronian *honestas* and be dishonest.[64]

Morton's brand of just expediency, though, once again contrasts with the teaching of More's poetry. One may approach the dangerous and changing nature of political life as Morton did or allow fortune to rule. In a poem titled "Death Unassisted Kills Tyrants," More comforts those that were abused by the hands of "unjust men" by invoking fortune:

> You who have been cruelly persecuted at the hands of unjust men, no matter who you are, take hope. Let kindly hope alleviate your sufferings. A turn of fortune will improve your state—like the sun shining through scattered clouds—or the defender of liberty. Death, touched by pity, will put forth her hand, while the tyrant rages, and rescue you. Death will snatch him away too (the more to please you) and will lay him right before your feet. (*CW* 3.2, 145)[65]

A turn of fortune can be like the sun bursting through clouds; it makes death a source of hope. Turned into a servant of fortune, death will set free those who are suffering from tyranny, and, in revenge of the innocent, death will come for the tyrant.

More would seem to emphasize the teaching of his poem by nar-

63. Machiavelli's formulation is that "it is necessary for a prince, if he wishes to maintain himself, to learn to be able to be not good, and to use it and not use it according to the necessity" (*Prince*, 93).

64. As Quintillian writes against those who allege that rhetoric "makes use of vices" in "speaking falsehoods and exciting emotions": "Neither of these is disgraceful when it is done for a good reason.... To tell a lie is something occasionally allowed even to the wise man; and for rousing emotions, the orator is bound to do this if the judge cannot be brought to give a fair judgment by other means" (*The Orator's Education*, vol. 1, ed. and trans. Donald A. Russell [Cambridge, Mass.: Harvard University Press, 2001], II.xvii.27–28).

65. *Duriter es quicunque uiris oppressus iniquis, / Spem cape, spes luctus leniat alma tuos. / Versilis in melius uel te Fortuna reponet, / Vt solet excussa nube nitere dies. / Aut libertatis uindex frendente tyranno, / Eruet iniecta mors miserata manu. / Auferet haec (quo plus tibi gratificetur) et illum, / Afferet atque tuos protinus ante pedes* (No. 80, *CW* 3.2, 144/1–9). The title is *Sola Mors Tyrannicida Est.*

rating the deaths of the princes and Richard in quick succession. First, the princes are jailed and guarded by likely assassins, after which time the elder prince never tied his laces, nor took care of himself, "but with that young babe hys brother, lingered in thought and heauines til this tratorous death, deliuered them of that wretchednes." Next, More describes how Miles Forest and John Dighton, upon orders from Richard, came upon the children at midnight and so "wrapped them and entangled them keping down by force the fetherbed and pillowes hard vnto their mouthes, that within a while smored and stifled, theyr breath failing, thei gaue vp to god their innocent soules into the ioyes of heauen " (CW 2, 85/8–23).[66] Such vivid description parallels the sudden fast-forward to the grisly images of Richard's ultimate demise, which immediately follows the episode of the princes' murder. More writes of King Richard: he was "slain in the fielde, hacked and hewed of his enemies handes, haryed on horsebacke dead, his here in despite torn and togged lyke a cur dogge" (87/5–6). The pathos that More evokes in both scenes of death may not be merely striking, but also indicative of his political thought. Rather than an instrument of fear wielded in the hands of a tyrant, death becomes a weapon against him, an ally upon which the persecuted may rely. As Fox suggests, fortune's changing ways transform into a figure for the slow machinations of time and justice. Behind fortune is the finger of God.[67]

Yet again, if fortune rights injustices, it may also wrong the innocent; as such, it seems a poor metaphor for God's agency in human affairs. It is for this reason that More turns to the figure of Morton. Instead of following the medieval commonplace of fortune, More shows fortune in light of man's capacity to manage events, turning them, as More surely judged the results of Morton's actions, toward better prospects. Although More may have viewed fortune as a trope for God's providence in his poetry, in the *History* More con-

---

66. On the controversy of the princes, see Ross, *Richard III*, 96–104.
67. Fox, "Archetype and Antitype," 95–100.

sidered fortune more like its description in *The Prince:* as a raging
river whose damaging effects may be mitigated by strong embank-
ments.[68]

Indeed, in *Tyrannicida*, More juxtaposes two means of removing a tyrant: the first is wrought by fortune and the gods, but the
second refers to a "resourceful man," one who is "able in stratagem
rather than in force; one who knows how to lay ploys, hide his traps,
make the most of opportunities." Only the resourceful man is worthy of praise. Prudential means, in other words, surpass the fortune
praised in More's poetry. More writes: "If one who has undertaken
a business of this sort attacks the tyrant himself by means of some
clever stratagem, overpowers him when attacked, and slays him
when overpowered, and does not desist from his work, once begun,
until it is finished—this man may boldly demand the reward for tyrannicide" (*CW* 3.1, 109/28–37). A "turn of fortune" may improve
"fate," but "clever stratagem" provides less uncertain means.

More's declamation is an *argumentum fictum,* but the corollary
between More's depiction of a stratagem versus chance is in his presentation of Morton and Hastings. Morton is the resourceful man,
deserving credit for his wiles, whereas Hastings represents the general results of all those who trust in fortune. Hours before Hastings
is falsely accused of treason and condemned to death by Richard,
More writes of him that he "was neuer merier nor neuer so full of
good hope in his life." So impressive is Hastings's confidence in his
own innocence and in his friendship with Richard that More's narrator confesses, "I shall rather let anye thinge passe me, then the
vain sureti of a mans mind so nere his deth" (*CW* 2, 51/10–14). In
fact, More proceeds to describe all the instances of Hastings's blindness to danger. Whether in explicit warnings from his friend, the
Lord Stanley, or by insinuations of danger from the man who accompanies him to meet Richard, Hastings disregards everything that

68. Compare More's treatment of fortune to Machiavelli, *The Prince,* 146–50.

ought to have made him cautious. When Richard condemns Hastings to death, More breaks into the account to deliver this epitaph
on Hastings: "O good god, the blindnes of our mortall nature, when
he most feared, he was in good suerty: when he rekened him self
surest, he lost his life, & that wᵗin two howres after." Hastings is a
man "very faithful, & trusty ynough, trusting to much" (52/14–22).
Though Hastings does not plot against Richard, his character illustrates how a change of fortune corresponds with a gullible disposition found within human nature.

Hastings and Morton, then, provide two opposing replies to fortune. In Morton's eventual success, More emphasizes stratagem,
following what Skinner identifies as a humanist pattern of thought,
beginning with the Florentine histories of the fourteenth century,
wherein "the idea of equating Fortune with Providence and treating
it as a lawlike force ... begins to give way to a sense that Fortune
amounts to little more than chance, and to a corresponding sense
that human responsibility and choice play a far greater role in the
flux of events than earlier historians had supposed."[69] Such an understanding of fortune is why Morton, a wise man with knowledge
of the "deep drifts" of political affairs, may help to remove a tyrant
such as Richard, as the virtue of prudence now appears to monitor
and control unfortunate developments of fortune.[70] In the figure of
Morton, More illustrates what Erasmus would not: a wedding of utility and nobility through deceptive means, which is a rare though
necessary posture to rebuke the advances of an evil *fortuna* in the
form of a tyrant.[71]

69. Quentin Skinner, *Foundations*, 1:97; see also 94–112 for a general discussion of fortune.
On fortune and a pre-Machiavellian moment, see Strohm, *Politique*, 1–5, 90–104, 114–16.

70. Strohm, *Politique*, 115, writes, "a flood of fifteenth- and sixteenth-century commentaries
and treatises—many prior to or independent of the influence of Machiavelli, who in this sense
may be seen less as an innovator and more as a exemplar of a general tendency—effect a sever-
ance of God's purveiaunce on the one hand and the exercise of practical and wordly decision
making on the other."

71. Erasmus does advocate "benign deception" in his *Education*, but he qualifies it as tool
for those in power, not for those who seek to unseat others in power, adding that such deception
should be used only "if the people are obstinate and resist what is to their own advantage" (73).

AGAIN: WHY A HISTORY?

In answer to Pollard's problem, mentioned at the beginning, More's "motive of conception," I have used the context of More's poetry to examine the *History*. In each case, More's poetry presents an ideal—kingship as fatherhood, kingship bestowed by enlightened consent, governance by deliberative assembly, and fortune as a means of distributing justice—that the *History* enacts and undermines or qualifies. Where kings should rule like fathers, they are rapacious, or imprudent. Though consent of the governed should provide a forum for communal deliberations, it may invite the opportunity for sophistry instead, for Buckingham is "neither vnlearned, and of nature marueilouslye well spoken" (69/8–9). If providence should govern affairs through fortune, men of cunning appear to be able to manipulate events to their liking. Imaginatively constructing past events to better suit his own purpose, More appropriated the rumors and facts of Richard's reign into a narrative meant to raise the same questions about political life he attempted to think through in his poetry.[72]

As a work that follows the *Life*, the *History* indicates how the ideals we have seen More uphold—*scientia, virtus,* and *pietas*—may be transformed by self-interested politics. Where power remains the ultimate horizon, learning becomes applied only with reference to *utilitas, virtus* begins to resemble Machiavellian *virtù,* and *pietas* becomes a subject for dark humor. In imagining history so, More represented aspects of political rule that he may have considered as ancient as the Roman emperors in whom he found his models, but that we may understand as part of his emerging realism about political life.

---

72. There were stories of Richard's tyranny in circulation before the *History* was ever composed. See Michael Hicks, "The Making of a Monster" in *Richard III: The Man behind the Myth* (London: Collins and Brown, 1991), 142–60.

3

SI MORO CREDIMUS
The "Dialogue of Counsel" in *Utopia,* ca. 1516

Given the political limitations the *History* demonstrates, the question of More's ideas of social reform appears best addressed in the debate over counsel from book 1 of *Utopia* rather than in the revolutionary ideas of an ideal regime like the kind Hythloday describes.[1] Because of the appetite of kings for power, unless a courtier abides in Utopia, reform will be of an incremental and prudential nature, consisting of modest measures like the kind More proposes at the end of book 1. In this crucial part of the text, which J. H. Hexter refers to as the "dialogue of counsel," More ostensibly provides his own statement of political philosophy, a principle of accommodation and compromise.[2] In challenging Hythloday, More advocates an "in-

This chapter expands upon and revises my earlier "Humanist Lawyer, Public Career: Thomas More and Conscience," *Moreana* 46, no. 176 (June 2009): 77–96.

1. No other text by More is as contested as *Utopia,* and critical commentary illustrates the "humanist More" referred to in my introduction. In such studies, More becomes an Aristotelian, Platonist, or Augustinian; a reformer or a medievalist; an ancient or a modern. See Fox, *History and Providence,* 50. For a survey of criticism on *Utopia* with reference to the question of More as a social reformer, see Guy, *Thomas More,* 84–105. For analysis of recent critical studies, see George Logan, "Interpreting Utopia: Ten Recent Studies and the Modern Critical Traditions," *Moreana* 31 (1984): 203–58.

2. For an introduction to the problem of counsel in the period, see John Guy, "The Henri-

direct approach," which is part of "another philosophy," a method More claims is better suited to politics because of its practical benefit. Accommodation to the realities of court assuages evils rather than solving them, but the latter is impossible, given imperfect humanity (*CW* 4, 99/1–101/4). As is often remarked, book 1's statement of compromise, the English context of its examples, and the method of dialogue it employs provide a counterpoint to the second book's principled monologue of Hythloday on the imaginary Utopians.³ The character of *Morus* or "More" in the dialogue of counsel and Raphael's monologues within book 2 represent competing, starkly contrasting, approaches to politics.

To seek one Thomas More in the question of humanist social reform, this chapter will investigate how the "More" of the dialogue represents the author's own position.⁴ Apart from the implications of the *History* for why the modest approach of "More" from the dialogue should be privileged, there are excellent biographical reasons for doing so. Hexter shows that More wrote *Utopia* in two segments: book 2 is first, written during More's mission to the Netherlands, from early May to late October 1515, and the majority of book 1 follows, including the dialogue of counsel, which More writes upon his return to England and up to the point when he sends the manuscript to Erasmus in September 1516. That very same year Henry VIII offers More a pension, and by 1518 More accepts a position on the privy council. The passages in which More most directly under-

---

cian Age," in *The Varieties of British Political Thought, 1500–1800*, ed. J.G.A.Pocock, Gordon J.Schochet, and Lois G.Schwoerer (Cambridge: Cambridge University Press, 1996), 13–22.

3. Richard Sylvester, "'Si Hythlodaeo Credimus': Vision and Revision in Thomas More's *Utopia*," in *EA*, 290, goes further, writing that "a conservative school" favors book 1 and a "radical" interpretation privileges book 2.

4. Because I side with "More" in the dialogue and identify a practical agenda for reform in equity, book 2, by implication, is not a serious statement of systemic political reforms. For a short bibliography on the question of *Utopia* as "ideal" or "idyll," see Skinner, *Foundations*, 1:257n1. Of more recent commentary, the case against taking book 2 as a serious program of reform is best made in T.S.Dorsh, "Sir Thomas More and Lucian: An Interpretation of Utopia," *Archiv fur das Studium der Neueren Sprachen und Literaturen* 203 (1967): 345–63; Gerard Wegemer, "*Utopia* 2: Augustinian Realist," in *More on Statesmanship*, 128–49; and Peter Iver Kaufman's "Utopia?" in *Incorrectly Political*, 153–84.

mines Hythloday's refusals to serve, then, are all later additions, including the conclusion to book 2.[5] Hexter, in effect, proposes what George Logan calls a "thoroughly disintegrative" reading by dividing the books according to the times in which they were written.[6] Such a division, though, accurately reconstructs the dialogue as a dilemma Thomas More addresses himself, at the age of thirty-eight: whether or not he should become a councilor.[7] More's final answer to that question is known, of course. As John M. Headley writes, when "More" claims the ship of state cannot be abandoned, "Morus becomes Thomas More," a humanist who will enter royal service despite its perils.[8]

Even so, how may the dialogue reveal how More approached this decision? The existential context, after all, contributes nothing to how More reasons through the question of counsel. So, too, the question of whether or not More was reluctant or eager to join the king's service has proven controversial.[9] Why did More decide to serve Henry VIII, especially if Erasmus opposed it? Traditionally, More has been viewed as a reluctant councilor; Elton, however, portrayed More as enthusiastic to serve.[10] Indeed, recent and perspicacious commentaries by Quentin Skinner, George Logan, and

5. Hexter incorporates the insights of his earlier *More's Utopia: The Biography of an Idea* (Westport, Conn.: Greenwood Press, 1976) into his introductory section to *CW* 4; see, too, Hexter, "Thomas More and the Problem of Counsel," in *Quincentennial Essays on St. Thomas More*, ed. Michael J. Moore (Albany, N.Y.: Appalachian State University, 1978).

6. Logan, *The Meaning of More's Utopia*, 15. Hexter, however, writes: "The greatness of a book which does this lies not in its harmony but in its intensity" (*CW* 4, xxvii).

7. For Hexter on how the offer of royal service moved More, see *CW* 4, xxxiii–xli.

8. John M Headley, "The Problem of Counsel Revisited: More, Castiglione and the Resignation of Office in the Sixteenth Century," *Moreana* 40, nos. 153–54 (2003): 104. For the argument that More decided to enter the King's service in 1516, see Jerry Mermel, "Preparations for a Political Life: Sir Thomas More's Entry into the King's Service," *Journal of Medieval and Renaissance Studies* 7 (1977): 53–66. Mermel's case indicates how New Critical divisions between author More and character "Morus" on the question of service are implausible.

9. Elton proposed that More had lied to Erasmus about when he joined the king's service as councilor, an accusation refuted by Guy, *Thomas More*, 42–61; on More's entry to court, Guy believes the traditional accounts seem more accurate. See Stapleton, *Illustrious Martyrdom*, 76–77 and Chambers, *Thomas More*, 154–56.

10. For a review of this question, see Yoshinori Suzuki, "Thomas More's View of Politics as a Profession," *Moreana* 24, no. 93 (1987): 29–40.

Brendan Bradshaw situate the dialogue in a humanist context of competing *otium* and *negotium*, but with different appraisals of what More means to emphasize.[11]

This chapter first addresses the positions of Skinner and of Logan with reference to what we have already discovered in the *Life of Pico* and the *History of Richard III*. In this way, I will challenge both the notion of More as neo-Roman in Skinner's sense and Logan's idea of More as a political philosopher after the model of Plato especially. Afterward, I will elaborate upon Bradshaw's defense of More's position from the dialogue, but in terms of how More as lawyer and judge envisioned practical reforms. Bradshaw assumes and argues from the importance of authorial intention, yet he isn't interested in detailing More's legal career, advertising a context of authorial intention that too many ignore. As John Guy notes, More's legal and commercial work between 1510 and 1517 was already "at least a limited form of commitment to a career in politics."[12]

In regard to More's legal work especially, I will show how attention to More's understanding of jurisprudence demonstrates his belief in the interrelation of equity with the virtue of prudence and the art of rhetoric, a teaching that may be located in the dialogue itself. As eventual chancellor of the realm, of course, More would become responsible for the Chancery and the Star Chamber courts, which employed the principle of equity or conscience, a standard and a coercive power that enabled judges to apply the sometimes ambiguous common law to particular cases.[13] That later practice of equitable jurisdiction, however, would agree with the philosophical understanding of equity More had already learned in his study of rhetoric and

---

11. Brendan Bradshaw, "More on *Utopia*," *Historical Journal* 24, no. 1 (1981): 1–27; Logan, *Meaning*, and "*Utopia* and Deliberative Rhetoric," *Moreana* 31, nos. 118–19 (1994): 103–20; Quentin Skinner, "Thomas More's *Utopia* and the Virtue of True Nobility," in *Visions of Politics*, vol. 2: *Renaissance Virtues* (Cambridge: Cambridge University Press, 2007), 213–44 and *Foundations*, 1:217–18, 222–24, 233, 246, 255–62.

12. Guy, *Thomas More*, 58.

13. "Equity" and "conscience" are used interchangeably during this period. See J. H. Baker, *An Introduction to English Legal History*, 4th ed. (London: Butterworths Tolley, 2002), 105–8.

formulated in his *Utopia*. The dialogue of counsel, in fact, does reveal how and why More, ultimately, decided in favor of service to the king for himself, indicating and particularizing "not the way of declamation but the way of calculation" and "job-oriented" rather than "status-oriented" service (lxxxv). For More, such a decision to serve was obviously existential, but the reasons and analysis by which More came to his decision were informed by a political philosophy of accommodation, and that philosophy, conversely, encompassed his personal experience of studying the law.

MULTIPLE *MORI*: SKINNER, LOGAN, BRADSHAW

Let us return to the Mores of Skinner, Logan, and Bradshaw. The contrasts and agreements between these three readers particularly illustrate the "humanist More" approach I describe in my introduction. Skinner, Logan, and Bradshaw all recognize the dialogue's relevance to the author's own dilemma of whether or not to serve, yet each considers the question within the context of humanist philosophy. For Skinner, More follows Cicero, favoring *negotium* over *otium*, wedding *officia* with *virtus*, "restating the case for a humanist ideal to which the courts of northern Europe were proving increasingly inhospitable."[14] "More" represents the ideal of civic self-government based upon an active and educated citizenship, making authorial More an eager and willing councilor. Logan, however, thinks More applies systemic analysis to political problems but in a humanist, rhetorical mode of expression. Hence, More's fundamental methodology is holistic and rational. More, contrary to Skinner's view, follows Aristotle and Plato, not Cicero.[15] The question of good counsel, in particular, is the "most serious of all systemic problems" because the "malfunctioning of councils nearly precludes the implementation of solutions of other problems."[16] Only Bradshaw takes "More"

14. Skinner, "More's *Utopia*," 223.

15. In Logan's reading, More's approach constitutes what may be called practical Platonism by offering a model to test results. See Logan, *Meaning*, 130.

16. Ibid., 56.

at his literal word, arguing for a More who sincerely advocates practical reforms for actual political life. Here More is a willing councilor, as Elton originally suggested, though for philosophical reasons rather than simply ambition.[17] For Bradshaw, More's motivation stems from an ideal of faith and learning combined in the active life, following Erasmus's *Enchiridion*.[18] Thus, the question of "humanist More" arises in the dialogue of counsel, with More as neo-Roman (Skinner), or Platonist (Logan), or a practical reformer (Bradshaw) who follows the imperatives of Christian humanism.

The particular differences between these readers of the dialogue deserve careful attention. For Skinner, the focus of the dialogue belongs to the debate between *otium* and *negotium*, contemplation versus action, and a related concept, *virtus vera nobilitas est*, or virtue as true nobility. Like Bradshaw, Skinner takes More's support of the active life as authentic rather than ironic, but Skinner stresses how More argues for *negotium*, following Cicero's attack upon Plato. Here Hythloday is a Platonic figure, whose concern with the truth mandates candor, a transparent discourse unpracticed by courtiers. More replies by proposing the good of the commonwealth, which may be enhanced by good advice. Such a duty Skinner notes as an "almost word for word" recapitulation of *De Officiis*, which teaches that such service represents the greatest responsibility incumbent upon men of virtue.[19] A life of action requires "greater abilities" and is capable of "bringing us greater fulfillment and happiness"; hence true nobility lies in its pursuit. For *otium* to be acceptable at all, "it must be because it helps to improve the life of *negotium*."[20] The active life places preeminent value upon *honestas* as crown of the cardinal virtues and the "most honorific term" for one who discharges his or her office with a well-ordered life.[21] *Virtus*, in short, mandates service, and More's view of the active life employs "precisely the vocabulary which, as we have seen, Cicero had originally put into cur-

---

17. Bradshaw, "More," 24; see n69.   18. Ibid., 8–14.
19. Skinner, "More's *Utopia*," 222.   20. Ibid., 219.
21. Ibid., 218.

rency in his defence of the active life."[22] In Skinner's reading, More's position becomes identical to that of Cicero.[23]

Logan agrees with Skinner's emphasis upon Ciceronian contexts, arguing that More uses deliberative rhetoric especially in the dialogue,[24] but the ultimate end is not to defend an active life. Instead, the point is to speculate on the nature of and problems involved in giving counsel, an issue that is itself "a product of flaws in the structure of society."[25] On the question of service, Hythloday combines Plato's critique of oligarchy (from the *Republic*, book 8) with Aristotle's assessment of tyranny (from the *Politics*, book 5) to show how and why philosophers should not enter politics. More, thereby, iterates the perspective of Greek political philosophy in Hythloday. In Logan's reading, More becomes a reluctant councilor indeed, a picture compatible with how Erasmus originally portrayed him, as a man who inclines toward contemplation instead of action.[26]

Accordingly, Logan believes the dialogue as a whole illustrates More's own philosophic method, wherein "the theorist first determines the best life for the individual, and on that basis determines the goals of the polis" and all that pertains to the realization of such goals.[27] At its core, this method assumes "social problems have causes that may lie at some distance from the actual manifestations of the problems, and that these causes can be ascertained by rational analysis."[28] Of particular importance, "comparative political study is highly instructive in the formulation of solutions." So, too, compara-

22. Ibid., 221.

23. Skinner's position on the importance of Cicero for More's role in the dialogue is elaborated well yet extended in a different direction for book 2 in Gerard Wegemer, "Ciceronian Humanism in More's *Utopia*," *Moreana* 27, no. 104 (1990): 5–26.

24. Logan, *Meaning*, 51–53; "Deliberative Rhetoric."

25. Logan, *Meaning*, 56. Logan later emphasizes Ciceronian *topoi* of *honestas* and *utilitas*, but is clear that Hythloday remains "not a rhetorician but a philosopher" ("Deliberative Rhetoric," 110).

26. See Erasmus in *TMSB*, 10, who writes: "for no man was ever more consumed with ambition to enter a court than he [More] was to avoid it."

27. Logan, "Deliberative Rhetoric," 106.

28. Logan, *Meaning*, 53–54.

tive political study represents what More accomplishes in having Hythloday provide examples of success from other polities and Morton apply such solutions to local cases, tailoring and experimenting with models (real or imagined) to suit new situations.[29] Such a method belongs to the philosopher, not to the statesman or orator; philosophers speculate about but do not enter politics.[30] Instead, a philosopher may "instruct receptive men about the best state of the commonwealth,"[31] which appears to be Hythloday's motive in returning to Utopia and what More does in writing his *Utopia*.

Logan, thus, counters the Ciceronian contexts of Skinner by pointing to a different passage of *De Officiis* that claims philosophers provide better service to the state by teaching people how to become better citizens,[32] a point that agrees with Seneca's position on the importance of "wise men." Plato, Cicero, and Seneca, then, provide "eminently respectable and obviously relevant precedents for Hythloday's position," which "seriously undermines the currently fashionable view that More means us to regard Hythloday's refusal to join a counsel as a dereliction of duty."[33]

Though arguing from different vantage points—Cicero versus Plato, Roman versus Greek—both Skinner and Logan privilege classical contexts and isolate *Utopia* from More's other writings. Indeed, Skinner and Logan ignore More's emphasis upon the mixed life from *The Life of Pico*, though this text directly bears upon the question of active and contemplative lives. In chapter 1, we saw how More revised the correspondence between Corneus and Pico to indicate a mixture of action and contemplation, suggesting a Christian context

---

29. Ibid., 61; and see 62–66.

30. Logan cites Plato's Epistle VII in glossing Raphael's refusal to serve as a court councilor: "But in the case of those [states] who altogether exceed the bounds of right government and wholly refuse to proceed in its tracks, and who warn their counselor to leave the government alone and not disturb it, on pain of death if he does disturb it, while ordering him to advise as to how all that contributes to their desires and appetites may most easily and quickly be secured forever and ever—then, in such a case, I should esteem unmanly the man who continued to engage in counsels of this kind, and the man who refused to continue, manly" (ibid., 101).

31. Ibid., 102.   32. *De Off.*, I.xliii.155–xliv.156.

33. Logan, *Meaning*, 103.

for the debate rather than a Ciceronian or Platonic one. Pico, at least, failed at both contemplation and action, with moral ramifications in the next life and in this one. Purgatory awaited Pico because of the service he had denied the Church, but Pico's faulty household management—his failure to behave responsibly in the most rudimentary of political spheres—created opportunities for injustice in this world too.

Here the difference between an Augustinian and a Ciceronian or Platonic political context becomes acute. For Skinner, Hythloday's position is a foil to More's civic humanism, and for Logan, More approves an ancient Platonic tenet, that of educating citizens, which Hythloday represents. Yet More's Pico wishes to remain his own master and irresponsibly loves "liberte" above all else so that he may be free for the "study of philosophy" (69/21–23). So, too, the description of Pico matches Hythloday's desire to live as he pleases—*vivo ut volo* (*CW* 4, 56/1). Such desires for autonomy, as we saw, prevent Pico from serving the Church.[34] Pico's letter to Corneus, finally, specifically invokes not the terms of *otium* and *negotium* but the types of Mary and Martha (86/5–9). Instead of service as manifestation of *honestas* or a project of educating citizens by teaching philosophy, More's *Life* privileges charity toward God and neighbor through service and an active life mixed with contemplation.

More's early inclination toward combining action and contemplation as an answer to a Christian vocation suggests that Raphael's monolithic disavowal of the active life does not represent More's own position, augmenting Skinner's general point against Logan, though from the standpoint of Christianity rather than Ciceronian thought. For the same reason, the *Life* detracts from Logan's emphasis upon a Platonic context. As we saw, Augustine or Hilton was More's probable source in reconstructing the *Life* to indicate how Pico should follow a vocation to the mixed life. The extension of the debate over *otium* and *negotium* to a distinctively Christian afterlife

34. For Pico's denial, see *CW* 1, 73/24–74/8.

in the *Life* pertains to salvation, not to republicanism or to platonic philosophy.

Skinner's reading of Cicero's sense of duty, too, requires qualification. For Skinner, Cicero's *De Officiis* and Machiavelli's *The Prince* represent two absolutely distinct and opposing ethics on the question of justice.[35] Cicero believes fraud or force may inflict harm contrary to justice; hence it follows that *fides* and *clementia* are "indispensable requirements of justice." The *vir virtutis*—or man of virtue, what Skinner translates as "the man of true manliness"—may be identified by his avoidance of "beastly ways," either that of the fox (fraud) or that of the lion (force).[36] Early humanists contrast *virtus* and *vis,* "manly qualities and brutal force," but Machiavelli's *Prince* conflates the distinction between them.[37] Machiavelli thereby fails to distinguish between two modes of acting: one proper to men, another to beasts. Significantly, a prince must have an understanding of beastly ways. Appropriating Cicero's imagery to his own purpose, Machiavelli recommends that the prince be able to imitate both the fox and the lion.[38]

Skinner eloquently summarizes these basic differences between Cicero and Machiavelli, yet Cicero's overall position on *honestas* versus *utilitas* is less than monolithic, as we saw in chapter 2. In *De Partitione Oratoria,* Cicero writes that necessity "must take precedence in public policy of all the remaining considerations, alike of honour [*honestatibus*] and of profit."[39] Here "a necessity [*necesse*] is something

---

35. Skinner writes: "It is true that Machiavelli's analysis differs from Cicero's in one immensely important respect. He silently makes one alteration—small in appearance but overwhelming in significance—to the classical analysis of the virtues needed to serve the common good. He erases the quality of justice, the quality that Cicero in *De Officiis* had described as the crowning splendor of virtue" ("The Idea of Negative Liberty" in *Visions,* 2:207).

36. Quentin Skinner, "Republican Virtues in an Age of Princes," in ibid., 125.

37. Ibid., 144.

38. Ibid., 145. For Cicero's earlier use of the same image, see *De Off.*; I.xiii.41, which reads: "While wrong may be done, then, in either of two ways, that is by force or by fraud, both are bestial: fraud seems to belong to the cunning fox, force to the lion; both are wholly unworthy of man, but fraud is the more contemptible."

39. Cicero, *De Partitione Oratoria,* trans. and ed. H. Rackham (Cambridge, Mass.: Harvard University Press, 1942), xxiv.83–84.

that is an indispensable condition of our security or freedom."[40] Reasons of necessity, then, take precedence over *honestas*. So, too, "circumstances ... very often bring it about that utility is at variance with moral value" [*ut utilitas cum honestate certet*].[41] The key for a good speaker in making political proposals is the ability "to place considerations of expediency and necessity in front of those of morality, or vice versa," depending on the situation and audience.[42] Even in *De Officiis*, Cicero addresses apparent conflicts between *honestas* and *utilitas* by remarking how "it often happens, owing to exceptional circumstances, that what is accustomed under ordinary circumstances to be considered morally wrong is found not to be morally wrong."[43]

Those "exceptional circumstances," I suggested in chapter 2, are present in how Morton dupes Buckingham to the latter's destruction but in service of removing a tyrant. Erasmus claims More possesses a "special hatred" for despotic, absolute power,[44] and More's own writing on tyrannicide confers merit on those who deploy deception—upon one who knows how to "lay plots, hide his traps, make the most of opportunities"—in eliminating tyrants (*CW* 3.1, 109/31–32). Removing a tyrant is by definition virtuous, but any act of tyrannicide, also by definition, requires dissimulation. Unless one may announce and plot and execute tyrants in broad daylight, deception remains necessary, a conspiracy orchestrated by a person whom More calls a *hominem artificem* (108/27). More's conception of conspiracy indicates how acting *pro bono publico* in the matter of tyrannicide includes such things as ambush, plots, false adulation, breaking trusts, and so on. Hence what may appear as a conundrum for *honestas* and *utilitas*: the performance of a virtuous action, removing a tyrant, entails a variety of other unseemly acts in order to be successful.

---

40. Ibid., *necesse autem id est sine quo salvi liberive esse non possumus.*

41. Ibid., xxv.89

42. Ibid., xxvii.96.

43. *De Off.*, III.iv.19. Italian humanists Patrizi, Platina, and Pontano all precede Machiavelli, advocating similar notions that distinguish a good man from a good prince. See Logan, *Meaning*, 108–9.

44. Erasmus is cited from *TMSB*, 6.

Yet at such a point, the absolute difference Skinner identifies between Machiavelli and Cicero on the virtue of justice appears more circumstantial than substantive.[45] For Cicero, the nobility of tyrannicide is architectonic: "What more atrocious crime can there be to kill a fellow-man, and especially an intimate friend? But if anyone kills a tyrant—be he never so intimate a friend—he has not laden his soul with guilt, has he? The Roman People, at all events, are not of that opinion; for of all glorious deeds they hold such an one to be the most noble [*pulcherrimum*]."[46] The beauty or nobility of a tyrant's execution brings enough glory to destroy any *fides* of friendship and renders *clementia* irrelevant. If Machiavelli would welcome the dispensation of *fides* and *clementia*, Erasmus, at least, would not—even in the case of prolonged subjection to tyranny. Erasmus's longanimity is such that, rather than remove tyrants, he only hopes to avoid more than one: "In some ways it is a more acceptable situation for the state when the prince himself is bad than when his friends are: somehow or other we put up with a single tyrant."[47]

Though Skinner knows the history of resistance theory, he does not consider its ethical ramifications philosophically enough and he does not associate More with tyrannicide. That is because, for Skinner, More's *Utopia* indicates More's political thought. Skinner couples More with Erasmus's *Education of a Prince*, but the example of Morton from the *History* undercuts such a view.[48] In the complex, dense history of tyrannicide and Christian teaching, at least, Cardinal Morton's work upon Buckingham shows how greatly More's own answers could deviate from those of Erasmus.[49]

---

45. For a helpful discussion of parallels, see Marcia L. Colish, "Cicero's *De Officiis* and Machiavelli's *Prince*," *Sixteenth Century Journal* 9, no. 4 (1978): 81–93.

46. *De Off.*, III.iv.19.

47. Lisa Jardine, ed., *Erasmus: The Education of a Christian Prince with the Panegyric for Archduke Philip of Austria* (Cambridge: Cambridge University Press, 1997), 71.

48. Skinner, *Foundations*, 1:249–50.

49. Aquinas writes that sedition is always a mortal sin, but resistance to tyrants does not have the nature of sedition, for tyranny is rule that is not directed to the common good (*ST*, 2,2, q.42, art.2). Aquinas rejects tyrannicide, however, in *De regimine principum*. For an introductory bibliography and review of sources on tyrannicide, see *CW* 3.1, 149–155.

Contrarily, Logan acknowledges the point of expediency in Cicero but affirms its union with *honestas* in *Utopia*. Hythloday represents the identification of the moral and the expedient, a position that Logan at some points argues is More's own, especially as represented in the *History*.[50] Yet Logan also believes that "More" believes in yielding to expediency,[51] distinguishing him from Hythloday— and from Erasmus.[52] Logan writes: "The theory that the politically prudent and the moral are identical is Hythloday's, not More's, and we cannot tell from the argument of Book I exactly how far the author of *Utopia* thought the harmony between them extended. It is, however, certain that he wished it to extend very far."[53] Later, however, Logan argues that *Utopia* as a whole critiques both "Christian" and "secular" humanists. The *"realpolitisch* tendencies of secular humanist theory" learn that the "dictates of political prudence, though not always identical to those of morality, do not differ from them as much, or as often, as the secular theorists imagine."[54] So, too, instead of functioning as simple moralists, Christian humanists "must consider not only what should be but what *can* be; consider, that is, the design of plausible means for implementing ideals, and questions of the degree of compatibility of his ideals and of the trade-offs that it may be necessary to make in realizing them."[55] In turning from platitudes to political solutions, the unique method of systemic analysis becomes imperative, but what it teaches is an "inescapable trade-off" between security and freedom for citizens and justice in foreign policy.[56] Therein a problem occurs because trade-offs are other words for *utilitas,* but *utilitas,* as Logan himself shows, best represents the position of "More" in the dialogue of counsel.[57]

As we have seen, Logan suggests that "More" from *Utopia* does

---

50. Logan, *Meaning*, 53, 111.

51. Ibid., 129.

52. Ibid., 113.

53. Ibid., 157; cf.121–22.

54. Ibid., 258.

55. Ibid., 249.

56. Ibid., 258.

57. On "More" and Hythloday's positions, see Logan, *Meaning,* 41–42; cf. 106, and Logan, "Deliberative Rhetoric," 110–12.

not speak for himself in arguing for service because Hythloday best represents the voice of philosophy that authorial More wishes to promote. Yet philosophy employs the method of systemic analysis that, it turns out, emphasizes expediency. Hence, by Logan's own argument, the words of "More" from the dialogue in favor of *utilitas* or "trade-offs" *would be indicative* of authorial claims. The overall argument that Logan finds in favor of expediency is the same kind of case that "More" gives as to why Hythloday should serve. Thus, Hythloday's disavowal of expediency means he could not represent systemic philosophy, but the arguments for service made by "More," at least, do not contradict the logic of compromise. If a form of prudential expediency becomes the lesson for both sets of readers—secular and Christian humanists—whom More ostensibly aims to address, Logan's conclusion about *Utopia* as a whole appears very different from his former statements cited in chapter 2, which associate More's political thought with a condemnation of Richard in the name of rejecting expediency. The method of systemic analysis, by implication, seems less convincingly demonstrated. The expediency finally elevated in the account of rational analysis could exist as simply another manifestation of deliberative rhetoric.

Bradshaw alone among the three employs an approach that seems compatible with teachings already found in the *Life* and *History*. For Bradshaw, More views the Christian vocation "as a call to perfection in which the classical ideal of *humanitas* was subsumed under the Christian ideal of the *imago Dei*."[58] Sanctification through grace is commensurate with human development achieved through cultivating a life of reason. Bradshaw's position confirms much of what chapters 1 and 2 of this study demonstrate by other means. Religion and morality, as in the *Life*, have an integral relationship, and More's position of engagement in political life—as in his position on tyrannicide—essentially constitutes a moral imperative.

<hr />

58. Bradshaw, "Controversial More," 566.

Thus, in addressing *Utopia,* Bradshaw combines the emphasis of faith with the problem of counsel. When More adjusts Plato's metaphor of the ship of state, argues Bradshaw, we see the "moral obligation of the intellectual towards the commonwealth."[59] Plato's first mistake—and that of Hythloday—assumes a freedom from politics that is unavailable from a moral viewpoint. Hythloday's second error is that the best is the enemy of the good; that utopian schemes, if impossible, would entail an abandonment of status quo politics. The philosopher or intellectual, after all, may still aid the ship of state by minimizing the damages of unjust or intractable problems.

So, too, Bradshaw observes what we have already seen in More's treatment of Morton, a more politic method. What Plato would condemn as sophistry, More condones as decorous adaptability applied to the realities of political life.[60] Where politics is governed by horizons of expediency, reformers must adjust and adapt, following the imperative of what More calls the "little bad," improving things by not worsening them and working incrementally upon those reforms that seem possible if not ideal (*CW* 4, 101/2). Systemic answers to political problems represent philosophical endeavor without ameliorative effects, a scenario that compares well with More's description of Pico's contemplation as harmful neglect. Similarly, engagement and accommodation applied toward modest goals resonates with the charity or love Pico owed his community, but failed to provide, and with Colet's own call for action that releases *amor Dei in nobis* through *viva sapientia.* Significantly, though, More now moderates these early imperatives with the limitations of political life he explored in his *History.*

Indeed, when Hythloday mentions the court of the French king, we see the foreign policy analogies to the sort of problems that occur domestically in England during Richard's rise. In Hythloday's account, states are termed friends yet suspected as enemies, treaties

59. Bradshaw, "More," 23.
60. See ibid., 24.

with false intentions are sought, exiled nobles from other states are cultivated as rivals to seated kings, and all proposals on behalf of war are advocated. As in More's depiction of Richard's own character, appetites for power are supreme here, whether in aspiring to a throne or by attempting to increase the dominion of any particular king. In Hythloday's account, kings vie against kings as councilors compete with each other. With words that recall More's own epigram on the lust for power, Hythloday wonders aloud how he would be viewed—as a councilor of philosophic candor—if he were to argue that "the single kingdom of France" is too large to be governed well by one man and, therefore, one shouldn't dream of adding other dominions (89/27–31).[61] The example of the French court illustrates Hythloday's propositions against service: monarchs prefer to pursue war and acquisition of riches, not peace and a common good (57/25–30), and councilors' self-aggrandizing manner privileges sycophancy instead of wisdom. They advise to please, anticipating what kings desire (57/31–59/16). If not a continuing picture of Richard as king and Buckingham as councilor, the chicanery and homogenous self-interest at court that Hythloday's describes correspond with the harrowing realism of political life More presents in the *History*.

Yet against Hythloday's position, the successes of Morton from the *History* also reemerge. The example Hythloday uses before the one of the French court is a recollection of his dinner with the cardinal. On that occasion, the penalties for theft are discussed, and Hythloday argues death is far too severe for the crime. As a political solution, such a penalty fails to address the societal causes of theft, which stem from nobleman who live idly with their attendants (63/5–25) and from the fact that all of these indulge themselves with a taste for luxury and horde goods (69/23–71/17). Though Hythloday's analysis is highly unconventional, the cardinal, in fact, does listen. More than

---

61. More's epigram reads: "Among many kings there will be scarcely one, if there is really one, who is satisfied to have one kingdom. And yet among many kings there will be scarcely one, if there is really one, who rules a single kingdom well" (*CW* 3.2, 257).

that, Morton silences Hythloday's opponents at one point (71/30–32) and he proposes experimenting with Hythloday's ideas, cautiously accepting and implicitly approving them (81/7–18).

The eulogy of Morton with which More opens the scene, too, praises the cardinal for prudence, virtue, eloquence, knowledge of the law, authority, and "ability incomparable" *(ingenium incomparabile)* and, running counter to Hythloday's complaints about kings, identifies Morton as one upon whom the "king placed the greatest confidence" (59/21–61/6). The identification of Morton's prudence here, like the deep insight into political affairs for which he is praised in the *History*, contradicts Hythloday's overall position against service. The prudence Morton employs against the violent instability of Richard's reign corresponds to the more delicate maneuvering of the state through counsel. Morton's style of prudential maneuvering seems intrinsic to More's politics of accommodation, suggesting a reconfiguration of the ideals from the *Life* into a moral commitment to service with moderated expectations about success, thereby confirming Bradshaw's general reading in the context of More's own writings. Even so, Bradshaw isn't concerned with addressing More's role as legal reformer, preferring a more general formulation. The possibility of "constructive social and political progress resides neither in moral idealism of the intellectual alone nor in the skeptical pragmatism of the politician, but in a constructive and continuing dialogue between the two."[62] Bradshaw doesn't consider here how the lawyerly vocation may be related to the role of "public intellectual." Yet the principles of accommodation and of service from the dialogue may be understood in tandem with More's own training and practice of considering common law cases according to equity. To see why this may be so, and how More refers to equity in explaining his political thought in the dialogue, we must review humanist jurisprudence and speculate upon More's own view of it.

62. Ibid., 27.

EQUITY AND HUMANISM

To read the dialogue in terms of equity and humanist jurisprudence, however, entails questioning recent assessments of More. In
traditional sources such as Roper's account, More remains a legal reformer, following the practice of conscience or equity. As a lawyer and
later chancellor, More understands how the Chancery and the Star
Chamber courts function, employing the principle of conscience, or ·
equity, a standard and a coercive power that enables judges to administer the sometimes ambiguous common law to particular cases.[63]
Despite the humanist context of equity, with the absence of new,
Utopia-like legislation, or radical reforms of law in More's political record, notable historians such as John Guy conclude More's traditional
reputation as reformer is a myth. Such a characterization agrees with
the general view of F. W. Maitland, which suggests only a slight influence upon England from humanistic reforms on the continent.[64]
Maitland still provides what Mike Macnair calls "the current orthodoxy," which teaches that, rather than provide equity through judicial
decisions on the basis of humanist principles, only "miscellaneous
defects" in common law were corrected by the chancellor's office.[65]

Though the practice of humanist jurisprudence does not appear
pervasive in England, the premise of its philosophical methodology
remains as straightforward as More's understanding of it: the interpretation of the law should begin with the application of historical
and philological criticism to ancient Roman laws. Skinner explains

63. For sources other than Baker above and Guy below on equity, conscience, and the court,
see Stuart E. Prall, "The Development of Equity in Tudor England," *American Journal of Legal
History* 8, no.1 (1964): 1–19; E. W. Ives, *The Common Lawyers of Pre-Reformation England: Thomas
Kebell, A Case Study* (Cambridge: Cambridge University Press, 1983), 189–221; P. Tucker, "The
Early History of the Court of Chancery: A Comparative Study," *English Historical Review* 115
(2000): 791–811; Mike Macnair, "Equity and Conscience," *Oxford Journal of Legal Studies* 27, no. 4
(2007): 659–81; for a broader reception history of Aristotelian equity, see Darien Shanske, "Four
Theses: Preliminary to an Appeal to Equity," *Stanford Law Review* 57, no. 6 (2005): 2053–86.

64. For a general statement, see F. W. Maitland, "English Law and the Renaissance" in *Selected Historical Essays of F. W. Maitland* (Boston: Beacon Press, 1962), 135–51; cf., Donald R. Kelley, "History, English Law and the Renaissance: A Rejoinder," *Past and Present* 72 (1976): 143–46.

65. Macnair, "Equity and Conscience," 664.

well the humanist intention: "They wanted to challenge the orthodox scholastic approach to the interpretation of the Civil Code, above all the deliberately unhistorical assumption that the main aim of the jurist should be to adapt the letter of the law as closely as possible to fit existing legal circumstances."[66] That approach, too, includes prominent proponents who are associated with More. Moving from Italy northward, Guillaume Budé, commentator upon *Utopia*, produces his *Annotationes in XXIV libros Pandectarum* (1508), "the earliest and greatest manifesto of legal humanism to be published north of the Alps."[67] As the method migrates, it also expands, such that Ulrich Zasius, praised by Erasmus, employs the *studia humanitatis* to medieval jurists and feudal law, thus becoming, according to Skinner, "one of the earliest civil lawyers to apply the techniques of humanist jurisprudence to the study of a legal system other than that of Rome."[68]

Scholars such as Budé know that feudal or princely laws of the day are different from those of antiquity, but the traditions of current practice at that time are considered derivative of Roman ones. In this way, *civilis sapientia* connects study of the humanities within civil law.[69] Accordingly, we find Peter Giles, writing on the sources of the Justinian code, Vives writing notes on Cicero's *De legibus,* and Budé writing *Annotationes* on Roman law. Giles and Budé are part of *Utopia's* publication, providing important prefatory letters, and Vives once stays in More's home.[70] Vives, too, addresses juristic humanism while at Oxford, arriving from the University of Louvain at the invitation of Cardinal Wolsey. And at Cambridge, the first Regius professor of Civil Law—Thomas Smith (1513–77)—praises humanist jurisprudence as well.[71]

---

66. Skinner, *Foundations*, 1:202.   67. Ibid., 205.

68. Ibid., 207.

69. Donald R. Kelley, "Law," in *The Cambridge History of Political Thought: 1450-1700,* ed. J. H. Burns (Cambridge: Cambridge University Press, 1991), 77.

70. These points are made by R. J. Schoeck, "Thomas More, Humanist and Lawyer" in *EA*, 569–79.

71. See Vives and Smith in Martha A. Ziskind, "John Selden: Criticism and Affirmation of the Common Law Tradition," *American Journal of Legal History*, 19, no. 1 (1975): 26.

More's connection to Budé deserves special mention because of Budé's letter recommending More's *Utopia*, which emphasizes social justice with regard to property rights and inheritance, advertising a sense of equity.[72] Comparing the complexities of the law to the simplicity of Christ's commandments, Budé claims lawyers are no longer concerned with the ancient virtue of justice, defined as giving each his due, but with the distribution of wealth and land according to technicalities of law. In short, legal positivism dominates the profession of More's day, a positivism that creates "Gordian knots and charlatan methods" in service of the strong, who may accumulate most of the wealth. Does God direct men to hoard goods, Budé asks, separating rich from poor? If so, why do the apostles teach that all goods should be held in common? Budé finds a formulaic set of legal rules very far from the Christian ideal of a just society and presents ancient teachings on the virtue of justice as commensurate with Christ's teaching: the way to a more just and, therefore, more Christian society is through correcting the positive law.[73]

Budé, in this way, projects a similar tone and theme to that of Hythloday. In arguing over the penalties for theft, Hythloday clarifies that the hoarding of goods constitutes a fundamental inequality, which represents what Logan calls the systemic problem of crime, a societal cause behind theft and one in contradistinction to "that strict justice" *(rigidam illam iustitiam)* of the law (*CW* 4, 60/8–9).[74] The reference to "strict justice" illustrates how Hythloday's assessment corresponds to Budé's demands of equity to reform the common law. As Guido Kisch comments generally in regard to a his-

---

72. The letter is published in the second edition of *Utopia*, and as Schoeck, "Humanist and Lawyer," 573, comments, it lends "Budé's legal prestige on the Continent to More's great publication."

73. My summary is from "William Bude to Thomas Lupset" in *CW* 4, 4–11. On Budé's argument and its significance for *Utopia*, see Peter R. Allen, "Utopia and European Humanism: The Function of the Prefatory Letters and Verses," *Studies in the Renaissance* 10 (1963): 91–107. For a reading of the letter as a response to Utopia on the issue of equity, see Andrew J. Majeske, *Equity in English Renaissance Literature: Thomas More and Edmund Spenser* (New York: Routledge, 2006), 64–69.

74. See Logan's treatment in *Meaning*, 48–51.

tory of ideas, "it is to the humanist-jurists that modern legal thought owes the theoretical opening up of the wide domains of *epiekeia* and equity," who illustrate to us "the varied evolution of legal-dogmatic ideas from Aristotle to Budé."[75]

Less than an illustration of More's own thought, Budé's letter provokes the question of whether the humanist emphasis upon social justice would augment the legal practice of equity in England by way of influencing the attitude of a judge like More. Given More's associations with Vives and Budé especially, however, his acquaintance with humanist jurisprudence seems certain. Apart from equity's presence in the debate over theft, the principle of equity—*ex aequo bonoque*—was a phrase he used elsewhere, thereby implying the context of humanist legal reform.[76]

Indeed, a fundamental principle of the rhetoric of legal reform in England was equity or "conscience," an obvious observation, yet one too often detached from critical discussion of More's humanist studies. Such an omission occurs because, in searching for More's own thoughts on equity, legal theorists and archival historians underestimate the importance of rhetoric for the study of equity in sixteenth-century England. "Such questions as More's reading in rhetoric, one of the liberal arts but one directly contributory to the practice of the law, and one in whose development during the sixteenth century common lawyers played a very large role, have scarcely been asked": though Schoeck wrote this in 1964, and much work has been done since on the use of rhetoric in early modern England, his observation largely stands with regard to More's legal thought.[77] As Schoeck argues, "lawyers in England studied their classical rhetoric long before the time of Thomas More, and in fact the relation between law

---

75. Guido Kisch, "Humanistic Jurisprudence," *Studies in the Renaissance* 8 (1961): 80.

76. For More's use of *ex aequo bonoque*, see *CW* 5.1, 278/1 and Headley's comments on this passage in *CW* 5.2, 755. Though not in regard to equity, More applied the exegetical method of "positive theology" to determine the meaning of a Church decree by way of examining a pope's intention in *A Dialogue Concerning Heresies*. See *CW* 6.1, 356/5–358/25.

77. Schoeck, "Thomas More, Humanist Lawyer," 576.

and rhetoric may already have a firm tradition before Chaucer (who studied both) and John Gower." When More cites Cicero in the *Utopia*, Schoeck observes, it occurs with reference to the law, implying that "More was richly aware of the extent to which Cicero was concerned with the study of law, as well as with legal argument."[78]

To Schoeck's more general points about an education in rhetoric, Andrew J. Majeske adds the emphasis upon equity: "More's familiarity with equity (as *aequitas*) would have begun in his grammar school education, probably when he encountered Cicero's uses of *aequitas* in the *De Finibus*, the *Topica*, and the *Pro Murena*, texts typically drawn upon for rhetorical exercises and translation practice."[79] But also, after finishing at Lincoln's Inn, More studied Greek with Grocyn and Linacre. The latter had just returned from Italy after helping publish Aristotle's works, where equity would have been addressed especially in the *Rhetoric*.[80] Majeske concludes that *Utopia*, too, shows a knowledge of "the relevant texts"—ranging from Plato's *Republic* and the *Laws* to Aristotle's *Rhetoric*, *Ethics*, and *Politics*—for identifying equity.[81]

The connection between equity and rhetoric illustrates how legal studies were combined with liberal learning, suggesting the vocation of a humanist lawyer.[82] Here the Inns of Court were important, a point difficult to grasp, because "our culture and our public life," argues R. S. White, "have lost the equal valuing of literature, law, politics and religion in the tight knit which could be fostered in

78. Richard J. Schoeck, "Lawyers and Rhetoric in Sixteenth-Century England" in *Renaissance Eloquence: Studies in the Theory and Practice of Renaissance Rhetoric*, ed. James J. Murphy (Berkeley: University of California Press, 1983), 279, 284. See, too, Lorna Hutson and Victoria Kahn, eds., *Rhetoric and Law in Early Modern Europe* (New Haven, Conn.: Yale University Press, 2001), 1–25 and 55–72.

79. Majeske, *Equity in English Renaissance*, 64–65.

80. On studying Greek, see *SL*, 2. For a bilingual presentation, see *CW* 15, 129/49.

81. Majeske, *Equity in English Renaissance*, 65. Majeske adds that at Oxford More would have read Aquinas's account, and at New Inn, Fortescue's interpretation in *De laudibus legume Anglie*.

82. On British common law and Renaissance rhetoric, see Peter Goodrich, "We Orators: Review Article of Brian Vickers' *In Defense of Rhetoric*," *Modern Law Review* 53, no. 4 (1990): 546–63.

the environment of the Inns of Court."[83] Legal associations, such as the kind formed at Inns, included exposure to rhetoric and poetry.[84] Though late, the examples of George Puttenham and Thomas Wilson are suggestive. Puttenham, author of the influential *The Art of Poesy*, was a student at Middle Temple beginning in 1556. He compared a poet's craft to that of an advocate "because our maker or poet is appointed not for a judge but rather for a pleader."[85] And Thomas Smith, professor of civil law at Cambridge, praised the eloquence of common lawyers who spoke in the vernacular.[86] Indeed, a student of Cambridge, Thomas Wilson, would write the *Art of Rhetoric* (1560), which presents and teaches rhetoric as complementary to law. The *Art of Rhetoric* includes equity as one of seven "places of confirmation"—that is, subjects in which "the state of right or wrong" may be argued.[87] Such rhetorical manuals are often cited by scholars to provide context for Shakespeare's plays, to show the importance of rhetoric to poetry, or, more recently, to demonstrate the presence of republican thought in the early modern period, but they emerge, as from their sources in Cicero, as texts that incorporate law with rhetoric.[88] "Books of rhetoric," argues White, were mostly "aimed particularly at either lawyers or poets" because both, "the one through oratory and the other through writing, shared a professional, vest-

83. R.S.White, *Natural Law in English Renaissance Literature* (Cambridge: Cambridge University Press, 1996), 75.

84. On the Inns of Court and rhetoric, see ibid., 73–87; see, too, Schoeck, "Humanist and Lawyer," 573–75 and his "Lawyers and Rhetoric," 280–82.

85. Puttenham, *Art of English Poesy*, 239; see, too, Schoeck, "Lawyers and Rhetoric," 288–89.

86. Peter Medine, "Introduction" to Wilson's *Art of Rhetoric* (1560), 5.

87. Wilson, *Art of Rhetoric*, 131.

88. On how classical rhetoric was received in Renaissance England and was part of the humanist ideal of *vir civilis*, see Quentin Skinner, *Reason and Rhetoric in the Philosophy of Thomas Hobbes* (Cambridge: Cambridge University Press, 1996),19–211; on the related issue of republicanism, see Markku Peltonen, *Classical Humanism and Republicanism in English Political Thought: 1570–1640* (Cambridge: Cambridge University Press, 1995), 1–17, which address republicanism before the civil war. On rhetoric and education, see Peter Mack's "Rhetoric in the Grammar School," in *Elizabethan Rhetoric* (Cambridge: Cambridge University Press, 2002); on rhetoric, politics and education, see Heinrich R.Plett, *Rhetoric and Renaissance Culture* (Berlin: Walter de Gruyter, 2005), 47–52. For an example of Shakespeare's use of classical rhetoric, see Miriam Joseph's *Shakespeare's Use of the Arts of Language* (New York: Hafner Publishing, 1966).

ed interest in the classical strategy of rhetoric to move hearts and minds in a certain direction through language."[89] In short, the examination of classical rhetoric that inspired humanist reforms in education, poetry, and politics came from the same texts that dealt with the law.[90] Though More is an expert in rhetoric and a pioneer in humanist education, the relationship between these interests and law does not pervade discussion of his public career, which suggests that much of the current picture about More's legal work is viewed anachronistically, following modern divisions between disciplines.

The connection between rhetoric and jurisprudence indicates not just the importance of humanist exegetical techniques but an educative vision that emphasizes prudential judgment. More demonstrates his own understanding of how legal and liberal learning contribute to shaping judgment in the *Dialogue Concerning Heresies*, which specifically associates the liberal arts with law. More writes: "so is it no doubte / but that reason is by study / labour and exercyse of Logyk / Phylosophy and other lyberall artes corroborate and quyckened / and yᵉ iudgment bothe in them and also in oratours / lawes & storyes moche ryped" (*CW* 6.1, 132/6–11). Along with the study of oratory and poetry, "lawes" are a means by which "iudgment" ripens or matures. Liberal arts may "quicken" reason, giving it life, animating reason, but More also views "judgment" as distinct from the sharpening of reason that occurs with an education in the *trivium*. Judgment would mature over time, or ripen, as it advances by studying orators, laws, and stories or poetry. Cultivating "judgment" through the study of law, then, suggests the literal sense of "to sit as judge" and the more figurative "to pass judgment upon" (*OED*, 1.b) but includes, too, other denotations of the word, which More proposes as fruit from the study of *humanitas*, such as an "ability to form an opinion" (*OED*, 8.a) and "discernment, discre-

89. White, *Natural Law*, 79.
90. "Lawyers and poets, together with preachers, shared the common heritage of classical rhetoric, and, since the sixteenth century saw a great revival of classical rhetoric in England, the common links were reinforced" (ibid., 78).

tion, wisdom" or "good sense" (*OED*, 8.b).[91] To be a judge at court not only would entail technical expertise of the law but should mean exercising mature judgment.

Philip Melanchthon, who would disagree with More on matters of religion, supports the same idea about the liberal arts as More does and in very similar language: "And there was no way that men, who were ignorant of the more refined sorts of literature, could have devised something sensible in the study of law, justice, and equity, because that particular discipline comes right from the humanities, and the works of the lawyers of antiquity are full of erudition that is both ancient and true."[92] Melanchthon, too, writes of "prudential judgment" that is sharpened by studying rhetoric and the "humanities." By imitating ancient authors, who were "involved in handling and managing the greatest of affairs," students may "contract a certain capacity for judging" as they are "tanned" by the ancients "just as people are who walk in the sun."[93]

In these contexts, rhetoric does not constitute merely power delivered by persuasion but informs prudential judgment, a necessary attribute in delivering equity. As Germain Marc'hadour observes of More's own inclusion of law in humanist studies, "the adding of law in a noble place between rhetoric and history may reflect the experience of More as Chancellor of the Duchy of Lancaster, in duty bound already to apply the humanizing categories of equity, or *jurisprudence*, to the letter of the statute."[94] Here the judicial experience of More leads him to elevate law, but more likely it was the opposite; the humanist studies, especially rhetoric, already prepared More to think of jurisprudence as an intellectual virtue.

In contexts such as these, the interrelation of prudence, equity,

---

91. Definitions of "judgment" are from *The Oxford English Dictionary*, 2nd ed., 1989, *OED Online*, Oxford University Press, June 1, 2010, http://dictionary.oed.com/cgi/entry/50124506.

92. Philip Melanchthon is cited from *The Praise of Eloquence*, in *Renaissance Debates on Rhetoric*, ed. and trans. Wayne A. Rebhorn (Ithaca, N.Y.: Cornell University Press, 2000), 110.

93. Ibid., 103.

94. Marc'hadour, "Basil the Great," 45.

and rhetoric emerges in More's climactic discussion of decorum at the end of book 1 in *Utopia*. As More debates Hythloday over what philosophy is best suited to court, Hythloday maintains that ideals should be clearly and bluntly stated. More responds, "in the private conversation of close friends this academic philosophy [*philosophia scholastica*] is not without its charm, but in the councils of kings, where great matters are debated with great authority, there is no room for these notions" (*CW* 4, 99/5–8). More advocates decorum here, as is often noted, following the Ciceronian formulation as "the form of wisdom that the orator must especially employ," adapting himself "to occasions and persons," for "one must not speak in the same style at all times, nor before all people."[95] That decorum is intrinsic to the practice of *honestas* I discussed in chapter 2, examining the behavior of Morton, a character we have seen More exalt further in having Hythloday laud Morton for his speaking ability. Most important, though, Morton's decorum constitutes a form of Ciceronian "wisdom," a prudential judgment of what will be heard or understood, given a particular group of interlocutors. The political concomitant to decorum is More's indirect approach, urging your case tactfully, and thus "what you cannot turn to good, you must at least make as little bad as you can" (101/1–2). Finally, as Majeske shows, equity is the legal collateral teaching to both the rhetorical and political positions.[96] Hythloday's own reply to More emphasizes equity by asking how customs of men may ever be changed for the better without the use of challenging candor. Christ himself did not adjust his teaching to the way men were living, though subsequent crafty preachers did. Here Hythloday calls More's decorum a "rule of soft lead" (101/34)—more literally, a *regulam plumbeam* or "leaden ruler" (100/26)—a term that significantly alludes to Aristotle's

95. Cicero, *Orator*, trans. H.M.Hubbell (Cambridge, Mass.: Harvard University Press, 1952), XXXV.123.
96. Majeske, *Equity in English Renaissance*, 82–84. Majeske provides a reading of both books of *Utopia* in light of equity, 63–91.

Nicomachean Ethics. For Aristotle, as Macnair summarizes, equity is "like the lead ruler allegedly invented in ancient Lesbos, which adapts the fixed measurements (the terms of the law) to the irregular stone (the particular situation)."[97] Law as a universal will never be sufficient unto itself because it cannot account for all the diversity of particular cases that may emerge; hence, to attain justice, a flexible application of the law must occur. The Cambridge editors of *Utopia* recognize that Hythloday refers to the Lesbian ruler but view it incorrectly as a "metaphor for adaptable moral standards."[98] Aristotle, more precisely, is discussing equity, and the allusion provides Hythloday a transition to a wonderful, wise Utopia, where laws are few. What finally emerges in the dialogue, then, is prudence as a governing virtue for speech, politics, and law, such that decorum, an indirect or tactful method, and equity are advanced against philosophy, force, and laws rigorously applied without exception.

JUDGE MORE

The most famous evidence of equity, conscience, and prudential judgment occurs in William Roper's account of More and common law judges. The injunctions granted by More, as chancellor at the time, were "misliked" by the judges, and so More directed a clerk to collate "the whole number and causes of all such injunctions." More invited those judges with complaints to dine with him, and afterward, when More "had broken with them what complaints he had heard of his injunctions, and moreover showed them both the number of causes of every one of them," the judges "were all enforced to confess that they, in like case, could have done no otherwise themselves." More advised them that "the reformation of the

---

97. Macnair, "Equity and Conscience," 660.

98. Thomas More, *Utopia*, ed. George M. Logan and Robert M. Adams (Cambridge: Cambridge University Press, 1996), 37n74; cf., *CW* 4, 376, where Erasmus's sense of adapting laws to morals is cited. For the passage from Aristotle on equity and the Lesbian ruler, see Aristotle's *Nicomachean Ethics*, trans. Hippocrates G. Apostle (Grinnell, Iowa: Peripatetic Press, 1984), 1137b10-32.

rigor of the law" could be accomplished by their own "reasonable considerations" and "discretion" because they, too, were "conscience bound."[99] Applying the law equitably would mean administering it in conscience, and in advising the judges to do what he himself had done, More claims both a difference from and a similarity to the common law magistrates. On the one hand, the chancellor's courts obviously have an appellate function according to conscience, but on the other, there need be no appeal, if common law justices implement judgments according to conscience. In other words, it is within the purview of the common law to implement conscience as well. The rigor of the law, not the law itself, should be reformed. If accurate, Roper's account fails to claim any sweeping, Utopian legislation because More's ideas of reform, such as they were, deal with the application of equity through conscience.

Yet even if More's actual agenda of reform simply corrects "miscellaneous defects" of the law, equity by way of judicial arbitration reveals a humanist context rather than an "anti-law" environment for resolving conflict. For Macnair, expanded injunctions through equity constitute a kind of "anti-law." Macnair interprets John Guy's archival research as an indication that Chancery and Star Chamber courts would "receive almost any claim." Because the increase in judicial accessibility could not be processed, most cases were sent "for compulsory arbitration by local worthies." This practice seems like "anti-law" or "alternative dispute resolution"; hence, if conscience simply meant dispute resolution under a new aegis, the term should mean anything or nothing at all.[100] Arbitration, however, is precisely the sort of equity Cicero speaks of in *De Officiis*. Though the example below concerns a negative outcome, the following passage is commonly cited as one that illustrates the Roman concept of equity as justice—and it is one that illustrates how arbitration aids the process:

99. Roper, *Life*, TMSB, 37–38.
100. MacNair, "Equity and Conscience," 670.

Injustice often arises also through chicanery, that is, through an over-subtle and even fraudulent construction of the law. This it is that gave rise to the now familiar saw, "More law, less justice." Through such interpretation also a great deal of wrong is committed in transactions between state and state; thus, when a truce had been made with the enemy for thirty days, a famous general went to ravaging their fields by night, because, he said, the truce stipulated "days," not nights. Not even our own countryman's action is to be commended, if what is told of Quintus Fabius Labeo is true—or whoever it was (for I have no authority but hearsay): appointed by the Senate to arbitrate a boundary dispute between Nola and Naples, he took up the case and interviewed both parties separately, asking them not to proceed in a covetous or grasping spirit, but to make some concession rather than claim some accession. When each party had agreed to this, there was a considerable strip of territory left between them. And so he set the boundary of each city as each had severally agreed; and the tract in between he awarded to the Roman People. Now that is swindling, not arbitration.[101]

Arbitration should deliver equity. The same point is made in Aristotle's *Rhetoric,* which argues that arbitrators should mitigate the law's rigor by deciding matters with a view to equity.[102] Equity achieved through arbitration should involve the same standards of good judgment we have already seen More define. Nor am I sure the first part of Macnair's argument—that of increased accessibility to litigants— validates his conclusion that conscience meant nothing other than a rationalization by which one would increase the scope of equity courts.

Indeed, Margaret Hastings's study of More as chancellor of the Duchy shows how equity as arbitration constitutes an attitude of reform. Reviewing the Decree and Order Book, bills of complaint and pleadings, depositions, and examinations of witnesses from More's tenure, she finds his proceedings as judge according to "equity and conscience" the "nearest approximation" to fulfillment of humanist hopes for justice.[103] Hastings's examples of More's implementation

---

101. De *Off.,* I.x.33.

102. See Aristotle's *Rhetoric,* trans. W. Rhys Roberts, in *Rhetoric and Poetics* (New York: Modern Library, 1954), 1374b10-25.

103. Margaret Hastings, "Sir Thomas More: Maker of English Law?" in *EA,* 105.

of equity are significant. In one case Thomas Hesketh's legitimate wife remains childless, and his will provides for his four illegitimate sons, with the eldest receiving the greatest portion. After Thomas's death, however, the "nearest legitimate heirs"—the four grandsons of Hesketh's four sisters—bring suit. More rendered settlement in 1526. There is no decree because the matter was settled by arbitration, but More's decision may be inferred by the fact that Thomas's eldest illegitimate son inherited everything given to him by his father's will. Hastings observes how unusual it was for a Chancery court to hear such a case and then replies: "An allegation of riot put in by the executors" may explain why.[104] "Riot" was one of the customary causes for appeal to Chancery courts. The addition of an allegation to change jurisdiction corresponds with Macnair's notion that an "anti-law" of a sort is at work, an easily manipulated means of finding courts to apply injunctions. Yet if the Hesketh case shows how arbitration often became the business of equity courts, it also resonates with Guy's general point that Chancery courts expanded accessibility by offering more flexible means of appeal.

WHAT UTOPIAN REFORM MEANS

An important part of the argument over whether More was a true legal reformer, then, emerges as a matter of prejudicial adjectives. Hastings concludes her review of More's work by acknowledging there is only insubstantial evidence for the claim that More was a "maker of law," but enough of the Duchy record exists to show a "hard-working administrator," a "peacemaker," and an "astute lawyer who could cut through a mass of detail to the heart of the matter at hand."[105] What Macnair calls "anti-law" by way of mere arbitration, Hastings terms "peacemaking," an ability to find "what is essential."

104. Ibid., 116–17. Cf. Christopher St. German, *Doctor and Student*, ed. T. F. T. Plucknett and J. L. Barton (London: Seldon Society, 1974), 51, 55, 57.
105. Ibid., 118.

So, too, John Guy's highly influential books on More credit Wolsey, not More, for legal reform, yet acknowledge More's "philosophical approach." In Guy's *Thomas More* (2000), More's "independent achievements" as lord chancellor provoke "the question of whether he [More] was still a Utopian reformer in 1529."[106] In this book, Guy finds the evidence "inconclusive" but "unpersuasive" that More was a reformer. He argues: "If equitable jurisdiction is itself to be equated with Utopian reform, then Wolsey was as much a Utopian reformer as More."[107] More recently, in *A Daughter's Love: Thomas and Margaret More* (2008), Guy asserts that More's own practice of equitable jurisprudence results from his "philosophical approach" to the professional practice of law, though Wolsey is still named first in legal reform.[108]

Yet the absence of new, Utopia-like legislation or radical reforms of the common law need not make More a mere follower of Cardinal Wolsey's innovations in regard to equitable jurisdiction. More's understanding of equity should involve a historiography that depends less on More's and Wolsey's work in the Star Chamber. As John Gueguen writes of Guy's earlier work on this subject, *The Public Career of Thomas More* (1980), Guy believes archival records "provide our best window to reality," thereby elevating whatever occurred at the Star Chamber and diminishing More as Church apologist, humanist, author of prayers and spiritual exercises. Guy, in other words, provides a "narrow understanding of what constitutes a man's 'public career.'"[109]

Gueguen's observation may be applied to Guy's treatment of Wolsey as well because, as Bradshaw writes of Guy, "he seems little

106. Guy, *Thomas More*, 127.

107. Ibid., 140.

108. To survey Guy's assessments of More as follower of Wolsey, compare the following: Guy, *The Cardinal's Court: The Impact of Thomas Wolsey in Star Chamber* (Totowa, IN: Rowman and Littlefield, 1977), 124; Guy, *Public Career*, 14, 50-1; *Thomas More*, 127, 140; and *A Daughter's Love*, 56, 86-7. See, too, chapter 5 of this text.

109. John A. Gueguen, review: *The Public Career of Sir Thomas More, Sixteenth Century Journal*, Vol. 14, No. 2 (Summer, 1983): 248-249.

interested in the mental attitude which the cardinal brought to his work in Star Chamber." For Bradshaw, "Wolsey was exposed to what might loosely be called an ideology of reform," which privileged a commonwealth and "reacted against the self-interested pursuit of power and glory on the part of rulers."[110] Bradshaw traces the "ideology of reform" back to Greek political philosophy, which, in part, "provided the source from which the demand for political and social renewal urged by Christian humanists derived moral force."[111] In this way, More could be initiating ideas of reform in his dialogue of counsel before he followed them as Wolsey's successor.

What Bradshaw addresses in regard to Wolsey's "mental attitude" should be applied to More, which reveals the importance of why More heard cases expeditiously and applied the law with equity. The "two Mores" thesis divides humanist More from the later lawyer and statesman of practical and political affairs. In the case of legal reform, this putative division appears plausible when "humanism" is defined exclusively in terms of a Utopian legislative agenda, by which many mean an implementation of a radical egalitarianism. Such an understanding, however, ignores or unduly diminishes the incremental approach of making political matters "less bad" that *Morus* espouses. It renders Thomas More into a failed Hythloday instead of a modest *Morus* or "More" from the dialogue of counsel. In this way, the question of whether More was a Utopian reformer appears slanted because there may be an attitude of humanist reform of the law that does not prefigure Enlightenment philosophy or represent radical progressivism.

By demonstrating the connection between rhetoric and law on the points of "equity" and "jurisprudence" and by locating that connection in More's own writings, the imperative of radical or Utopian reform emerges as the creation of critics who believe Hythlo-

---

110. Brendan Bradshaw, "The Tudor Commonwealth: Reform and Revision," *Historical Journal* 22.2 (June 1979): 458.

111. Ibid., 459.

day. I have suggested More as a humanist reformer by examining the importance of equity to his legal and rhetorical studies and by showing how More viewed the law as part of the liberal arts.[112] What emerges, as a result, is the potential for harmony between More's humanist studies and his legal work. In the above reevaluation, equity is not simply a function of Wolsey's legacy, but one of More's priorities, especially given the context of humanist jurisprudence. Such jurisprudence need not be read as a detached, philosophical statement upon the relationship of an intellectual to the polity, and indeed a program of reform that exists only in principle would be ironic. More's sense of equity remains part of a larger constellation of ideas, including equity in light of liberal learning, the liberal arts as part of developing the virtue of prudence, and statecraft as more than a matter of making a city in speech.[113]

112. On rhetoric and law, see Hutson and Kahn, *Rhetoric and Law in Early Modern Europe.*
113. On liberal education and virtue, see More's *Letter to Oxford* in *CW* 15, 139.

4

HUMANISM, HERESY, AND THE ONE
THOMAS MORE, CA. 1523–33

If *Utopia* is Thomas More's most contested humanist text, how More
addresses heresy proves the most difficult issue of his controversial
writings, a topic that degrades the "man for all seasons" in the minds
of some. Jasper Ridley accuses More of turning from a "brilliant intellectual" to "a sycophantic courtier and then into a persecuting big-
ot," an "intolerant fanatic."[1] So, too, David Daniell asserts that More
lost his "Erasmian lightness" in writing against heretics because "he
was so desperate to destroy heresy that what balance he once had was
eaten away."[2] Daniell sympathizes with Tyndale and other English
reformers who must have felt that "More had sold himself" by abandoning humanism for power with Henry.[3] Most recently, Brian Moynahan imagines that More commissioned "Tyndale's destruction," a
plot More orchestrated from prison, and thus, he became a villain

---

1. Jasper Ridley, *Statesman and Saint* (New York: Viking Press, 1982), i.

2. David Daniell, *William Tyndale: A Biography* (New Haven, Conn.: Yale University Press,
2001), 276. This biography shows "open partiality" according to John A. R. Dick, "Review: *William Tyndale: A Biography*," *Renaissance Quarterly* 50, no. 2 (1997): 596–97. James Hitchcock,
"Review: *William Tyndale: A Biography*," *American Historical Review* 101, no. 2 (1996): 478, believes Daniell presents "Tyndale's theology as self-evidently true."

3. Daniell, *Tyndale*, 272.

who sends the true man of conscience, William Tyndale, to martyrdom.[4] Even the popular television show *The Tudors* (1997–2010)
depicts More with a wild look in his eye as he gazes into a fire that
consumes a man.

Yet behind such depictions are important if uneven critical studies. First, with regard to More's intellectual biography, Richard Marius argues that More's theological concerns began as early as 1521 with
More's work on the *Responsio ad Lutherum*. Eventually, More moves
from a "theological councilor" to a "public defender of the faith" in
1525.[5] Marius's division of More's writings augments the "two Mores" thesis, emphasizing a "humanistic period (1500–20)" from a
"theological period (1520–35)" with the latter devoted to polemics,
especially from 1523 to 1533 (*CW* 8.3, 1144).[6] The years from More's
work as the king's secretary to his service as chancellor roughly constitute a single period of focus upon theology, a time during which
More solidifies his notion of ecclesial "consensus" that would determine his later refusal of the Act of Supremacy.

Second, though John Guy does not introduce new findings on this
question, he precisely and yet with broad scope reviews the ebb and
flow of the debate over More as "heresy hunter," carefully distinguishing fact from fiction in authors ranging from Foxe to Marius himself,
and Guy iterates two important points of emphasis. He affirms the
substance of Chambers's original position that defending the Church
was a "secular" duty incumbent upon More, following from *De Hereti-*

4. Brian Moynahan, *God's Bestseller: William Tyndale, Thomas More, and the Writing of
the English Bible—A Story of Martyrdom and Betrayal* (St. Martin's Press, 2003), 352. See Moynahan's connection to Daniell at 392, 403. Ridley and Marius provide "excellent modern biog-
raphies" at 399.

5. Marius, *Thomas More*, 276–91; 325–50.

6. Cf. *CW* 8.3, 1265, where Louis A. Schuster adds: "It should be observed, however, that the
comparative inaccessibility of More's English polemical works over the centuries help account
for the theory of two Mores: of the early humanist who had assumed positions fundamentally
inconsistent with the older More's stand on the catholic church, its clergy and its practices." For
Schuster, billingsgate and harsh words, often interpreted as More's rage and fury by revisionists,
show More's appeal to commoners: "When More's vernacular controversy is approached from
this perspective of audience-orientation, most of its formal characteristics are explainable by
function."

co Comburendo, which was passed by parliament in 1401.[7] And Guy stresses that Henry directed More to the anti-Lutheran campaign, and so in attacking heresy, More was continuing the king's policy.[8]

One important reason More's polemical tracts against the Reformation remain dismissed and unpopular is because his critics often define humanism in ways that undervalue or misrepresent its religious character.[9] Such a representation of humanism directly corresponds to the divisions of More's writings into categories of humanism and religious controversy. To challenge the "two Mores" thesis, this chapter will examine the very text singled out by Alistair Fox as a paragon of More's humanism, the *Letter to Oxford* (1518), in hopes of showing how the concerns of that letter remain present in More's later polemical tracts, especially in the *Dialogue Concerning Heresies,* a text that More composes ten years after *Oxford.*[10]

More's 1518 *Letter to Oxford* follows shortly after the publication of *Utopia* and before his public engagement with Luther. Thus, *Oxford* falls within the category of "humanist" writing and is reviewed as such by Fox. Because of its categorization, the letter should reveal evidence of More's humanist credo in contradistinction to his later polemical theology. Yet a close reading of the letter will show that More proposes a harmony of faith and liberal learning in the virtue of *pietas,* following the thematic emphasis of the *Life.* So, too, the arguments More provides in *Oxford* I will locate in his later antiheretical tracts.

Like Eamon Duffy's recent defense of More's polemical performance, I see More's response to heresy as closely related to his previous humanist scholarship, what Duffy refers to as a "humanist vision" that More "never repudiated."[11] Lucianic character types, philology and translation, and especially the relationship of theology to the lib-

---

7. Guy, *Thomas More,* 120, and see Chambers, *Thomas More,* 281.
8. Guy, *Thomas More,* 122.
9. See the introduction and Brendan Bradshaw's "Controversial More," 535–69.
10. On the historical context of More's dialogue, see *CW* 6.2, 455–72.
11. Duffy, "'The comen knowen multytude of crysten men,'" 212.

eral arts, I will argue, work in concert with More's vision of authority within the Church. More suggests that Luther is a "mad grammarian" *(insanus grammaticus)*, but the comment is not simply a polemical one (*CW* 5.1, 467/22–25). For More, the semantic content of Scripture is determined by a set of agreed-upon definitions provided by an authoritative discourse community, what More calls the whole corps of Christendom.[12] Still further, More's "articulation of a faith rooted in ecclesiastical rather than scriptural truths"[13] leads him to develop a distinctly Catholic system of signs, which he believes should govern all Christian terms and practices, and Scripture's interpretation. The ultimate arbiter of these religious signs is the Catholic Church and, in particular, its traditional teachings.[14] To be outside this authoritative discourse reveals not just "heretics" but people who resemble Lucian's morally frail braggarts, liars, false philosophers, and poets. Such a reply to heresy emerges rather than deviates from More's humanist pursuits, harkening back to his translation of the *Life of Pico* and his letters *To Dorp* (1515) and *To a Monk* (1519).

TROJANS, GREEKS, AND HERETICS

The occasion for More's *Letter to Oxford* was a homily, which pitted the liberal arts against piety. In this way, the preacher contradicts the formula we have seen More maintain in the *Life*, where *pietas* and learning exist in relationship to one another. The homily was part of a conspiracy led by the "Trojans," a faction of the university set against Greek learning (*CW* 15/133). More calls the sermon evidence of laziness, envy, and pride, an object lesson in claiming praise for ignorance (139). Against the homilist, contemplation and action constitute More's theme, and both indicate not a rupture of faith and liberal learning but a synthesis of them.

12. More often combines questions of grammar with "common senses" that are derived from the early Church Fathers. See my section on "Common Sense" below for discussion.

13. Rogers, "Thomas More's Polemical Poetics," 388.

14. For a full treatment of More's idea of the Church and the importance of tradition to achieve "consensus," see Brian Gogan, *The Common Corps of Christendom: Ecclesiological Themes in the Writings of Sir Thomas More* (Leiden: E.J. Brill, 1982).

More writes to Oxford that students will acquire "prudence in human affairs" *(rerum humanarum prudentia)* from liberal studies, advertising his sense that studying history and literature sharpens the capacity for judgment (138–39). Yet the liberal arts also show how sanctity and piety, virtue and learning, agree with the mixed life suggested in More's reworking of Pico's letter to Corneus. More connects the practical advantages of liberal studies with a defense of a union between *pietas* and the new learning. He writes: "Indeed, some plot their course, as it were, to the contemplation of celestial realities [*supernarum contemplationem*] through the study of nature, and progress to theology by way of philosophy and the liberal arts (all of which he condemns under the name 'secular literature'), thus despoiling the women of Egypt to grace their own queen" (138–41). The biblical allusion (Ex 3:22) represents an early patristic commonplace of "despoiling the Egyptians"—or learning from pagan teaching—to enhance the "queen" of theology. That theology would be the crown of humanist endeavor iterates Augustine's position from *De Doctrina* that humanistic studies are propaedeutic to theology.[15]

Addressing the same passage, however, Fox writes of More: "While acknowledging that *others* construct such a ladder, More refrains from stating that *he* does." More employs such equivocation because "if one looks at his own humanistic writings, it appears that he never tried to use his humanism tendentiously in the cause of piety as Erasmus did."[16] Indeed, Fox believes that any "Morean Christian-humanist synthesis" contains trajectories that are "centrifugal and well as centripetal," a synthesis that was crumbling even before the "Lutheran explosion."[17] Yet the Oxford homilist More attacks is the one who condemns pagan literature in the name of piety, and More maintains the reverse position: piety and learning should ac-

15. See also the commentary on 138/25–140/1 in *CW* 15, 549.

16. Fox, "Interpreting English Humanism" in Alistair Fox and John Guy, *Reassessing the Henrician Age: Humanism, Politics, and Reform 1500–1500* (New York: Basil Blackwell, 1986), 29.

17. Fox, *History and Providence*, 4. Fox does not think Christian humanism involves a "harmonious synthesis." See *Reassessing the Henrician Age*, 28–31.

company each other. So, too, the "others" who construct such a ladder of learning are likely the same persons More mentions at his letter's end: the king, Chancellor Wolsey, and those scholars at Cambridge, all of whom value liberal studies. More writes of the king, especially:

Finally, what of our most Christian prince [christianissimus princeps]? His sacred majesty has shown as much favor for all sound learning [bona artes] as any prince ever did.... With his limitless prudence [pro immensa prudentia] and great piety toward God [tantaque in Deum pietate] he will undoubtedly never permit the endeavors of wicked and slothful individuals to abolish the pursuit of sound learning [bonarum atrium] in a place ... with a long roll of learned alumni who have been ornaments not only to England but to the entire Church [totam Ecclesiam]. (CW 15/146–47)

As a paradigm, whether ultimately correct or not, Henry illustrates a combination of liberal learning with the virtue of piety, a mixture that enriches the Church and a formula that More originally advanced in the *Life*.

In praising the king, too, More reminds his audience of those influential patrons of liberal learning after the manner of a veiled threat. If the preachers at Oxford will question the orthodoxy of humanist scholars and studies, they will challenge England's own king. The whole listing of proponents—from Augustine to King Henry VIII—suggests that those who condemn the liberal arts under the guise of piety may themselves be accused of insufficient orthodoxy by those in power, auguring how More would deal with later and more severe opponents such as Luther and Tyndale. Erasmus, in fact, reports of the Oxford episode that the king, a "supporter of the humanities," heard of the incident from "More and Pace" and then declared scholars welcome to study Greek. "And so," concludes Erasmus, "those rascals were put to silence."[18] More's letter, in context, defends the liberal arts against those who would

18. Erasmus, *Letters 842-992: 1518-1519*, trans. R.A.B. Mynors and D.F.S. Thomson and annot. Peter G. Bietenholz, Wallace K. Ferguson, and James K. McConica, vol. 6 of *The Collected Works of Erasmus* (Toronto: University of Toronto Press, 1974), 317.

maintain these studies are impious, suggesting already how in his mind the liberal arts and Christian faith constitute a unified whole. In this manner, More writes that "secular learning" *(seculars literas)* prepares the soul for virtue and for theological study, even if, he adds, such learning is not necessary for salvation (*CW* 15/138–39).

What the emphasis upon piety in the *Letter to Oxford* shows is that More favors the new learning, but with an emphasis upon the teaching of *fides et ratio* within the Catholic tradition.[19] As More is sympathetic to Aquinas's teaching without admiring Scholastic methodologies in the *Life*, he defends wedding the liberal arts to orthodox doctrine against conservatives in *Oxford*. In this way, his arguments against the Trojans anticipate those More would use against Luther and Tyndale in his *Dialogue Concerning Heresies* (1529). Though the *Dialogue* is the same text that Guy identifies as the transition point from "theological councilor" to "public defender of the faith," it actually connects the "humanist" of 1518 to the controversialist at work in 1529.[20]

DIALOGUING WITH HERESY

In the *Dialogue*, "More" debates a "messenger," who is a university student captivated by the teachings of Luther and Tyndale. The same topics of *Oxford*, the importance and place of the liberal arts, are introduced by the messenger's accusation against them. According to the messenger, apart from Latin, which is necessary for Scripture study, there is little else that should be examined. Liberal arts may have useful applications—arithmetic for merchants or geom-

---

19. Fox, *Reassessing the Henrician Age*, 29, believes More's criticism of philosophy in the *Dialogue of Comfort* further illustrates the position he alleges More held in his *Letter to Oxford*, a skeptical sense about how faith and learning correspond. Yet the pages from *Comfort* that Fox cites state that we should not "fully receve" those philosophers who address pain without reference to "the fynall end of their comfort vnto god," providing a local qualification about philosophy rather than a universal statement about a life of reason. Even on the question of suffering, More writes that we should *not* "vtterly refuse" philosophical studies, but "vsyng them in such order / as shall beseme them," which, in turn, entails accepting philosophy with reference to the "high great & excelent phisicion," God (*CW* 12, 10–11).

20. Guy, *Thomas More*, 119.

etry for masons—yet where they provoke important questions about human nature there are deleterious effects. For the liberal arts cultivate reason rather than faith, thereby harming a true Christian understanding of man's nature. That is why philosophy and logic are especially useless, even harmful. They destroy theology with "the subteltyes of theyr questyons / & babelynge of theyr dyspycyons," building everything upon reason, which gives blindness instead of light (CW 6.1, 33/29–33).

The messenger is not Daniell's "airy-headed nitwit" in making these points, an "anonymous small mind" that More creates for easy refutation.[21] The messenger's concerns are as a continuation of previous humanist objections against Scholasticism. The complaint against "subtleties of questions" refers to the Scholastic method employed at the Sorbonne, what More calls *istae argutae quaestiunculae*—those sophistic little questions—in his *Letter to Oxford*.[22] Erasmus criticizes the method by listing some actual questions debated by Scholastics, including "whether the following proposition is possible: God the Father hates the Son." And "what Peter would have consecrated, if he had consecrated, during the time Christ was hanging on the cross? And whether during that same time Christ could be called a man?"[23] Francois Rabelais would make the same critique through the tales of his giant, Gargantua, who is educated in Scholastic dialectics, reading books such as *Petty Doctrines* and *What's What,* a "charming discourse set in question and answer form."[24] In Rabelais's library of Saint-Victor, we find the names of Scholastics attached to fictional works, such as Peter Tartaretus, an actual authority at Sorbonne, now listed as author of *De modo ca-*

21. Daniell, *William Tyndale,* 264. For a different picture of More and the messenger, see *CW* 6.2, 456.

22. *Priusquam argutae istae nascerentur, quae iam prope solae uentiliantur, quaestiunculae* (*CW* 15, 140). For More's own critique of scholastic dialectic, see the *Letter to Dorp,* ibid., 26–36.

23. *The Praise of Folly,* trans. Clarence Miller (New Haven, Conn.: Yale University Press, 1979), 88–89.

24. François Rabelais, *Gargantua and Pantagruel,* trans. Burton Raffell, in *The Norton Anthology of World Masterpieces,* 7th ed. (New York: W. W. Norton, 1999), 1:1886.

candi.[25] More began composing the *Dialogue* in 1528, ten years after Oxford and about three years before Rabelais's first installment of *Gargantua and Pantagruel,* but just one year after the University of Paris condemned thirty-two of Erasmus's propositions. In More's account of pilgrimages to St. Valery in the *Dialogue,* a merry tale not unlike those found in *Gargantua,* he slights the University of Paris by claiming that the institution, still full of Scholastics, remains worthy of judging bizarre or ridiculous religious practices (*CW* 6.1, 234/31–33). Daniel Kinney, More's editor, writes of More that "by 1526 he begins to sound considerably more tolerant of the *quaestio* method in theology," but More hardly seems disposed to Scholasticism in the *Dialogue* (*CW* 15, xci).

The messenger's prejudice against a classical curriculum, too, restates another humanist criticism against exponents of Scholasticism, an accusation previously alleged by Erasmus. In the *Antibarbarorum liber,* Erasmus complains of Scholastics who are "planning for the eternal ruin of the republic [of letters] under the appearance of devotion." Such devotion, like the kind employed by the preacher at Oxford, becomes a mask for neglect of study, an instrument of envy, and a sign of pride.[26] In the *Dialogue,* More focuses Erasmus's critique into a description of the pride he finds in heretical preachers, who use the "pretext of symplycyte / and good crysten deuocyon" in claiming to love "holy scrypture alone," but the "spyryte of pryde that vnware to them self lurked in theyr hartys" actually motivates them. Under the praise of Scripture alone, these preach-

25. M. A. Screech, *Rabelais* (Ithaca, N.Y.: Cornell University Press, 1979), 61, identifies the allusion of *De modo cacandi* with "Peter Tartaretus, a pillar of the Sorbonne and an authority on Aristotle and on the dethroned, old-fashioned, scholastic philosopher Peter of Spain," though Screech suspects Rabelais was mostly interested in Tartaretus because of the pun on "tarter," a slang term that means "to defecate."

26. *Antibarbarorum liber,* trans. Margaret Mann Phillips, in *The Erasmus Reader,* ed. Erika Rummel (Toronto: University of Toronto Press, 1990), 54. The *Antibarbarorum* is a source for More's *Dialogue* in other places that concern the liberal arts as well. More tells the messenger, without poetry, "all learning is half lame," which mirrors Erasmus's formulation, where we are told without the humanities, "all learning is blind." See *CW* 6.1, 132/11–16 and *Antibarbarorum,* 53.

ers long to appear marvelous to others by setting out "paradoxis and straunge oppynyons / agaynst ye commen fayth of Crystes hole chyrche," favoring their own "fonde gloses" against the "olde connynge" of the Church Fathers (CW 6.1, 123/1–16). More speculates that heretics, like the Trojan homilist he condemned, are motivated by the "scabbed ytche of vaynglory," which preaching to the people satisfies, granting them notoriety and distinction by way of idiosyncratic, unstudied opinion. These "longe to be pulpetyed," and More writes of them: "And this I say hath comen of some that haue with contempte of all other lernynge gyuen them to scrypture alone" (125/37–126/7). In such passages as these More connects the desire to be "pulpetyed" with "pryde," "slouth," and ignorance, creating a character type for heretics.

Rather than a new position specific to More's controversialist writings, the desire to be pulpited indicates a literary type that More first developed in his studies of Lucian. "There are many thumbnail sketches of special types of frail morality scattered through Lucian," observes Benjamin Boyce, "in addition to his full-length exposures of the rhetorician and of the illiterate bibliomaniac."[27] More proposes such a frail character type in explaining and defending his translation of Lucian, justifying a scornful kind of humor directed at those with an "inordinate passion for lying" (CW 3.1, 5/14).[28] Like the stories told by those who love lying, More writes, false devotional practices and fanciful theology—fables—contaminate "truth unadorned" (ipsa veritas), the truth of Christian doctrine. Indeed, More suspects the architects of pious stories and false miracles are heretics who are attempting to undermine rightful authority (7/3–22).[29] As early as

---

27. Benjamin Boyce, The Theophrastan Character in England to 1642 (Cambridge, Mass.: Harvard University Press, 1947), 36n48.

28. On the rhetorical function of humor, see Cicero, De Oratore, II.lviii.236: "Then the field or province, so to speak, of the laughable ... is restricted to that which may be described as unseemly or ugly; for the chief, if not the only, objects of laughter are those sayings which remark upon and point out something unseemly in no unseemly manner."

29. Instead of a humanist period in which More condemns miracles and a religious time in which he supports them, then, More's position remains consistent: He writes that we ought to

1506, therefore, More provides an instance of how he associates traits such as bragging, ignorance, and lying with heresy.

More condemns this self-aggrandizing type not just in the Oxford case but later, too, in his 1519 *Letter to a Monk*, where More recycles the Lucianic figures. In telling of a visit to Coventry, More describes a "most holy" and "learned" friar, who teaches that any who said the psalter of the Blessed Virgin Mary every day could not be damned (*CW* 15, 287). More ridicules the teaching and is promptly rebuked by the friar himself. The people applaud the friar, More writes, because of his *persona pietatis,* a mask of holiness. The friar's teaching, in other words, allows the people to indulge in vice, so long as they keep the office of the Virgin Mary (288–89). For More, the problem is not with prayer to the Virgin Mary or with the religious orders themselves, but with those who enjoy the epithets of "blessed" and "saintly" because these prefer self-adulation to truth (291).

As More points out the relationship between the people and the preaching in Coventry in terms of mutual corruption, he would later identify the sedition of Lutherans in relation to the men who inspired them. The friar in Coventry enjoys his status as will Tyndale take pleasure in his, but more generally, faction in the Church emerges from pride, from the belief that nothing is more holy than that which we do ourselves (278–79). That fundamental position—*nihil est sanctum, nisi quod faciunt ipsi* (278/12–13)—predicates More's metaphor of *persona* piety, emphasizing a characterological rather than a doctrinal assessment. Such *persona* piety More applies to Scholastics or to those who advocate fantastic religious practices before the Reformation and, later, to "heretics." Like the Theophrastan character of "Petty Pride," a person with a "vulgar appetite for distinction,"[30] both More's early depiction of foolish clerics and later accounts of proud heretics illustrate men who thirst for attention.[31]

---

believe the miracles in Scripture and test others according to the Christian teaching (*ad Christi doctrinam*) (*CW* 3.1, 6/18).

30. Cited from Boyce, *Theophrastan Character,* 6.

31. On "pride" throughout More's work, see Wegemer, *More on Statesmanship,* 30–34.

In the *Dialogue*, Thomas Bilney becomes paradigmatic of this proud attitude. More articulates plainly his principle of distinguishing well-intentioned but uneducated preachers from malicious, self-aggrandizing ones: "I speke but of those / whose erronyous oppynons in theyr prechynge / and theyr obstynate pryde in the defence of theyr worldly worshyp well declareth theyr myndes" (*CW* 6.1, 124/10–13).[32] More, then, claims that Bilney first accepts correction and admits his heretical opinions are "erronyous." Later in "secrete pryde" Bilney reverses himself because he hopes to avoid shame in front of the people who admired his previous teachings. Bilney would experience a "passion of shame" if the people should hear his retraction, especially because before they had held "his sermons in great estymacyon." And so "at the first sight of ye peple," Bilney reverses his recantation (125/7–31). More later expands upon Bilney's fault of pride in a general way, explaining it as a "hygh mynde to be in the lykyng of the people," which becomes a frantic impulse in heretics because they "delyte to thynke how they be take[n] for holy." Assertive, spirited claims for singular and personal holiness lead heretics to "deuyse new fantasyes in our fayth because they wolde be syngular among the peple" (423/3–23). Those with "moch lesse than meane lernyng so sore to long to seme far better lerned than they be" that they create new teachings for the pleasure of "newe fangle folke," who, in turn, place such preachers in authority (423/30–35).

Marius investigates the Bilney case in terms of whether or not he actually and finally recanted, sorting through the different eyewitness accounts of Bilney's last hours, but More's point, whether about the religious he criticizes in his so-called humanist letter or here in the *Dialogue,* is that just as clerics condemn learning out of arrogance at Oxford, Bilney rejects correction out of pride.[33] From

32. Heresy, thus, appears as a function of "frowardnesse" or "vayne pryde" more than a matter of asking any particular theological question (*CW* 13, 28/16–32).

33. Marius, *Thomas More,* 397–401.

Trojans to reformers, Lucianic "lovers of lies" appear. More calls Pico proud for his heresy and later Scholastic theologians proud in attacking the liberal arts; finally, More transfers the same defect to reformers. More's application of a character type from his humanist studies to his controversial writings illustrates cohesion rather than discontinuity.

REASON AND AUTHORITY

More emphasizes Bilney's case in terms of rightly interpreting Scripture and in doing so returns to the relationship between faith and the liberal arts. As James Simpson argues, all the points of the *Dialogue*—the case of Bilney, the use of witnesses in heresy trials, the translation of Scripture, the place of religious images and pilgrimages—press More's cardinal argument: the need for "faith-dependent practices" that govern how we should understand Scripture.[34] Though Simpson correctly identifies the importance of "faith-dependent" reading, I think More's aim extends beyond texts. Put otherwise, authority of some kind always guides reason for More. A related inquiry to the importance of authority for reason is that of how authority and liberal arts inquiry may coexist, and, in one sense, questions such as these address the essence of the "two Mores" or "real More" theses. Yet how may humanism and religion coherently coexist?

That question the messenger poses in the *Dialogue*. As More develops the discussion, the messenger makes his case against liberal learning pointed: "And as for reason / what greter enemy can ye fynde to fayth than reason is / whiche counterpledyth fayth in euery poynt" (128/ 25–27). In contrast, More proposes a synthesis of faith and reason. Christians "haue reason in theyr heddys" and

---

34. James Simpson, *Burning to Read: English Fundamentalism and Its Reformation Opponents* (Cambridge, Mass.: Belknap Press of Harvard University Press, 2007), 245. For Simpson, see ibid., 264–71, More's *Dialogue* is different from other anti-polemical tracts, which illustrate More's devolution to a "defender of a dead traditionalism." I argue, however, that the *Dialogue* conceptually agrees with More's other arguments on authority.

"the lyght of fayth in theyr soulys" (56/13–14), More writes. Reason is "well gyded" by faith, a virtue personified, who walks with faith as "her handmayde" and should never go without her (131/18–31). For More, reason cannot "dysdayne to here ye trouth / of any poynt of fayth / then to se ye profe of many thynges naturall / wherof reason can no more attayne to ye cause than it can in ye artycles of ye fayth" (129/24–27). Thus, a natural phenomenon, such as the attraction of metals to magnets, which could not be explained in More's time by way of cause, may be believed without defying reason. People may wonder about a "secrete proprete of the stone," but without knowledge of cause, speculation amounts to "I wote nere what," or "I know not what." More states "reason can byleue" in the power of magnets, despite the lack of causal knowledge (129/31–130/9). By analogy, reason may believe in the truths of faith. The doctrine agrees with Scholastics such as Aquinas, yet its articulation avoids the format of *istae argutae quaestiunculae* (CW 15, 140).

More elaborates his defense of faith and liberal arts study by addressing how the realm of suprarational opinion remains contingent upon authority. What if an Ethiopian man, More posits, never left his country and received no foreign visitors, might he not surmise that it were against "the nature of man to be whyte" (CW 6.1, 65/6)? Such a one would reason no differently than those who infer all men are reasonable, arguing from induction, and yet the messenger would hold the Ethiopian is incorrect, and the proposition on the reasonable nature of man, accurate. Why the distinction? If the messenger interjects that an educated Ethiopian would know man's nature is not the same as the color of his skin, More replies that the same may be said of the reformers: "yf they had some lernyng that they lacke / [they] sholde well perceyue that of reason they sholde gyue credence to credable persones / reporting them thynges y^t seme farre against reason because they be farre aboue reason" (66/1–4). As an educated Ethiopian would find it reasonable to believe reports from abroad about skin color, so, too, theologians should accept credible information about what is beyond reason. In both cases, what is credible follows from an antecedent trust in some form of authority. The messenger himself assents to arguments from authority, as More shows in these examples: from accepting the identity of his father as whomever his mother may indicate to him as such (63/28–64/6) to believing in certain practices of metalworkers, who may separate gold from silver with "fayre water," a liquid that we know as nitric acid but that appeared mysterious to Londoners at that time (66/28–34).[35] The messenger accepts authority because it seems reasonable to do so, More insists. The case is the same with deferring to the Church on matters of divine action, from the working of miracles to the conveyance of wisdom through revelation. More argues: "yf ye byleue no man in suche thyngys as maye not be / than must it follow that ye ought to byleue no man in many thyngys that may be / for all is one to you / whyther they may be or may not be / yf it seme to you that they may not be" (70/9–12). Based upon what principle does something seem acceptable? Argument makes no difference about credibility where the first premise already declares a matter believable or not. So, too, what "may be or may not be" illustrates the need for authority in thinking about questions of faith. Events like miracles or teachings above reason cannot be affirmed by rules of reason alone. In matters where reason is not the authority, it is reasonable to defer to another authority. Rather than fideism, More teaches respect for the limits of reason. To do otherwise allows reason "to renne out at ryot" and "wax ouer hye herted and prowde," inviting reason to "to fall in rebellyon towarde her maystres fayth" (131/26–28).

Returning to the subject of magnets, the messenger rejects More's argument, but clumsily: because one may witness the power of magnets, their power must exist. The empiricism here gives More an easy rebuttal. More responds that sight may be deceived and think it sees what it cannot, if reason gives over its hold. More

---

35. On "fayre water," see commentary on 66/28–30 in CW 6.2, 619.

then asks whether the messenger would believe a magician's trick that turns "a plum into a doggys torde" (130/18). Passages like this one question Germain Marc'hadour's general assessment that "a healthy instinct ... supported by experience, prompts us to trust our eye, despite the tricks it occasionally plays on us" (*CW* 6.2, 534).[36] A healthy instinct formed by experience, in More's presentation, includes an epistemological trust in an authority that indicates where and how God acts. After distinguishing the examples of magnets and magic, More draws attention to their similarity: "Nowe ye se that reason is not so proude a dame as ye take her for. She seeth done in dede by nature that she can not perceyue how / and is well contentyd therwith" (130/27–30). That assessment belongs to the case of magnets, and it parallels the one for magic: "She [reason] seeth a fonde felowe deceyue her syght and her wyt therwith and takyth it well and meryly / and is not angry that ye iugeler [magician] wyll not teche euery man his craft" (130/30–32). We hold belief in the magnet's function as reasonable, and in the magician's trick as unreasonable, because of shared assumptions about plausibility. More, then, emphasizes reason's liabilities without faith, increasing the importance of what he calls "common sense."

COMMON SENSES

Sensus communis plays a specific role for More. He uses the term in addressing Scholastic dialectic, especially its emphasis upon formal logic, in his 1515 *Letter to Dorp*. Scholastic dialecticians, More writes, win obscure arguments because they "have secretly agreed to construe our own words," defining words against "all common sense" *(contra communen omnium sensum)* (*CW* 15, 36–37). Yet words, More writes in the *Dialogue*, are conventional instead of natural signs, conveying signification because of human agreement (*CW* 6.1, 46–47). "All these names spoken / and all these wordes wrytten," More

36. Marc'hadour thinks that in natural theology "More is attuned most strikingly to Aquinas" (*CW* 6.2, 534).

asserts, "be no naturall sygnes or ymages but onely made by consent and agrement of men / to betoken and sygnyfye suche thynge" (46/26–29). More here follows Augustine's *De Doctrina*, which defines a sign as "a thing which of itself makes some other thing come to mind." Augustine distinguishes between "natural signs," such as smoke that signifies fire, and "given signs," which "express and transmit to another's mind what is in the mind of the person who gives the sign."[37] Augustine's context shows how More's earlier use of "common sense" should include the context of shared understanding by human convention.[38] That definition—common sense as agreed-upon knowledge—accounts for More's distinction between magnets and magicians. Philological common sense, like other forms of knowledge acquired by shared experience, provides a basis for judgment. We may rightly "know" without scientific demonstration that magnets work, as we may "know" men are reasonable.

Similarly, the truths of faith function as fundamental agreements within the tradition of the whole Corps of Christendom, guiding our thinking about the significance of images (47/11–15), or reverence of saints, who stand for God's honor (48/27–34), or identifying certain places as special for God's presence, such as pilgrimage sites (54/32–59/34). More's overarching point in each of these cases may be best illustrated by his discussion of sacraments in his *Confutation of Tyndale's Answer* (1532–33). In addressing the sacraments as signs, More criticizes Tyndale because the latter had posited a "bare sygne voyd of any frutefull effecte" (*CW* 8.1, 99/9). "Bare" signs are those conventional ones mentioned above, signifiers that translate mental conceptions from one to another through speaking or writing. Hence More's characterization of Tyndale's position is that "the sacraments be but sygnes and tokens that betoken and preache the promises" (96/3–4). Sacraments, for Tyndale, are like any other name, a sign,

---

37. Augustine, *On Christian Teaching*, 30. For an account of how Augustine's semiotics are employed by More's polemics and affect the aesthetics of his controversial writings, see Rogers, "Thomas More's Polemical Poetics," 387–407.

38. For a different view, see *CW* 15, lxn3.

what More calls only a "bare dede token" (101/26). Tyndale inherits his basic position from Luther because both believe "god gyueth all the grace by the fayth alone" (98/24–27).

To explore the sacraments as efficacious signs, More first proposes a "lyuery gowne" of his household, which signifies the promise, "I wyll take the[e] for myn housholde seruaunt," thereby granting room and board to whoever dons the gown. The sign of the garment entails a promise and therefore transfers a "frutefull effecte" (99/9–18). Sacraments may be the same kind of effectual sign. Alternatively, the sacraments themselves are "workers and instrumentes" in the cleansing of souls, not simply a promise of that purging (105/19–20). The water of baptism, for example, by "the secrete sanctyfycacyon of god," contains a "strength of spirytual lyfe infounded in to that corporall element," which constitutes not merely a sign, but also a "quycke lyuely workynge medycyne, meane, and instrument" (101/21–28).

As in the case of language, sacraments constitute signs that are not natural but "given." For More, a traditional, ecclesial discourse governs not just the *res* of a sacrament, but also the *signum*, illustrating how divine action corresponds with semantics. All "holy ceremonyes" are not superstitious practices but what "Crystes chyrch hath receyued" from the days of the "blessed apostles" (110, 28–34). Hence, the sacraments are effectual because the Church tradition proves them to be so, even if More may play with the rationale by which such efficacy occurs. Because of this commitment to traditional teaching and language, More believes reformers reject a necessary epistemological trust in the Church, an intellectual framework that is essential to reason well about theological questions. More writes of this trust in his *Dialogue:*

For yf a knowen lyar tell you a knowen trewe tale / ye wyll byleue him bycause he telleth you trouth. But nowe if a knowen true man tell you an vnknowen trouth ye byleue not him / bycause yᵉ thyng is trouth / but ye byleue the thyng to be trouth bycause ye byleue yᵉ man to be true. *And so byleue you the chyrche / not bycause it is trouth that yᵉ chyrche telleth you / but ye beleue the trouth of the thynge bycause the chyrche telleth it.* (*CW* 6.1, 251/7–13, my emphasis)

Elsewhere, More contrasts what one feels is written in the heart by God with teaching from what "all the olde holy sayntes" and "all chrysten people besyde" have believed the past 1,500 years (*CW* 8.2, 816/28–35). The passage above, though, appears striking because of its clarity: belief about what is true in theology exists exclusively as a function of ecclesial discourse, not independently.

Rather than change his earlier position on the place of reason from the *Letter to Oxford,* More's polemical theology expands upon it by specifying reason's "handmaid status." The early enemies of More are theologians or clerics who privilege decadent forms of Scholastic inquiry or religious fable over and against reason, thereby devaluing authentic piety. The reformers, conversely, reason from a different faith, and in so doing, redefine authority and, ultimately, the parameters of reason itself. As More summarizes later in his *Apology:* People first fall into "doutynge of the trouth"; after accepting "false bylyefe," they become "very neglygent & vnreasonable" (*CW* 9, 9/29–37). Doubting the truth means rejecting the accepted doctrine of Christendom, a first step that is followed by accepting a "false" belief or account of Christian revelation, after which men become "unreasonable." More concludes that from rejecting the doctrine and discourse of traditional, ecclesial consensus within the Catholic Church, reformers lose the capacity of reason.[39] Revisionist critics fail to take seriously the alleged loss of the latter. Indeed, they cannot do so and advance the existence of "two Mores," a reasonable humanist and a religious fanatic, or a "real More," who, in Elton's assessment, cannot cross the "abyss" between "theocentric Christianity" and "humanocentric humanism."[40]

---

39. Cf. *CW* 7, 37: "Reverence is not lost if in the course of a dispute reason seems to run counter to truth, for it is absolutely certain that since faith is sustained by divine revelation, it far surpasses the reason of mortal men."

40. Elton, "Humanism in England," 228.

EPISTEMOLOGICAL TRUST AND
TRANSLATING SCRIPTURE

For More, the reformers' questions of redefined authority and reason erupt in the controversy over retranslating Scripture. When Moynahan writes that the "real horror" of Tyndale's testament is not "the words themselves" but that they are "English words" capable of infecting the multitude with heresy, he only partially captures More's point; in fact, the words Tyndale used are a crucial focus for More.[41] In the *Dialogue,* More singles out three terms especially from Tyndale's New Testament: "priest" or "senior" (from *presbuteros*), "church" or "congregation" (from *ekklesia*), and "charity" or "love" (from *agape*). In each case, More favors the former while Tyndale supplies the latter. Daniell questions whether More had "ever seen Tyndale's translations for himself" but later claims More's own translations of Scripture are close enough to Tyndale's "to argue for dependence."[42] Better arguments from Daniell are in the following claims: Tyndale's goals of translation "were always accuracy and clarity," and his efforts significantly aided the later composition of the King James Bible.[43] Daniell's assessment, though, that Tyndale provides "the Bible in English, England's greatest contribution to the world for nearly five hundred years" seems hyperbolic.[44] Even so, the King James revisers would side with More twice on these contested words, exchanging "church" for Tyndale's "congregation" and "charity" for Tyndale's "love"; Tyndale himself changes "senior" to "elder."[45]

More believes Tyndale is guilty of discursive violence in making these changes because the new translations erase traditional teaching from Scripture. For More, words are signs, as we have seen,

41. Moynahan, *God's Bestseller,* 106.

42. Daniell, *Tyndale,* 267; David Daniell, *The Bible in English: Its History And Influence* (New Haven, Conn.: Yale University Press, 2003), 171.

43. Daniell, *The Bible in English,* 158.

44. Daniell, *Tyndale,* 280.

45. For Tyndale's defense of his translation of these words, see his *An Answere Unto Mores,* 10–20. Tyndale admits to More's critique about the word "senior" at 15/9–13.

which remain essential to an extra-scriptural tradition. "Chyrche" denotes not simply any congregation of people, but a "congregacyon of crysten people / whiche ... hath ben in Englande alway called and knowen by the name of the chyrche" (*CW* 6.1, 286/29–31). Charity should mean "a good vertuous and well ordred loue" (288/5–6), but that meaning remains unspecified in the more general term "love."[46] The words "elder" and "senior," too, eliminate the distinctive office of a priest in dispensing sacraments (289/14–31). For More, changing such terms undermines traditional consensus, reconfiguring previously held definitions.

More did favor an English translation of the Bible, as is often noted, but as in the case of sacraments, he wants a translation in which the English language corresponds with Catholic doctrine.[47] For More, the authority of tradition exists before Scripture, and, indeed, the Church provides Scripture. "I praye you tell me what scrypture hath taught the chyrch to knowe whyche bookys be the very scrypture?" More asks (253/21–22). The Church determines what books of Scripture are canonical or inspired; thus, it creates Scripture through the "holy spyryte," which first "inspyred that consent / qui facit vnanimes in domo / whyche makyth the chyrche all of one mynde and accorde" (253/30–33). After arguing for Scripture alone, More reasons, Tyndale's translation would effectively replace the Church as the preeminent Christian authority about all matters of doctrine. "So that it is eth [easy] to se," More concludes of Tyndale, "what he ment in the turnynge of these names" (290/9). The implication of Tyndale's work argues that "prechers haue all thys .xv.C. yere [1,500 years] mysse reported yᵉ gospell ... to lede the people purposely out of the ryght way" (290/34–36). Lurking behind the

---

46. See Anne M. O'Donnell, "Agapē and Synonyms in New Testament Translations of St. Thomas More," *Moreana* 45, no. 175 (2008): 121–46.

47. More values Scripture just as much as the messenger, but he thinks the liberal arts contribute to understanding Scripture: "There was neuer thynge wrytten in this worlde that canne in any wyse be comparable with any parte of holy scrypture. And yet I thynke other lyberall science a gyft of god also / and not to be cast away / but worthy to wayte and as hande maydes to gyue attendaunce vpon dyuynyte. And in this poynt I thynke not thus alone" (*CW* 6.1, 126/16–19).

scriptura sui ipsius interpres concept—Scripture itself is its own inter-preter—More recognizes a revolutionary overthrow of 1,500 years of consensus.

More's objections to Tyndale's translation, however, are not new or alien to his previous "humanist" writings on translating Scrip-ture, but rather directly follow from his defense of Erasmus's trans-lation of the Scriptures, which, More emphasized, was approved by the pope and permissible according to the teaching of the Church Fathers. Responding to an unnamed "monk" who criticized Eras-mus's translation of the first verses from John, More defends Eras-mus's use of *sermo*, or speech, instead of Jerome's *verbum*.[48] More stresses that Erasmus's translation is in harmony with the Church Fathers. Jerome used *verbum* but indicated that *logos* had other meanings as well, a teaching that Gregory of Nazianzus supported in claiming Christ as Word and Speech because he "is Reason and Wisdom" (*CW* 15, 237). For More, *ratio, causa, verbum,* and *sermo* may all indicate *logos* (241), an etymological position of the Church Fathers and one that leads More to suggest that "if any word should be so revered as to be kept in its original form," such as in the case of "Amen," it should be done with *logos* (237). The Church again functions as a community of discourse in which consent is achieved over time and with deference to its traditional teachings. The differ-ence between *sermo* and *verbum*, then, is like that between *vxorem* and *coniugem* (248/3–5).

So More writes in 1519, but he returns to the issue of translat-ing the Gospel of John again in addressing Tyndale. More takes is-sue with Tyndale's 1525 version, which reads: "In the begynnge was *that* worde, and *that* worde was with god, and god was *that* worde" (*CW* 8.1, 236/18–19, my emphasis). More argues for "the" instead of "that" because "*the* god and *the* worde that is *the* synguler god

48. The monk was John Batmanson, Carthusian of London (*CW* 15, xli). Erasmus had *In principio erat sermo, & sermo erat apud deum.* See *Novum Testamentum*, Basel, 1519, sig.q₅ in *CW* 15, 237–38.

and *the* synguler worde, that is to wyt *the* worde of god" (*CW* 8.1, 236/27–28, my emphasis). As the Yale editors gloss this dispute, "Tyndale's 1525 version, here accurately reproduced, became in 1534, 'In the beginnynge was the worde, and the worde was with God: and the worde was God,' thus incorporating More's suggestions for correction."[49] Even so, without referring to More, Moynahan brings his own recent account of Tyndale to a close by citing the *revised* lines from John as a final tribute to "Tyndale's genius."[50] In the *Confutation*, however, More jokes about Tyndale's mistake, playing upon the words "beginning," "that" and "word": "I meruayle why he translated *In principio erat verbum,* In the begynnyng was that worde / for surely that worde that, was not to begynne with all nor to stande there, but yf Tyndale entended to mokke" (*CW* 8.1, 237/3–6). The word "that," More argues, is erroneously supplied by Tyndale, but More's own parody of the gospel lines indicates that Tyndale's translation makes an unconscious parody of the reformers' claim that scriptural verses ought to explain themselves.

In both cases—from the *Letter to a Monk* to the *Confutation*—More privileges tradition as the authority to adjudicate disputes of Scripture. For external signs emerge from invisible, interior ones; all of these are created and driven by the Holy Spirit within a visible and historical Church.[51] More writes that the "worde vnwryten" of the Church's tradition is equal to and as strong as the "worde wryten" (*CW* 8.1, 132/32–34). The Church, though "not aboue the scripture," is "so taught by the spyryte of god and his holy secrete inward worde vnwrytten" that it cannot be deceived in interpreting Scripture (133/33–34).

That context of the "holy secrete inwarde worde" seems crucial in determining whether there were "two Mores" or for resolving how More's religion impacted his previous thought. Daniell argues,

49. Commentary on 236/18–19 in *CW* 8.3, 1553.
50. Moynahan, *God's Bestseller*, 388–90.
51. On the visible Church, see *CW* 8.1, 480/35–481/18.

"Tyndale can only have wondered what had happened to the Christian humanist who had been so scathing in *Utopia* about prejudice." More should have been enough of a "scholar" to recognize Tyndale's "fine piece of work," which carried "the torch of the Greek and new Latin" of Erasmus.[52] Daniell's argument here updates the revisionist theory by incorporating it into his hagiographical narrative of Tyndale's life. In the *Confutation*, however, More writes that the Church, as custodian of traditional teaching, provides a definitive understanding of Scripture, "for yf you take you to yͤ gospel then wyll I take me to the chyrch, by whose commaundement I byleued the gospell" (*CW* 8.2, 737/32–33). For More, the "consente of the olde holy doctours of Chrystes chyrche" may prove the "knowen catholyque chyrche is the very chyrche" (740/27–29). The consent of those Church Fathers protects Erasmus but not Tyndale. The monk's concerns about Erasmus's translation ignore those "holy doctours" who employed the notion of *duplex sensus literalis,* a word whose literal sense provides more than one meaning, as with translating *logos* into either *sermo* or *verbum,* but tradition cannot justify Tyndale's English version of the same lines.

Because of More's commitment to Christendom's common senses, he acknowledges Erasmus's "errors" even in those passages where he appears to explain them away. So when Tyndale taunts More over defending Erasmus's translation of "thys worde *ecclesia*" into *congregatio,* calling Erasmus More's "derlynge," More replies:

I haue not contended wyth Erasmus my derlynge, bycause I found no suche malycyouse entent wyth Erasmus my derlynge, as I fynde with Tyndale. For had I fownde with Erasmus my derlyng the shrewde entent and purpose that I fynde in Tindale: Erasmus my derlynge sholde be no more my derlynge. But I fynde in Erasmus my derlynge that he detesteth and abhorreth the errours and heresyes that Tyndale playnely techeth and abydeth by / and therfore Erasmus my derlynge shall be my dere derlynge styll. (*CW* 8.1, 177/15–23)

---

52. Daniell, *William Tyndale,* 272.

The above explanation about malice corresponds with the philological account More gives: Erasmus translates Greek into Latin, not Greek into English; he could not use the English term "church" (177/27–32). More's defense again iterates a shared way of translating that privileges respect for the tradition as much as innovative scholarly acumen. Some changes are permissible not because Erasmus makes them instead of Tyndale but because they are in accordance with the tradition. As Simpson explains, "faithful, unwritten intuitions about the pre-textual truths that produce meaning as we read are not in the least nonevidential" because "all knowledge is dependent on faith of one kind or another." Simpson's "pre-textual truths" mean there can be no Scripture alone, but only competing reading strategies, ways of reading that emerge from different faiths.[53] Names and words, like other symbols, are not natural but *given* signs. The question is who should give them.

HUMANISM AND COMMUNITY

Sensus communis, then, indicates another understanding beyond philological shared senses: it illustrates the ideal of an authentic and authoritative interpretive community.[54] Words entail contexts and contexts involve interpretations, but rival interpretations require a community of consensus for adjudication. Thus, more than correct translation is at stake for More, whether he debates Scholastics or reformers. In the *Letter to Dorp*, More claims Scholastics are unable to sustain the faith or encourage virtue. Scholastics are removed from poetry and rhetoric, too, just "as they are from theology proper; and from nothing, apart from ordinary common sense, are they further removed from that" (*CW* 15, 49). For Kinney, this passage defines "common sense" after the interrelation of *ratio* and *proprietas*, dia-

---

53. Simpson, *Burning to Read,* 247.

54. On translation and the need for an authoritative interpretive community, see *CW* 5.1, 477/20–23: "And who does not see how wide a window for blaspheming the king has opened to all heretics and enemies of faith once it is admitted that the authority of scripture relies on slippery and deceptive words?"

lectic and grammar, an assessment following Quintilian's instruction on style (CW 15, lx). Referring to the same passage, however, Richard Sylvester glosses *communi hominum sensu* with a better understanding, what he calls the "common feelings of humanity."[55] Though late, Sylvester's translation accords with the *OED* definition of "common sense" in usage, at least, by 1598: "The general sense, feeling, or judgment of mankind, or of a community."[56] This "general sense" suggests a judgment not only *by* mankind but *of* mankind. In this way, the kind of theology More wants Dorp to support should include the same liberal arts that More defends in his *Dialogue*, a program of study that emphasizes especially poetry but also history and oratory because these "moche helpe the iudgement," providing what More calls the "one specyall thynge / without whiche all lernynge is halfe lame"—a "good mother wyt" (CW 6.1, 132/11–16).

Of importance, More's formulation of a good mother wit, and the arts that cultivate it, echoes Cicero's teaching in *De Officiis*, which proposes an understanding of human nature obtained through the study of *bonae litterae*. Cicero writes: "We are invested by Nature with two characters, as it were: one of these is universal, arising from the fact of our being all alike endowed with reason.... From this all morality and propriety are derived, and upon it depends the rational method of ascertaining our duty. The other character is the one that is assigned to individuals in particular."[57] Next, Cicero uses examples from history and poetry to elaborate, teaching, as Gerard Wegemer writes, "the best way of life is known by reason's reflection on the comprehensive requirements of human nature."[58] After making the above point about human nature, Cicero emphasizes "individuals in particular"—from "Gaius Laelius, of unbounded jollity" to his close friend, Scipio, "who cherished more serious ideals

---

55. Sylvester, "Humanist in Action," 465.
56. *The Oxford English Dictionary*, 2nd ed., 1989 *OED Online*, Oxford University Press, June 27, 2007, http://dictionary.oed.com/cgi/00181778.
57. *De Off.*, I.xxx.107.
58. Wegemer, "On Statesmanship," 114.

and lived a more austere life." He lists "fascinating" characters such as Socrates and shrewd, deceptive political types such as Themistocles or Solon, who may serve their country through craftiness.[59] From the poets, we see that Ulysses endured long wanderings and humiliations by striving "to be courteous and complaisant to all," but Ajax would choose death over indignities.[60] The importance of self-knowledge becomes explicit: "For we must so act as not to oppose the universal laws of human nature, but, while safeguarding those, to follow the bent of our particular nature."[61] As a result: "Everyone ... should make a proper estimate of his own natural ability and show himself a critical judge of his own merits and defects."[62] A shared understanding of human nature, one that matures through the study of rhetoric, history, and poetry, will emerge in the ability to judge other types of character, other kinds of men, and develop self-knowledge. By following Cicero's example in the *Dialogue*, More confirms the earlier message of *Oxford*, which places the study of nature *before* that of theology (*CW* 15, 139). Common sense, in turn, should operate as a function of "a good mother wyt," indicating a general intellectual capacity *and* a shared anthropological sense.

Indeed, Sylvester sees a "temporal" and "spatial" meaning in the phrase translated above. The *communis sensus hominum* links "the new humanist position with what all wise men thought in the past," and it looks in the present for a "new community of spirit and feeling," a spirit that enables men to live in charity.[63] That broader notion of *humanitas* Poliziano had already articulated: "When I say 'humanity'[*humanitatem*], I intend learning no less than kindness. For to people who know Latin it clearly means both."[64] Poliziano's sense of "humanity" appears in the 1565 Latin dictionary of Thomas Cooper as well, a late date for More but an appropriate context for understanding Sylvester's gloss. Cooper defines *humanitas* under

---

59. *De Off.*, I.xxx.108.
60. Ibid., I.xxxi.113.
61. Ibid., I.xxxi.110.
62. Ibid., I.xxxi.114.
63. Sylvester, "Humanist in Action," 465.
64. Poliziano, *Letters*, 1:169; cf. Butler's commentary, ibid., at 343.

three categories: "the state of human nature common to us all"; "liberal knowledge, learning, humanity"; "courtesy, gentleness, humanity." The concepts are interrelated.[65] Knowledge of human nature occurs through study of good literature, and by such study we become humane or, in Sylvester's terms, acquainted with the "the common feelings of humanity." From Cooper's definition, we see how *humanitas* may relate to a *sensus communis* because these terms imply a shared understanding due to shared human nature. Such a broad educational approach stands in contrast to narrow disputes of Scholastics over how logic applies to semantic conundrums. That is why More's argument against Dorp suggests a comparison between the common sense acquired through the study of rhetoric and poetry or from true theology against the logic of Scholastic dialecticians. *Studia humanitatis* is more than a family of academic disciplines, emphasizing rhetoric, but a study of "secular letters" that opens a window into the human condition; it is a shared understanding and a way of life, and for More a way of life pursued within a community of belief. Sylvester's explication of More's humanism, in other words, appears like More's understanding of the Church.

In fact, a shared understanding of the human condition illustrates how humanist community parallels the Church. As More tells Dorp, the gospel was not a written text, but an inward one, "written" within the heart of humankind. More writes to Dorp that the meaning of Scripture should have recourse "to that living gospel of faith [*uiuum euangelium fidei*] which has been infused into the hearts of the faithful [*corda fidelium*] throughout the whole Church [*universam ecclesiam*]" (*CW* 15, 89).[66] Faith, the Church, and a conception of humankind are woven together and bound by charity. Defend-

---

65. Thomas Cooper is cited from Robin Headlam Wells, *Shakespeare's Humanism* (Cambridge: Cambridge University Press, 2005), 8, which Wells uses to argue for "the significance that humanists attached to the study of human nature" (9). For a fuller account of Thomas Cooper and the term "humanism," see Mike Pincombe, *Elizabethan Humanism: Literature and Learning in the Later Sixteenth Century* (London: Longman, 2001), especially 4–14.

66. For the Latin, see *CW* 15, 88/1–4.

ing Erasmus from Dorp and written before Henry's own *Assertio,* More speaks in his own voice here about a living, pre-textual gospel, which is "written" on the hearts of the faithful within the universal Church.

More recapitulates the point against Luther in 1522, elaborating upon Hebrews 8:10, "I will put my laws upon their hearts and upon their minds I will write them" (*CW* 5.1, 101/21–22). More notes that the new law is not on "stone" or "tables of wood," or any external thing, but "He [God] will write the new law inwardly by the finger of God on the book of the heart" (101/22–25). John M. Headley believes this passage "suggests typology, pertaining to the church in time," but cannot name a source.[67] I think More interweaves his commentary here by alluding to 2 Corinthians 3:1–8. Tyndale translates the opening verses without controversy:

Nede we as some other of pistles of recommendation unto you? or letters of recommendacion from you? ye are oure pistle written in oure hertes, which is understonde and reed of all men, in that ye are knowen howe that ye are the pistle of Christ, ministred by us and written, not with ynke: but with the sprete of the livynge god, not in tables of stone, but in flesshy tables of the herte.[68]

Headley's allegory of the Church is present in More's figure of the apostle Paul, who speaks of the people as a "letter of Christ" administered by him, a letter written by the spirit of God on human hearts. More proposes Paul as the conduit for the message of the Spirit so that Scripture itself may show how the Church and its apostles essentially convey Christ's message. Hence, More writes to Luther that *in corde* and *in ecclesia Christi* God writes the true gospel (*CW* 5.1, 101/31–34).[69] The heart of man, or his nature, and the Church of Christ become identical because God implants his gospel in both.

So, too, the Church, as in the humanist philological tradition,

---

67. Headley's commentary on 100/22–27 in *CW* 5.2, 883.

68. *The New Testament: The Text of the Worms Edition of 1526 in Original Spelling,* trans. William Tyndale, ed. W. R. Cooper (London: British Library, 2000), 381.

69. See the Latin phrases in *CW* 5.1, 100/25–26.

forms a discourse community in which texts are construed and glossed according to agreed-upon conventions and in pursuit of common goals. "Given signs" are *given by* the Church, especially those signs that constitute Scripture. Again, in the *Dialogue,* More writes: "the substaunce of our fayth it self / which oure lorde sayd he wolde wryte in mennes hartes / not onely bycause of the secrete operacyon of god and his holy spyryte ... but also for that he fyrste without wrytynge reueled those heuenly mysteryes by hys blessyd mouth / thorowe the eres of his appostles and dyscyples in to theyr holy hartes" (*CW* 6.1, 143/6–14). The word of God is more than Scripture; that word was before Scripture; it was "inwardely infused in to saynt Peter his harte / by the secrete inspyracyon of god / without eyther wrytynge or any outwarde worde" (143/15–17). To the contrary of an "invisible" church of true believers who ground faith on Scripture alone, More's living gospel abides in an imperfect Church that includes the visible sign of unity.[70] The "secrete operacyon of god" animates the Church in doing so, working upon individual "hartes" within and *through* a particular community, mirroring and elevating Sylvester's ideas of shared natures and aspirations.

As humanist *communitas* rejects alien understandings, so does the Church. More informs Dorp that those removed from a "common sense"—more properly, a shared sense—*exclude themselves* because they are "perversely convinced of their total omniscience," a characterization More applies to those who opposed the new learning, but one that resembles his later condemnation of reformers (*CW* 15, 49). More continues in this same letter to Dorp with words that are written in defense of humanism but sound like ones we might

---

70. As More writes against Tyndale: "The very chyrche is ... the comen knowen catholyke people, clergy, lay folke, and all / whych what so euer theyr lyuynge be (amonge whom vndowtedly there are of bothe sortes many ryght good and vertuouse) do stande to gether and agre in the confessyon of one trew catholyke fayth, wyth all olde holy doctours and sayntes, and good chrysten people beside that are all redy passed thys fyftene hundred yere byfore, agaynste ... erronious heretykes" (*CW* 8.1, 480/35–481/5). See, too, Simpson, *Burning to Read,* 249–50, who writes: "Scripture may be the letter, but the historically continuous institution of the Church is, as it were, the envelope in which the letter arrives, and which makes sense of the letter."

find in defense of the Church from More's antiheretical tracts. Addressing those who ignore the Church Fathers, More writes: "They think they alone can interpret the writings of all men, and even sacred scripture itself, in whatever sense happens to suit them" (49). More's emphasis upon interpreting Scripture from traditional consensus rather than as an idiosyncratic exercise does not change even if his disputants do.

More next illustrates his point for Dorp, telling him a story about a theologian and member of a religious order who cannot identify made-up scriptures as fictitious, even when cited in defense of having mistresses. Rather, this cleric debates the meaning of the made-up scriptures, replying: "You quote well ... but I understand that text as follows" (55). The theologian's pride and ignorance make a fool of him. For More, a similar dynamic applies to reformers. "Heretics are either learned or unlearned," More writes. The majority are unlearned and will not understand rebuttal; the learned ones, however, will never end disputing because they argue only about those particular issues they have studied. Hence, "the very problems with which they are assaulted afford them no end of material with which to strike back" (71). More would later formulate such dialogical hopelessness in terms of pride: "This pryde hath ere this made some lerned men to deuyse new fantasyes in our fayth because they wolde be syngular among the peple" (*CW* 6.1, 423/19–22). Learned "heretics" are narrow, proud readers and interpreters, but so are Scholastics. Both are motivated by the appetite for distinction we saw More describe at the beginning of the *Dialogue.*

For More, reformers are alien readers of Scripture, isolated from the "common sense" of the Church, and, most strongly, they strike against the original word of God implanted within their hearts, all of which explains More's sometimes vehement tone or language. Yet More's opinion is not derived from a conception of religion removed from his previous humanist studies. More believes *humanitas* includes a judgment *of* humankind, but the reformers, by renaming what God put in their hearts, do not just change the Church, but in another sense, they destroy a shared conception of selfhood and community. Pride's impetus toward singularity, more obviously, undermines a community of learning and faith. The rhetoric More employs, so often condemned, reflects not simply what our term of "religious intolerance" conveys, but his concern for *humanitas,* what it means or would mean to be considered a man or woman as an *imago dei,* a child of god, a member of the visible, historical, and unified Church.[71]

A CULTURE OF PUBLIC FAITH

After addressing the role of faith and reason in the *Dialogue,* More turns to humanities in a general way. He tells the messenger there is "no doubte / but that reason is by study / labour and exercyse of Logyk / Phylosophy and other lyberall artes corroborate and quyckened" (132/6–9). Reason, necessary to faith, receives training by studying liberal arts, a teaching that echoes the ladder of contemplation More advanced in *Oxford.* The liberal arts are just as important for More's humanist principles as they are for his religion because reason and faith need not be at variance with one another as the messenger mistakenly believes. In conjunction with the *Dialogue,* More's *Oxford* maintains the liberal arts prepare the soul for *virtus* and should be studied with *pietas.* So, too, in the letter to Dorp, More suggests how such a combination of learning and virtue teaches how to be associative, reasonable, and discerning men and women, an image of More's notion of humanist community and a concept that More cannot detach from his idea of Catholic Christendom. For More, those with such formed judgment will be able to judge Martin Luther, William Tyndale, Thomas Bilney, or Richard Hunne.

71. Gerard Wegemer explains the harsher language of More this way: "For present-day critics like Elton, Fox, and Marius to pretend that More should use the polite language of scholarly circles to counter individuals set upon tearing down all that he judged necessary for a civilization's survival seems utopian indeed, mistaking harsh political realities for the school room" (*More on Statesmanship,* 167).

The emphasis upon faith and reason under the auspices of "theology proper" indicates how More viewed Lutheran heresy not just as a civil disturbance, or an unraveling of the Church, but as another attack upon humanism, a far worse one than before. As Robin Headlam Wells writes, "Classic humanists shared a view of man's fallen nature, his vulnerability to temptation, and his capacity for improvement through the arts of civilization. There were two main challenges to this meliorist view of humanity and the power of the arts to repair our fallen nature: primitivism and Protestant fundamentalism."[72] Wells's general account conforms to Gerard Wegemer's examination of More's polemical works, which show how More viewed his writings as an attempt to protect "the survival of an entire cultural movement—Christian humanism—that was just promising to come to fruition."[73] Indeed, like the depiction of Bilney, More characterized Luther as person who, "sensing that he has been overcome by reason, turns wholly to wrangling" (CW 5.1, 7/10–12; cf. 305–7). Where revisionists highlight mockery and anger in More's polemics, Wegemer's rhetorical analyses illustrate how More viewed Protestant reforms as endangering advances in law, diplomacy, education, and even an emphasis upon a life guided by reason.[74] More sees Luther defying the unbroken faith of the whole Church (totius ecclesiae fidem), which was a public faith (fidem publicam) and an entire culture (CW 5.1, 468–69). To cast aside traditional teaching and its supporting humanist scholarship threatens the existence of and possibility for a "public faith." As historian Richard Rex speculates, More could not recognize nor like our label of "the Reformation" for this period of history, but "he would certainly have appreciated the reason we use it." Because More rightly understood religion as the basis of his society, that new doctrines established new orders, "the most important fact of his lifetime was the rise of

---

72. Wells, Shakespeare's Humanism, 14.
73. Wegemer, More on Statesmanship, 166–67.
74. Ibid., 161–82.

an alternative account of the very essence of Christianity" (*CCTM*, 111). Yet new orders should not be viewed just in terms of societal or political changes. More's understanding of humanism was in jeopardy.

ONE THOMAS MORE

The division between More's so-called humanist and theological writings should be reexamined, addressing, in broad terms, whether faith and liberal arts study are complementary or contradictory—the same point at the center of interpreting More's *Dialogue*. The entire structures of the two Mores and real More theories congeal around Elton's notion of a "true" humanism that excludes the possibility of faith and reason working together, a position transparently stated by Elton and one that influences contemporary condemnations of More as a "fanatic."

Indeed, John Carey applies Elton's perspective to the *Dialogue*. Less than a model of philosophical inquiry, Carey finds the *Dialogue* marred because "the entire logical superstructure rests upon an assumption (that the Church cannot be wrong) which renders the superstructure superfluous." The text presents "logic" as play, which keeps "commonsense from questioning the basic issue."[75] Carey does not address More's presentation of faith and reason, Catholic and humanist concerns. He means "commonsense" after the contemporary usage, without reference to More's specific usage of that term in the *Letter to Dorp*.

Yet Carey seems nearly correct. Logic is not play, but neither is it absolute. Thought should be directed by common senses as in shared senses—of what signs mean and convey in sacraments or in the Scriptures, or in regard to what religious images convey, or with respect to acknowledging what pilgrimage places maintain God's special presence. All these "signs" or images require an antecedent

---

75. John Carey, "Sixteenth and Seventeenth Century Prose," in *English Poetry and Prose, 1540–1674*, ed. Christopher Ricks (London: Barrie & Jenkins, 1970), 343.

epistemological trust, a faith in the Church. That commitment to traditional consensus within a visible, historical, and known ecclesial discourse connects More's humanist letters to his antiheretical tracts. In this way, there is only one Thomas More. From the *Life* to the *Dialogue*, More's writings on the liberal arts indicate how they should not be judged without reference to *pietas* or to the relationship of faith and reason or to concerns that Protestantism would unravel humanist *communitas*. Rather than abandoning "common sense," More believed he was saving Christian humanist principles.

5

INQUISITION, EQUITY, AND THE "BATTLE OF THE BOOKS," CA. 1532–33

Like the war of words between More and Tyndale, disputes between the laity and the Church, especially over how inquisitorial trials functioned in England, involve More in a "battle of the books" with the common law attorney Christopher St. German.[1] More's part begins with the *Apology of Sir Thomas More, Knight*, published in 1533, which replies to St. German's *A Treatise Concernynge the Diuision betwene the Spirytualitie and Temporaltie*, a text published as early as 1532.[2] St. German writes with the stated purpose of healing a "division" between laymen and clergy, but he attacks the clergy's character and the independent powers of the *Ecclesia Anglicana* especially. More's defense of the Church and counteraccusation of anticlericalism engages St. German's own reply, *Salem and Bizance*, and More follows with *The Debellacyon of Salem and Byzance* (1533).[3] As the argument

---

1. "Battle of the Books" refers to John Guy, "Thomas More and Christopher St. German: The Battle of the Books," in Fox and Guy, *Reassessing the Henrician Age*, 95–120.

2. On texts and dates, see *CW* 9, lxxxix–xciii. This edition includes St. German's text as the *Diuision* in Appendix A. Hereafter both texts will be noted internally as *CW* 9. After the first use of a book's title in these exchanges, I will use the following modernized and shortened titles: *Apology, Division, Debellation,* and *Salem*.

3. On texts and dates for *Debellation* and *Salem*, see *CW* 10, xcv–xcix. For a complete listing of St. German's published works, see ibid., xxxiii–xxxiv. The *Debellation* and St. German's original *Salem* are included in this volume, and both are cited internally as *CW* 10 hereafter.

progresses, the focus sharpens on *inquisitio ex officio* proceedings and whether ecclesiastical courts deliver equitable treatment to those suspected of heresy.[4]

In these controversies, too, the related questions of how to understand More's and St. German's authorial voices become equally as contested. As in the case of polemical theology reviewed last chapter, most recent descriptions of More's performance find it less than admirable. "Let us remember," Elton writes, "that More lost his polemical battles, both at the time and by any dispassionate later assessment." More the polemicist "was really a disaster, especially to himself," and St. German appears as best in terms of prose, tone, and argument.[5] Elton finds St. German thoughtful and able, but he carefully distinguishes the role of St. German from Thomas Cromwell, the real architect behind the Supremacy Act.[6] Though John Guy disagrees with Elton's claim that St. German was working independently from the king in writing for the supervision of the Church by the Crown, Guy enlarges the status of St. German as Henrician reformer, claiming him as "learned, relentless, concise, and with a razor-sharp mind" (*CW* 10, xxix), a lawyer whose propaganda justifies "the nature of the Henrician schism" (xxi–xxii).[7] Similarly, Marius calls St. German "the greatest English legal mind in the early sixteenth century," a man who but for his late age during Henry's schism and poor writing style "might be recalled today as one of the founders of modern political theory, less witty than Machiavelli but much more practical and profound."[8] For Marius, More's own "defense of the clergy and the canon law was to no avail." More replied

4. See William Rockett, "More and St. German: Ex Officio and Lay-Clerical Division," *Moreana* 34, no. 129 (1997): 21–43, who believes More purposefully turned the argument to focus upon *ex officio* proceedings to link St. German's *Division* with an agenda to increase heresy in England.

5. G. R. Elton, "Reviews," in *Studies in Tudor and Stuart Politics and Government*, vol. 3: *Papers and Reviews 1973–1981* (Cambridge: Cambridge University Press, 2002), 452.

6. Elton, *Policy and Police*, 173-74; cf., "The Political Creed of Thomas Cromwell," *Transactions of the Royal Historical Society*, 5th ser., 6 (1956): 69-92.

7. On refuting Elton, see *CW* 10, xxii and xxxix–xl.

8. Marius, *Thomas More*, 377, 380.

ineffectually to his opponent and must have known his *Apology* was mostly a "failure" almost "as soon as it appeared."[9] In short, More appears as belligerent or factious in contrast to the presiding calm and intelligence of St. German.

The work of Elton, Marius, and, in particular, Guy, represented an authoritative though not unchallenged view until Henry Ansgar Kelly, an expert on heresy proceedings, revealed such praises for St. German as overstatement in a landmark 2008 article.[10] Kelly demonstrated how St. German misunderstood the inquisitorial system, mistaking, among other things, elementary differences between accusation and *ex officio* trials. More "may eventually have had some inklings that St. German really was a dunce in these matters," but Kelly finds it probable that "More constantly underestimated the depth of his opponent's ignorance of canon law."[11] There were other items of related dispute, such as the manner of interrogation or definition of compurgation, but More corrected St. German on the key aspects of *ex officio* proceeding.

Kelly's findings challenge conventional characterizations of St. German and More in other ways that scholars have yet to grasp. To begin, if the reconstruction of *ex officio* disputes should be understood as erroneous, how More and St. German argue over the issue of equity may deserve reevaluation as well. Specifically, I will question Guy's narrative of how the legal issue of equity impacts their debate. Like Marius, Guy treats St. German as a significant political theorist, especially in finding a "brilliant, comprehensive, and intellectually satisfying attempt to construct a systematic theory of the

9. Ibid., 438.

10. On challenging the revisionist depiction, see Bradshaw, "Controversial More," 535–69. For Kelly on St. German, More, and inquisition, see Henry Ansgar Kelly, "Thomas More on Inquisitorial Due Process," *English Historical Review* 123, no. 503 (2008): 847–94; on inquisition generally, see Kelly's "The Right to Remain Silent: Before and after Joan of Arc," *Speculum* 68, no. 4 (1993): 992–1026; and "Inquisition and the Prosecution of Heresy: Misconceptions and Abuses," *Church History* 58, no. 4 (December 1989): 439–51;and *Inquisitions and Other Trial Procedures in the Medieval West* (Aldershot: Ashgate Publishing, 2001).

11. Kelly, "Inquisitorial Due Process," 849.

law within an English context" in *Doctor and Student* (xxxvi). Yet I will show how St. German's presentation of equity and conscience appears largely unoriginal, even contradictory, and, ultimately, a vehicle for anticlerical propaganda. In this way, equity represents an important corollary to Kelly's scholarship because combined reassessment of the debates over *ex officio* and equity best reveals why More's tone represents an acute voice rather than, as in recent assessment, a pompous or enraged one. If St. German's assault upon ecclesiastical courts shows neither a knowledgeable critique of canon law nor an application of a new and brilliant systematic legal theory of equity, More would be justified in finding in his interlocutor clumsy yet politically dangerous anticlericalism.

If the roles of More and St. German on *ex officio* and equity are recast, other questions about More's voice in these polemical writings may be reassessed, including the ways in which he thought of his opponent as "razor sharp" or "dunce" and, significantly, whether or not More employed a generally sincere or contrived *ethos*. The conventional view is that More knew St. German was the author of the *Division* and *Salem*, though these texts were published anonymously. That anonymity, so runs the argument, allows More an opportunity to oppose the king's propaganda with plausible deniability about doing so. More creates an "elaborate hoax," ironically calling his opponent "the Pacifier" and adding the persona of a simpleton priest from the countryside to that moniker (xxii–xxiv). More's deployment of a "hoax" fits well with a dramatic tale of political intrigue and "clash of legal titans," yet I think More is sincere in his stated belief that the Pacifier is corrupted by some other "wyly shrewys" (64/3).[12]

Emended accounts of *ex officio* and equity should cause a reexamination of *ethos* and tone in these exchanges. In this manner, More's general account of his opponent's character and intelligence

---

12. "Clash of legal titans" is the formulation in Guy, *Christopher St. German on Chancery and Statute* (London: Seldon Society, 1985), 35.

will emerge as essentially sincere, even accurate. Richard Rex argues against the revisionist view of More by countering that "there is at least as much of the 'real' More in his personal efforts to win men back by argument."[13] Rex's point refers to More's "attitude to heretics" yet, as we shall see, it may be especially true of More's exchanges with St. German.

EX OFFICIO: WITNESSES AND THE ACCUSED

Kelly's evidence that St. German scarcely knew canon law begins in the *Division*, which argued ecclesiastical trials of heretics consisted in a bishop calling up a suspect because of secret information, followed by conviction and punishment. Thus, according to St. German, a cause of division was *ex officio* suits in the "spiritual courtes of offyce" because "the parties haue not knowen who hath accused them" (*CW* 9, 188–89). Because of that system, in *Salem,* St. German proposed that heretics should be reported to the bishop by whoever heard the suspect's utterance; the bishop, in turn, would send the accuser to inquire of the suspect if he said such things. At this point, if the suspect concurred, the informant would take witnesses to the accused in order to admonish him. In case the suspect remained obstinate, the bishop would summon the accused and now rebuked man, not for punishment, but for further investigation (*CW* 10, 353). Hence, St. German's conclusion: "if he [the bishop] fynde it trewe by sufficient profe, or by his [the suspect's] owne confession, and he wyll not be reformed, then it semeth conuenient, that he, vpon the witnes of the other, be punished as he as deserued" (353/39–41). Such a system, St. German pressed, would be more charitable to the accused, granting more opportunities for remonstration and dialogue, but most importantly, it would eliminate the anonymity of the accusers. For that anonymity remains a great cause of division between temporal and spiritual men; it leads

---

13. Rex, "More and the Heretics: Statesman or Fanatic?" in *CCTM*, 105.

into coerced abjuration and subsequent unjust penance those suspected, who in turn blame the bishop, as accuser, for penalties of
penance or fines (*CW* 9, 188–89).[14]

Though contemporary evaluation often accepts St. German's
version of *ex officio,* Kelly shows how St. German operated with several erroneous assumptions in suggesting the above reform. The
ex officio proceedings in use before the 1534 Act for Punishment
of Heresy were actually different from how the *Division* portrayed
them, a misrepresentation that More rightly recognized.[15] At time
of summons, the bishop would call the suspect forth openly and
take depositions; if trial were necessary, the accused would hear all
the testimony from all the witnesses to the alleged heresy. Contrary
to St. German's allegation, the original accuser along with all witnesses, under oath and in front of the accused, would provide testimony (*CW* 10, 73–74; 108–9).[16] Such was the usual practice, though
it would not necessarily be the case that the original informer would
be a witness in the trial. Thus, in regular proceedings when the suspect denied the charge, anonymity was *not* granted to witnesses; the
charges were specifically named; allegations, too, must be corrobo-
rated with witnesses other than the accuser. St. German made no
distinctions between accuser and witness, failed to grasp that witnesses' identities could be disclosed to the accused, and did not even
know that there were no penalties for those cleared of suspicion by
purgation (355–56; cf. 89–93).[17]

Fama publica, in particular, involved witnesses, not just the

14. See Kelly, "Inquisitorial Due Process," 854–59. Kelly believes More found St. German
to be advocating accusatorial process over inquisitional; St. German advocates a procedure "of
his own invention," which resembled the *denunciatio* (855). For a historical review of inquisition proceeding and for actual cases of abuse, see Kelly's "Misconceptions and Abuses," 439–51.
Most of the abuses occurred in continental Europe. More challenges St. German to produce an
instance of similar abuse in England. Though St. German could not, Kelly does. See "Inquisitorial Due Process," 862–71.

15. The important heresy statutes in England from 1382 to 1414 are reproduced and translated in *CW* 9, 249–60. The 1534 act is carefully discussed in "Inquisitorial Due Process," 884–86.

16. See Kelly, "Inquisitorial Due Process," 857–59.

17. On purgation and penances, see ibid., 881, and see *CW* 10, 117.

original informant. *Fama* occurred after the bishop investigated the charged by interviewing a number of witnesses to determine whether or not there was a case; those witnesses could then be deposed as people who believed the suspect was guilty of heresy. Deposed witnesses could remain anonymous during the investigative period but would be identified in case of a trial. When the 1534 Act for the Punishment of Heresy specifies the need for at least two witnesses, then, it provides an affirmation of canon law. Neither did the 1534 act specify when witnesses would come forward to confront the accused, which means, Kelly writes, "the modern assessment that the 1534 Act discouraged confidential denunciations, because the trial was to be conducted in open court, is not accurate."[18] Secret accusation, in fact, would continue under the new law. St. German's proposed innovation of one accuser initiating a proceeding seems more charitable, but the old system of *publica fama* already required two witnesses.

Given the above, Kelly concludes, More wins the debate. "St. German scored no points at all," writes Kelly, but "it has been hard for modern readers to realize how completely More debellated his opponent, because of the tedious length at which he responded, and because most such readers are even more benighted about the principles of canon law than St. German was." More's mistake was "to overestimate St. German's knowledge of canonical procedure" by assuming his opponent had rudimentary knowledge of the basic process of inquisition.[19] In consequence, when Guy asserts "witnesses were not necessary in English heresy trials before 1534," Kelly accuses him of echoing St. German's misunderstanding.[20] Guy "failed to understand what More said about the difference between an accuser in an accusation process and a witness in an *ex officio* process, and he

18. Kelly, "Inquisitorial Due Process," 888.

19. Ibid., 894. More's own knowledge of canon law may be questioned. Kelly, ibid., 850, finds More "well-informed" but admits "More never drew specifically on the fundamental decretals in *Liber Extra (Decretales Gregorii IX)* setting forth the rules, not even the Fourth Lateran Council's decree on *inquisitio, Qualiter et quando*."

20. Ibid., 885.

mixed up the detection of heresy (the preliminary investigation, in which secret informants were used) and the actual trial."[21]

NARRATIVES OF EQUITY

Kelly's findings suggest a propaganda war, a controversy wherein both disputants emerge as sometimes confused polemicists. Yet St. German's performance, rather than that of More, appears exceptionally hapless. Such a characterization of St. German provokes other questions about the revisionist evaluation of his acumen, especially in regard to his formulation of equity and how it impacted his debate with More.[22] To examine the role of equity and its critical reception requires a review of Guy's foundational and thorough assessment of the issue.[23] Despite Kelly's critique, Guy's account of how equity pertains to these polemical exchanges remains necessary reading, yet he provides oscillating roles for More and St. German and, upon review, illustrates how speculative and changing are even the best narratives about St. German's contribution.

As Guy begins his treatment of equity, More and St. German are in agreement about the reforms of Wolsey. In *The Cardinal's Court* (1977), Wolsey's career as chancellor demonstrates how the Star Chamber becomes primarily a center of judicial activity, where conscience or equity guided the implementation of common law. The "essence" of Wolsey's design was "better enforcement of the law in the existing courts of common law, with the assignment of the council in star chamber of a firm supervisory and, if necessary, punitive role," which would then "ensure" an "impartial administration of the system."[24] Wolsey's Star Chamber, reconfigured as more

21. Ibid., 886; cf. *CW* 10, lxv–lxvi.

22. St. German appears as advocate of anticlericalism but with Guy's high estimation of him in recent studies such as Samuel Gregg, "Legal Revolution: St. Thomas More, Christopher St. German, and the Schism of King Henry VIII," *Ave Maria Law Review* 5, no. 1 (2007): 173-205; Wegemer, *More on Statesmanship*, 201–4; Rockett, "More and St. German."

23. Cathy Curtis, "More's public life," in *CCTM*, 85, most recently recapitulated Guy's thesis on More, Wolsey, and equity. See, too, 62n of chapter 3.

24. John Guy, *The Cardinal's Court: The Impact of Thomas Wolsey in Star Chamber* (Totowa, N.J.: Rowman and Littlefield, 1977), 123–24.

judicial, less executive, was the office More inherited, an office he did not change.

Such an assessment of More's significance as a reformer relative to Wolsey's Guy amplifies in *Thomas More's Public Career* (1980), which first surveys More's service, stating that "More was a councilor much concerned with administering two of Wolsey's favourite policies,"[25] both of which are presented in the same terms as found in *The Cardinal's Court*: the "impartial enforcement of law" and "popularisation of the council courts."[26] Right from when More became chancellor, he continued Wolsey's general policy of equitable procedure, and, hence, "the scope of the work discharged by More as lord chancellor was thus directly comparable to that undertaken by his predecessor."[27]

In *Public Career*, though, Guy illustrates More's idea of conscience by examining St. German's *Doctor and Student*, a text that advocates Aristotelian *epikeia*, or equity, "a method of interpreting positive human law in accordance with the presumed intentions of the legislator" in light of "conscience." Here conscience is defined as "an objective ideal implanted in man," which in practical terms provides the court its authority in law. Conscience, then, was "the moral principle which gave the chancellor the cognitive and coercive authority to pronounce decisions in his court and bind litigants to observe them."[28] In this way, St. German stands against conservative common lawyers and, in particular, in opposition to the anonymous author of *Replication*, a text whose "clear implication was that Thomas More, a common-law chancellor, was guilty of professional apostasy by exercising an equitable jurisdiction at all."[29] Though St. German later attacked canon law, he was an early ally of More's attempt to prolong the reforms of equitable jurisdiction begun by Wolsey. The problem for St. German's theory, and for More's im-

25. Guy, *Public Career*, 13–14.   26. Guy, *Cardinal's Court*, 124.
27. Guy, *Public Career*, 51.   28. Ibid., 43.
29. Ibid., 43–44.

plementation of it, was that some common law judges and lawyers preferred to follow the letter of the positive law, even if conscience opposed it.[30]

Yet Guy changes his presentation on conscience and equity vis-à-vis the relationship of More and St. German. In *Public Career,* St. German is proposed as "another ally" of More in fighting against common law judges because *Doctor and Student* is a "treatise which elegantly defended the equitable initiatives of More's time."[31] *Public Career,* however, is only a "beginning," which should prompt further research into St. German.[32] Guy's later opinion in "Battle of the Books" (1986) is that St. German's *Doctor and Student* made him a "dangerous man" because he, ultimately, "resolved the sixteenth century conflict of laws in favour of English common law and statute, and had simultaneously erected common law as the species of law which should properly govern the consciences of Englishmen in matters of equity."[33] Of note, the same reason why St. German was an ally—his formulations of equity contra other common lawyers—becomes the reason why he is More's ultimate enemy.[34] Accordingly, in Guy's more recent *Thomas More* (2000), the argument from *Public Career* in regard to St. German's "elegant defense" of the "equitable initiatives of More's times" is excised, which thereby undermines the original and theoretical account of conscience that was attributed to More.

In "Battle of the Books," the dispute between More and St. German *begins* as early as *Doctor and Student.*[35] How to read this text becomes crucial because in it "St. German had *already* conditioned

---

30. See Roper's *Life* in *TMSB,* 36–38, and Guy, *Public Career,* 87–89.

31. Guy, *Public Career,* 42, and see 88.

32. Ibid., ix.

33. Guy, "Battle of the Books," 102, 104. This chapter is a revised version of the one that appeared in *Moreana* 21 (1984): 5–25; a shortened version of the revision appears in *CW* 10, xvii–xxviii.

34. Guy finally claims, too, that Christopher St. German wrote the *Replication.* See *Chancery and Statute,* 56-63.

35. My text for *Doctor and Student* is St. German's *Doctor and Student,* ed. T. F. T. Plucknett and J. L. Barton (London: Seldon Society, 1974). Hereafter abbreviated as *DS* and cited internally.

his readers and More's to the *a priori* notion, as it would have appeared to More, that similar sorts of situations and types of legal case should result in similar solutions, whether these matters were adjudicated before royal or ecclesiastical courts."[36] The principle of equity, in other words, inclines one toward precedent within the common law, and that mindset creates an impetus whereby the ecclesiastical courts, too, may be reformed and controlled by the common law.

The interpretative key is the second part of the dialogue of *Doctor and Student*, which argues that when the "Church made laws pertaining to men's goods or property," men were not obliged to obey, essentially, because property rights fell under the jurisdiction of the human positive law.[37] Though the second part of *Doctor and Student* becomes explicit on jurisdiction, the first provides the principle of separation, which claims the creation of property rights belongs to political convention rather than to any divine institution; as such, all property should fall under the regulation of human law.[38]

A second and related issue to the significance of *Doctor and Student* pertains to sources, which Guy uses to distinguish between Jean Gerson and Thomas Aquinas. For Gerson, "Equity is justice [which] having weighed all the particular circumstances is tempered with the sweetness of mercy."[39] As merciful exception, equity could overrule even the divine and ecclesiastical laws. Gerson's teaching in combination with the position on property rights from *Doctor and Student* shows the radical nature of St. German's thought. The "issues debated by More and St. German between 1532 and 1534" sprang from St. German's general proposition in *Doctor and Student* that "no greater, nor less, favour should be shown to clergy or laity under the law."[40] That ideology would eventually establish peace by

36. Guy, "Battle of the Books," 108.   37. Ibid., 103.

38. Ibid., and see *CW* 10, xxxvi–xxxviii.

39. Gerson's *Regulae morales* is cited from John Guy, "Law, Equity and Conscience," in *Reassessing the Henrician Age*, 183–84.

40. Guy, "Law, Equity and Conscience," 104.

granting control to the Crown of most ecclesiastical functions other than the dispensing of sacraments.[41] Hence, *Doctor and Student*, even its points on conscience and equity, become part of the "battle of the books" between More and St. German.[42]

RECONSTRUCTING THE DEBATE

Yet such a battle of the books and corresponding depiction of St. German poses questions. The first dialogue of *Doctor and Student* was published in Latin in 1528 and then in English in 1531, and the second dialogue was published in 1530.[43] As Mike Macnair writes, "when St. German discusses the Chancery and similar jurisdictions, he is mainly reliant on Year Book Reports from the 1450 to 1517 period, not on contemporary practice."[44] Macnair's observation about the Year Book Reports suggests how St. German's 1532–33 debates with More need *not* include the first dialogue of *Doctor and Student*.[45] Or, more generally, without an explicit argument in *Doctor and Student* like those more radical ones found in texts such as *The Division*, claims for an early disguised polemic against the Church may represent anachronistic special pleading.

So, too, arguments for St. German's writings to be read as a

41. Guy summarizes the points from *Doctor and Student, New Additions*, and St. German's parliamentary draft to conclude: "There can be no doubt whatever that Christopher St. German was at work in 1531 on a program of parliamentary reform and propaganda designed to purchase peace between the church and state at the expense of the clergy's traditional privileges and jurisdictional independence" (*CW* 10, xxxix). See, too, "Law, Equity, and Conscience," 180.

42. Most recently Guy references his previous work on St. German and More in the notes to chapter 22, 314–15, in *A Daughter's Love* (2008).

43. Guy, *CW* 10, xxxiii, n2, suspects the 1523 Latin edition of the first dialogue is a "ghost." Barton, *DS*, xii, accepts St. German's authorship and writes "the original version of the First Dialogue cannot be described as an unorthodox work."

44. Macnair, "Equity and Conscience," 671.

45. Macnair, ibid., 670–71, believes that "from 1450 and 1517" the so-called English side of Chancery "began to have a perceptible shape" as a "jurisdiction in conscience." From 1517 and through More's tenure, however, the Star Chamber lapsed in a kind of "anti-law," a place of casual, informal arbitration. The work of Wolsey, by expanding accessibility, did not reform the laws, but deviated from them, producing methods for quick arbitration, ways around the law. For Macnair, St. German's thought upon "conscience" represents a real philosophical endeavor, but only as a following of medieval theology, especially Thomist theology. In this way, as proponents of "anti-law," neither More nor Wolsey were reformers.

seamless garment, including both the powers of the clergy and the king's divorce, are questionable. As William Rockett argues, the question of the divorce involves "the privilege of England," a separate policy matter and one that "receives no support" from St. German's 1531 publications.[46] Rockett shows that the *New Additions* to *Doctor and Student* in 1531 indicate that, for St. German, "it was not the divorce but, rather, the question of parliament's authority to rule in ecclesiastical matters that led him into controversy."[47] Even if St. German wrote the parliamentary draft of 1531 to expand the powers of the king and parliament over the Church, adds G. W. Bernard, in St. German's "consideration of how ecclesiastical legislation should be reviewed" he imagines "the authority of parliament, the authority of his proposed standing council and even the authority of the king were subject to significant limitations."[48] Instead of supplying the theory that would later become the Act of Supremacy, Bernard finds an escalation in anticlericalism from the parliamentary draft to the *Division* and calls for a "subtle evaluation" of that theme in St. German's work.[49] If *Doctor and Student* was a work of "reform," it was more with respect to how property rights should fall under the aegis of common law. Yet the degree to which that text conforms to the later exchanges between More and St. German or to the legislative development of the Act of Supremacy remains speculative.

Most important, a philosophic problem exists in Guy's account because it dissociates St. German from Thomas Aquinas in order to show how "controversial" was St. German's formulation that "equity is not outside of the law, but resides implicitly in it."[50] Guy's argument assumes that if St. German disavowed Aquinas's teaching on

---

46. Rockett believes St. German's thought dramatically changed with the 1531 appendage of *Newe Addycyons*. See "Temporal and Spiritual: Prolegomenon to the More–St. German Controversy," *Moreana* 37 (2000): 5–36.

47. Rockett, "Temporal and Spiritual," 5; cf. Guy, *Chancery and Statute*, 24–33.

48. G. W. Bernard, "Review," *Historical Journal* 31, no. 1 (1988): 174. The 1531 parliamentary draft is reproduced in Guy, *Chancery and Statute*, 127–35.

49. Bernard, "Review," 175.

50. "Law, Equity and Conscience," 184.

equity we may recognize St. German as a proponent of the more "controversial" teaching of Jean Gerson. For Aquinas, Guy argues, exceptions from the law only constitute "necessity," urgent rarity, calling for executive or unilateral action by those entrusted with the public good.[51] The Aristotelian notion—that equity should be configured in terms of the lawgiver's original intentions—operates in Thomas, but with the addition that such interpretation is the sole purview of the ruler. Equity is the business of the ruler, and as such, like any of the ruler's actions, it may be virtuous or vicious.

Because equity is so defined, Guy speculates, Aquinas is led to make "bald conclusions." Such conclusions are: "*Epieikeia* does not seem to be a virtue. One virtue does not displace another; yet *epieikeia* displaces virtue, doing away with what is just in law and seeming to be counter to severity. Therefore it is no virtue." And "To act under *epieikeia* seems to be to pass judgment on a law, namely in the decision that the law is not to be observed in a certain case. Therefore *epieikeia* is a vice rather than a virtue." Finally: "The application of *epieikeia* being unlawful, *epieikeia* is thus not a virtue."[52] Yet these lines cited by Guy come from the "objections" portion of the article from the *Summa*—in the very places where Aquinas represents erroneous positions that he later refutes. In both of these two articles under question 120 that address equity, in fact, Aquinas claims epikeia is a virtue. He writes:

When we were treating of laws, since human actions, with which laws are concerned, are composed of contingent singulars and are innumerable in their diversity, it was not possible to lay down rules of law that would apply to every single case. Legislators in framing laws attend to what commonly happens: although if the law be applied to certain cases it will frustrate the equality of justice and be injurious to the common good, which the law has in view. Thus the law requires deposits to be restored, because in the majority of cases this is just. Yet it happens sometimes to be injurious—for instance, if a madman were to put his sword in deposit, and demand its de-

51. Ibid., 185.
52. Ibid., 186.

livery while in a state of madness, or if a man were to seek the return of his deposit in order to fight against his country. On these and like cases it is bad to follow the law, and it is good to set aside the letter of the law and to follow the dictates of justice and the common good. This is the object of "epikeia" which we call equity. Therefore it is evident that "epikeia" is a virtue.[53]

Aquinas's discussion of equity cannot be relegated exclusively to unilateral decisions of kings; equity concerns the law itself. Aquinas later states, "epikeia corresponds properly to legal justice, and in one way is contained under it, and in another way exceeds it." Where legal justice regards the "letter of the law" or "the intention of the lawgiver," epikeia is the "more important part of legal justice." Epikeia, in short, may be part of legal justice, a guiding principle for the law, but a legal principle nevertheless.[54] As long as the regime does not merely hold to the letter of the law, the intention of the lawgiver along with the law constitutes "the more important part of the legal justice itself."[55] Equity as a principle of legal justice, too, is precisely the model St. German would seem to employ in the first part of *Doctor and Student*.

St. German discusses an example of a law that declares no man could open the city's gates before the sun rose and the case of a man who violates that law because fellow citizens are fleeing from enemies and in need of rescue. Such an offender does not violate the law, "for that case is exceptyd from the sayd general law by equytie." Equity justifies the exception because it "foloweth the intent of the lawe/ then the wordes of the lawe" (*DS*, 97–99).[56] In the case where the city's legislator intends the protection of his citizens by prohibiting the city's gates to be opened at certain times, the very violation of the law's letter—that the gates are not to be opened until the sun rises—results in the death of loyal citizens, if not violated. Hence,

53. Thomas Aquinas, *The Summa Theologica*, 2nd ed., trans. Fathers of the English Dominican Province, http://www.new advent.org/summa/, II, II, q.120, art.1.

54. Ibid., II, II, q.120, art. 2, reply to obj. 1.

55. Ibid.

56. In *Doctor and Student*, conscience, synderesis, and equity are the focus of chapters 12–16, with chapter 17 transitioning to equity and the laws of England. See *DS*, 77–107.

there is no offense because of the lawgiver's original intent. Second, each exception via equity is an "excepcyon of the lawe of god" or the "lawe of reason," the eternal and natural laws in Thomistic terms, from which the human laws emerge. Such an exception, then, is based upon the human law's derivative status from eternal and natural, a general rule that all "secretely vnderstande in euery generall rewle of euery postyue lawe" (DS, 97).

The above example, though common, may derive from Aquinas, who begins his own discussion of equity by iterating that "every law is directed to the common weal of men, and derives the force and nature of law accordingly" and by quoting "the jurist" who writes: "By no reason of law, or favor of equity, is it allowable for us to interpret harshly, and render burdensome, those useful measures which have been enacted for the welfare of man." This preamble gives way to a case in which "the enemy is in pursuit of certain citizens, who are defenders of the city." Because it would be a loss to the city to have the gates closed upon them, even if the "letter of the law" may mandate it, the citizens should be allowed to enter "in order to maintain the common weal, which the lawgiver had in view."[57] Guy treats this instance in Aquinas as one of rare urgency, calling for executive action, but the example in both Aquinas and St. German pertains to the "diversity of particulars" that are unforeseen by the law and that equity may correct by taking into account the intention of the lawgiver.[58] Equity as just exception, too, emerges from the hierarchy of law in which human law should reflect divine and eternal.

In fact, St. German's definition of conscience, instead of seeming the work of a thinker who might be called "one of the founders of modern political theory," rather resembles Aquinas's own notion.[59] For St. German, conscience is based upon *synderesis*, a quality that allows one to recognize self-evident propositions, which

---

57. Aquinas, *ST* II, I, q.96, art. 6, response.
58. "Law, Equity, and Conscience," 185–86.
59. The description of St. German belongs to Marius, *Thomas More*, 380.

guide one toward good, avoiding evil. As *synderesis* supplies the first principles of the natural law, conscience is the judgment that applies them to specifics. "Thus conscience," summarizes J. L. Barton, "which is the art of translating this general rule [do good and avoid evil] into specific rules of conduct to be followed in particular situations, is a form of applied knowledge."[60] That notion of conscience becomes part of the Aristotelian notion of equity. "To folowe the wordes of the lawe/ were in some case both agaynst Iustyce & the common welth," writes St. German; such cases, instead, require one "to leue the wordis of the lawe/ & to folowe that reason and Justyce requyreth" (*DS*, 97). So, too, a function of reason, already defined in *Doctor and Student*, "is the preceeding of the intellect from one point to another, from premise to conclusion," but in a way "conformable to the wyll of god" (85). "Conscyence," then, is an "applyenge or an ordering of any scyence to some partyculer acte of man" (89). "Science" denotes "knowledge" as conscience becomes an act of judgment. Reason functions in tandem with judgment, applying universal principles to particulars through an act of conscience. Aristotelian equity is achieved, in other words, by means of conscience. "If anybody," writes R. S. White, "created the opportunity for the reception of Natural Law principles into England, it was St. German," whose work White views as fundamentally Thomistic, and which "ensured respect for the Chancery," accommodating common law with "Natural Law content."[61] Rather than a modern political philosopher, St. German appears to follow Aquinas.

So, too, St. German's own presentation on conscience, though praised as progressive and brilliant, creates conceptual difficulties, involving a divide between theory and practice. For after invoking a hierarchical scheme of the law and corresponding faculties of reason and conscience in man like that of Aquinas, St. German subordinates conscience to the human law. Thus, when the second part of *Doctor and Student* places property under the common law in mat-

---

60. Barton, "Introduction," *DS*, xxvi.
61. White, *Natural Law*, 53.

ters such as tithes on wood, the philosophical framework from the first part of the dialogue cannot justify the arrangement.[62]

St. German's ambiguous allusion to Nimrod, a "mighty hunter before the Lord," marks a transition from holding goods in common to laws of property and from a smaller population to a larger one, which requires "a law of property lest the slothful and the wicked should oppress the good" (*DS*, 19). Property law, for St. German, originates as a human device subject to human law. Yet the article on the law of England that eventually follows the reference to Nimrod is preceded by a discussion of human law in general, and there the "law of man" is defined as following "the law of reason/ & of the lawe of god, for the due end of human nature" (27). The law of reason, already defined, is a participation in the eternal law, which is the reason of the supreme governor, God, and hence the Doctor states of human law that "orygnynallye it be made of god/ for lawes made by man/ that hathe receyued therto power of god be made by god" (11). St. German summarizes: "Therfore the sayd thre lawes: that is to saye/ the lawe of reason/ the lawe of god/ & the lawe of man the which haue seuerall names after the maner as they be shewed to man/ be called in god one lawe eternall" (11–13). Though property falls under the categories of secondary reason, and secondary reason divides into general and particular, each follows from the "primary reason" by which rational animals participate in the eternal law.[63] Conscience, as an application of reason, is not disengaged from such a hierarchy of law, but constitutes man's participation within it, which provides the problem: because the earlier sections of the dialogue maintain such a hierarchy of law, when later questions adjudicate property rights so that conscience is entirely bound by the positive law, "it must be

---

62. On tithes, see St. German, *DS*, 300–14.

63. On "primary reason" as a function belonging to rational creatures, see ibid., 37; cf. 11, where "almighty god maketh this lawe eternall knowen to his creatures reasonable." On property's connection to laws of secondary reason, and how both primary and secondary are two degrees of the law of reason, see ibid., 32–35. On the law of reason as man's participation in eternal law, see ibid., 12–13, which reads: "Hence the law of reason is nothing else than the participation or knowledge of eternal law in a rational creature, revealed to him by the natural light of reason, whereby he has a natural inclination to act duly, and to a due end."

confessed," as Barton writes, "that it would seem possible to do some pretty odd things with an untroubled conscience" (xxvii).

So, for example, in the "right of wreck," where a king may claim property lost by a ship at sea, "there may be cases where the law of man transfers the title of property from A to B, and yet B cannot retain the property with a clear conscience."[64] The Doctor argues that cattle which come alive to shore ought not to be forfeited to the king, ultimately, because by justice these goods should be restored to their owner and because, by divine law, a man should love his neighbor as himself—one may not take away his neighbor's goods (290–91). To put the problem another way, right of wreck as law in accord with reason would admit to a clear conscience for the king to claim goods washed ashore, though such a transfer would mean taking goods that are not the king's own.[65] If the king claims such goods, conscience should oppose the positive law, but that opposition is impossible given previous statements that property rights, as a human contrivance, govern conscience. The human law of wreck, without being declared against reason, violates natural and divine law, and as such, eternal law as well. Hence, Barton's understatement that "odd things" seem in accord with conscience.

The Student ultimately justifies the "right of wreck" because kings *may* incur costs from keeping the seas safe, but that argument, although the Doctor accepts it, does not adequately address the previous objections, and right of wreck, as Barton points out, is only one of many issues where conscience appears at variance with property law.[66] Of note, Guy would recognize how conscience may contradict common law, but he does not state the full significance of the conceptual contradiction St. German's hierarchy of law and definition of conscience provoke.[67] Guy believes *Doctor and Student*

64. Barton, "Introduction," xxvii–xxviii.

65. See *DS*, 33, where unlawful withholding of another man's goods violates the law of secondary reason general.

66. See Barton, "Introduction," xxvii.

67. Guy notes that "conscience, as derived from natural reason and moral calculation, might sometimes speak directly contrary to general rules of common law in specific instances"

provides "a brilliant, comprehensive, and intellectually satisfying attempt to construct a systematic theory of law within an English context," but St. German's synthesis includes an incoherent account of conscience vis-à-vis its relationship to human, natural, and eternal law (*CW* 10, xxxvi).

These points of contrast have significant implications for how to judge the later assessments of More's disputes with St. German. If Guy's interpretation of *Doctor and Student* involves inaccuracies, the degree to which it constitutes a battle of the books with More, or indicates a radical, single program of reform whereby the Church would be absorbed into the state, diminishes. Second, More's ideas of equity may never have consisted of an account of *Doctor and Student*, though Aquinas, as an influence upon St. German and as an author More would have read at Oxford, could represent a common source. Alternatively, if Guy's changes on the relationship between St. German and More are accurate—from early allies to early enemies—there is an absence of any theoretical context for Guy's earliest and still influential evaluation of More's practice of equity and conscience. Finally, recent commentary privileges a special status for St. German as a political theorist without demonstrating the high quality of thought in *Doctor and Student* that one should expect. St. German's writings on conscience and law, at least, share nothing of the imagination present in More's *Utopia,* the wit of Machiavelli's *Prince,* or the scope of educative vision and aspiration for universal peace found in Erasmus's *Education of a Christian Prince.* Instead, the treatment of conscience and law appears mostly derivative and uneven, which confirms Kelly's general assessment that More's opponent was less brilliant than is often claimed.

THE CLERGY AND EQUITY

Equity directly relates to the questions of heretical proceedings because St. German attacked the ecclesial judges' ability to deliver

---

before identifying "equitable interventions in the name of good conscience" as "key to St. German's theory" (*CW* 10, xxxvi).

it. What may be understood now in light of the above analysis is how More would find in St. German's assault upon ecclesiastical courts neither a knowledgeable critique of *ex officio* proceedings nor an application of a new and brilliant systematic legal theory, but instead crude anticlericalism.[68] More writes at the end of *Debellation* that St. German's case is based "vpon none other ground but onely that an innocent may happe to take harme by meane of false iudges" (*CW* 10, 230/2–3). Though St. German did not understand the function of accusers and witnesses, he alleges how clerics are unable to function as just judges; they cannot provide equity, even if the laws are just. Anticlericalism in the early sixteenth century remains a matter of legal reform because the question of judicial discretion becomes an argument about the moral character of bishops. In this way, instead of the picture that provides St. German as "possessing perhaps the best political mind in the country," he emerges as mostly an anticlerical partisan.[69] St. German, after all, refrains from attacking the 1534 act for the same practice of secret accusation he had denounced before.[70]

In the *Division*, "the Pacifier" attacks the character and competence of judges to administer the law. The proceedings of *ex officio* and the issue of subpoena, along with the jurisdictional questions

68. The related and vast topic of anticlericalism's overall significance for reform in the period is not my concern, but on this topic see A. G. Dickens, "The Shape of Anticlericalism and the English Reformation" in *Politics and Society in Reformation Europe*, ed. E. I. Kouri and T. Scott (London: Palgrave Macmillan, 1987), 379–410; cf. Christopher Haigh's *English Reformations: Religion, Politics and Society under the Tudors* (Oxford: Oxford University Press, 1993), pt. 1; cf. Ethan H. Shagan, "Anticlericalism, Popular Politics and the Henrican Reformation," in *Popular Politics and the English Reformation* (Cambridge: Cambridge University Press, 2003), 131–61; an excellent overview of how to discuss reformation models remains Haigh's "The Recent Historiography of the English Reformation," *Historical Journal* 25, no. 4 (1982): 995–1007.

69. Marius, *Thomas More*, 380. See, too, Alistair Fox, who writes: "More's opponent was avowedly Catholic, and the measures he was proposing are likely to strike the reader as eminently reasonable according to any modern norms of equity" ("Review of Debellation," *Catholic Historical Review* 75 [1990]: 848); cf. "Inquisitorial Due Process," 852, where Kelly criticizes Fox for assuming "More was not telling the truth." St. German's theological views by 1537—especially his undated "Discourse of the Sacraments"—would have been viewed as heretical by More in 1533. See *CW* 10, 405–17.

70. The *Additions of Salem and Byzance* (1534) do not address inquisition, but on this point see Kelly, "Inquisitorial Due Process," 894.

of church and state, all return to the alleged incompetence of ecclesiastical magistrates. The cruelty, or lascivious nature, or concern for honor in the spiritual judges prevents both mercy and equitable treatment for laymen. The problem here is not the laws per se but with the judges: "the prestes."

Chapters 7 and 8 in *Division*, where the character of judges is raised in light of their ability to deliver equity, clarify St. German's polemical intention. After St. German calls *ex officio* "daungerous lawe" that will probably cause "vntrewe and vn-lawfulle men to condempne innocentes, than to condempne offenders," he worries over whether mere tokens of suspicion will constitute evidence, a problem that would be exacerbated by unfair judges. "And yf the iudge be parcyall," he writes, "suche tokens may be soner accepted than truely shewed" (*CW* 9, 189). Rather than the laws, the clerical judges soon become the source of emphasis. In a passage from chapter 7, St. German makes the clergy his clear focus:

Neuertheles my entente is nat to proue the said laws all holly to be cruell & vnresonable, for I know well, y^t it is right expedient, that strayt lawes be made for punisshment of heresies, that be heresies in dede, more rather than any other offence, and that the discretion of the iudges spyrytuall may ryght well aswage the rygour of the sayde lawes, and vse them more fauorably agaynst them that be innocent, than agaynste them that be wylfull offendours, yf they wyll charytably serche for the truthe. (190–91)

Though the "strayt lawes" are necessary, the "discretion of the iudges spyrytuall" remains a problem. The rigor of heresy laws must be assuaged by judges who search for truth with charity. Only then may equity be achieved and the innocent protected. After describing how the law should function with lenient judges, St. German explores the alternative:

But surely yf the sayde laws shulde be put into the handelynge of cruell iuges, it myghte happen that they shulde many tymes punyssh innocentes as wel as offendours / but I trust in god, it is nat so. Neuer the les whether it be soo or nat / certayne it is that there is a great rumour amonge the peple, that it is so / & that spiritual men punysshe nat heresye only for zele of the faythe, and of a loue & a zele to the people, with a fatherly pietie to them that so offende / as they oughte to do / how greate offenders so euer they be, but that they do it rather to oppresse them that speketh any thynge agaynste the worldly power or ryches of spyrytuall men, or agaynste the greate confederacie, that (as many men say) is in them to maynteygne it. (191)

This picture of ecclesiastical magistrates corresponds with the other violations against justice committed by the clergy as portrayed in the *Division*. According to St. German, the moral failings of priests and religious mean that, where the law is concerned, "spyrtuall men" will fail to provide equity. Strict laws may be adequate, if the judges were. For St. German, "cruell" judges are punishing innocents independently from the law. The "discretion of the iudges spyrytuall may ryght well aswage the rygour of the sayde laws," but that does not occur—or, at least, that is what "some say." Instead, ecclesiastical judges act with a view toward consolidating Church power, contradicting the faith and love of the people that they should represent and enact.

St. German assumes the posture of one meant to reconcile divisions between Church and state, ecclesiastical courts of heresy proceeding and the laymen brought before them, but he attacks the character of "spyrytuall men" especially, writing that, although "many" such judges have "greate vertues and great gyftes of god," it will be "harde to fynde any one spyrytuall man, that is nat enfecte with the sayd desyre and affection to haue the wordily honoure of prestes exalted and preferred" (191). Because of vainglory, spiritual judges conceal the poor conduct of priests, silencing laymen who raise objections, though these judges know better and will not be excused before God. This is especially the case in heresy trials:

For as some haue reported, yf any woll wytnes, that a man hath spoken any thynge, that is heresie, though he speke it onely of an ignoraunce, or of a passyon, or if he canne by interrogatoryes and questions be dryuen to confesse any thynge / that is prohybyted by the churche: anone they wyll dryue hym to abiure, or holde hym atteyn-ted without examining the intent or cause of his sayenge, or whether he had a mynde to be refourmed or nat. (192)

Particularly notorious, then, are these judges who will not "examine the intent" or look for a "mynde to be refourmed or nat" in the accused. Such a practice has nothing to do with confronting the witnesses; it is simply judicial misconduct.

Thus, St. German cites from the *Summa Rosella* of Baptista Trovomara, a canonist's manual for confessors, the case of a man who may err not only without fault but with merit. A simple, unlearned man may hear the preaching of a bishop who speaks against the Church, but because the man believes the teaching out of obedience, such a one deserves merit, though he errs (192). In sum, it is "very peryllous" that spiritual men should have authority to arrest a man "for euery lyght suspection" or "complaynte of heresye" (192). It would be "ryghte expedient" for the King to look into this matter with "great diligence" in order that "pride, couetise, nor worldly loue be no iudges, nor innocentes punysshed" (193). However just the laws against heresy are, judges may corrupt them. The ultimate solution, then, must be a return to the powers of the crown.

So, too, in defending the clergy and the laws against heresy, More's arguments are not just "legal" in the narrow sense of the term. More addresses the rumors of misconduct by calling them "cherytable infamacyon of the clergyes crueltye," identifying the use of "some say" or "some haue reported" as a "fayre figure of lamentacion" disguising anticlericalism (146/34–38). More writes:

But surely some say agayne, that lyke as there is nothing so euyll, but that some maye happe to do it / so is there no thynge so false, but some may happe to saye it. And some other saye also that lyke as there is nothyng so false, but some man may happe to saye it / so can no man say any thing so false, but some man vnder pretext of pacyfyenge maye happe to repete & reporte it. (147/1–6)

Balanced antithesis and climax are More's own figures, employed against the "figure of lamentation" of the Pacifier. In particular, the use of "some say" deserves attention because the citation of anonymous, even fictional, accusers enables St. German to call witnesses to his own case, thereby creating a façade of indifferent assessment (56/27–35). More knows that "some say" functions like "hearsay," a potent weapon in the courts of public opinion. The function of St. German's "some say," argues More, creates a "vnyuersall lye," a series of false reports, which insinuate that the clergy are eager to find and punish men for heresy. Such a "gaye reported tale" would "make all laye men wene that those some spyrytuall men were so great a somme, that it were some great cause of all this great grudge and dyuysyon" (147/7–20). Hyperbole and trafficking in rumor raises the question of defamation, a legal and rhetorical matter. The Pacifier must prove "outragyouse dedes in the dealynge and myshandelynge of men for heresy," otherwise "the kynges hyghnes and his counsayle can se for al his holesome counsayle, no cause to chaunge those iudges that are all redy, but to leue them styll" (152/17–24). By distorting the proportions of corruption and operating under the guise of attempted reconciliation, the Pacifier, whether by malicious design or with good intentions, sows and increases discord between lay and spiritual men. Rhetorically, the issues of heresy, equity, and the competence of the clergy are bound up in St. German's attempts at self-fashioning, or establishing *ethos,* and More's counter-use of "redescription," or *paradiastole,* a figure of speech for reframing the moral context of subjects.[71]

On equity and judicial discretion, More argues that if the king will suffer no judge that "hath any spyce at all" of pride or love unto the world, no heretic will ever be convicted, for such pure judges do not exist (152/24–26). By St. German's own reasoning, no heresy trials will come to court, for he declared already that despite other virtues, it will be hard to find a single spiritual man not infected with a love of honor and through such pride "farre fro suche indifference & equyte" that judges should have (153/3–4). But if clerics cannot deliver equity, More counters, neither can the laity. Few laymen are

---

71. Skinner, *Reason and Rhetoric,* 138–80.

knowledgeable of the laws of the Church, and "yf any such men be so suffycyentely lerned / yet is it possyble that those men whiche are so lerned, are not those y^t are so pure and clene frome euery spyce of pryde, couetyse & worldely loue." As a result, "ye heretykes [are] likely thus to make mery a good whyle, before there shoulde be founden good iudges for them" (153/17–22). More suspects that St. German's "equity" becomes a euphemism for licensing or augmenting heretical activity.

What these exchanges illustrate is that the dispute between More and St. German is a matter not simply of heresy but of equitable relief, with St. German favoring "mercy" and More "justice." For St. German, corrupt judges condemn the innocent, such as those innocents who would convey information from a bishop's own heretical homily. Because St. German argues for standards to be applied to the ecclesiastical courts that could not apply to secular ones, More counters that St. German's point is not reasonable reform of heresy proceedings but an abolition of them. An inability to offer equity, after all, implies that the judges are *without* conscience.

Throughout, More believes that where heresy occurs judges should give punishment according to the law.[72] Mercy toward the innocent, as St. German defines terms, More views as a miscarriage of justice. Elton argues that More, the "persecutor of heretics," did in practice "deny those forms of toleration which he had incorporated in *Utopia*,"[73] and "the hammer of poor Christopher St. German" represents a very different More than the traditional man for all seasons.[74] Yet on the question of equity and the ability of ecclesiastical judges to deliver it, Elton's division of humanist More from opponent of St. German appears to substitute a reading of *Utopia*'s second book for More's actual record as chancellor. In fact, More did not change his position on equity: punishment of heretics was what

72. See Trapp, *CW* 9, at lxxxi.   73. Elton, "Thomas More," 346.
74. Ibid., 354.

he thought just.[75] Rather, St. German, who favored the rigor of the human law in property cases like the right of wreck from *Doctor and Student*, adjusted his position, arguing later for a version of equity as relief from the law in matters of heresy. Instead of his being a political theorist who created a "brilliant" systematic theory of the law, St. German used the issue of equity to attack the clergy—an observation already made in part. At least, Christopher Haigh writes: "St. German was no revolutionary theorist: he was drawing on established legal thought; but he was making it more explicit and public and so, for the Church, potentially more dangerous."[76] More seemed to think so as well.

WHOLESOME HOLY BABBLING

The characterization of More's polemical voice deserves final reconsideration. Elton finds More "full of contemptuous sneers," lacking "compassion," "pretty pompous," and missing the charity and mild manner of his opponent.[77] More's "passionate assault" reveals much about him because, as a "non heretical critique of the clergy," there was "nothing in St. German's treatise" that should have "compelled More to take up the cudgels."[78] Yet an important consequence of Kelly's research is that on the point of witnesses and secret accusation, More's words lack the tone Elton and others attribute to them. When St. German addresses secret accusation, More writes as if "the Pacifier" is taking the exception—hiding the name of the accuser in those unique cases where disclosing his identity would place his life in danger—for the rule. More writes: "in some case for drede of perell that may fall to the wytnesses, the ordynary shall not suffre the partie that is detected, to knowe who hath wytnessed

---

75. See *ST* II, II, q.11, art. 3, and compare with *CW* 6.1, 405–18.

76. Haigh, *English Reformations*, 87.

77. Elton, "Reviews," 451–52. Similarly, Marius believes the *Division* "enraged" More and comments on the "studiously calm and benign" tone of St. German's treatise. See *Thomas More*, 434.

78. Elton, "Reviews," 452.

agaynste hym." Yet such a case is rare. Hence, "wolde this good man bygyle his readers ... & make theym wene [know] that that specyall prouysyon in that one specyall case, whych prouysyon I wene was yet in Englande neuer put in vre, were a comen order in euery mannys case" (CW 10, 93/6–16). Kelly's identification of St. German's errors about anonymity contextualizes More's own replies, which iterate that the suspect "shall see theym [the witnesses] and shall here theyre deposycyons to" (106/22–23). Hence, it is "very shamefaste" where the Pacifier "maketh as though the lawe were made generall, to prohybyte all men that they sholde not haue knowledge of the wytnesses in no case" (109/7–10). In More's view, the Pacifier's false description of *ex officio* proceedings is a fiction that would harm the "catholyque fayth" (104/19–35). So More concludes his point about knowing witnesses by writing: "Vpon my fayth except this good man se better how to salue this sore than I se: I wolde not haue wryten such another poynt in my boke, for more than all the paper coste and the prentynge to" (110/4–7). Though the language is strong, demands for greater "compassion" or for a "mild manner" from More on these points appear as corollaries to confusion about how *ex efficio* proceedings functioned.

More writes as if the Pacifier is simply confused as well. In the same chapter 15 of the *Debellation* that provides More's arguments about witnesses, More questions whether the Pacifier has been a "recluse" all his life (102/34–35). The context in this passage again concerns open accusations. Because people "feare of harme from mennes hartes," More argues, they would much rather witness against the heresy and allow the Bishop the adversarial role of accuser (98/20). "Yet of many trew men that wyl detecte and bere wytnesse," More adds, "ye shold fynde but very few that wolde bycome accusers" (99/7–8). The Pacifier's collapse of witness and accuser not only indicates the confusion Kelly discovered in St. German's case but also shows how easily the Pacifier will defy the "the playne comen experyence" of those who have been involved in court proceedings (102/33).[79] In proposing the King as safeguard for accusers, St. German ignores the fact that no one wants to play accuser. More's reply here is based on the experience of practicing the law, but it augments his general picture of the Pacifier as removed from the norms of the legal profession.

Such a portrait of St. German is too often described in terms of More's feigning ignorance about St. German's identity, which More does as an "elaborate hoax" (xxii). Yet ignorance of what actually transpires during *ex officio* proceedings and naïveté due to isolation render More's sense of his interlocutor as plausible. More wonders if the Pacifier is a "religyouse recluse" who cannot "come abrode," and for this reason, his opponent exaggerates what "some say." Then again, More questions how a religious could be aware of so much gossip (*CW* 9, 94/3–10). The Pacifier writes of a division, but levels his criticism at the character of the clergy, ignoring faults of the laity, so More, again, considers the identity of his opponent: "Howe be yt bycause he is peraduenture of the clergye hym selfe / therfore leste he shoulde seme parcyall to hys owne parte, he rather speketh of theyre defautes then oures: wherin I wyll not myche stryue wyth hym." Even so, if More himself were a priest, he would preach against the Pacifier's "fame of indifferency," for the Pacifier "neuer sholde say more then treuth" for the pleasure of laymen (103/20–29).

More questions the case for and against the identity of his opponent as a cleric, and there are reasons for his suspicion. The Pacifier's reliance upon the *Summa Rosella*—a text that More refers to as "so straunge a boke to fynde ... that very few men hadde medeled wyth it byfore" (146/29–31)—implies that a common priest's handbook for hearing confessions should be used in addressing the complex legal matter of heresy.[80] The *Division*, too, abounds with allegations of mistreatment by ecclesiastical courts, but the Pacifier

79. See commentary on 103/15–18 in *CW* 10, 277–78.
80. See commentary on 146/29 in *CW* 9, 385–86.

cannot name a single, specific instance during the seven years he is addressing—he seems unable to argue the cases of Thomas Hitton, Thomas Bilney, Richard Bayfield, John Tewkesbury, James Bainham, and two unnamed heretics at Exeter and Lincoln. More cannot understand the "babelyng of generalty" instead of addressing an actual, recent, and extremely relevant record. Even if it is "holsome holy babelynge," More jokes, the Pacifier presents a "false fayned tale" about heresy proceedings, an account detached from actual cases (147/31–148/18). Because St. German neither knew canon law nor addressed contemporary events involving heresy cases, More's claims about his opponent may be sincere queries: the Pacifier, in any case, emerges like the man described by More, as one removed from the world, or perhaps a well-intentioned priest who wishes to address rumors of clerical misconduct with his confessor's handbook.

Though More explicitly claims not to know his opponent's identity, an important argument for distrust of More's claim is that he was chancellor when St. German was writing proposed parliamentary legislation in 1531 and the king's council presented government policy to parliament. Because of More's position, he must have known the author of the legislation, and because that author was the same one who wrote *New Additions,* More could identify St. German's later controversial works (*CW* 10, xxiii). More, too, "described one of his adversaries as by reputation 'one greate cunnynge man'" (xxiv; cf. 4/29), which adds credibility to revisionists' own high estimation of St. German.

Yet what may appear as the most persuasive point—that More's position would have necessitated acquaintance with the 1531 parliamentary draft—remains speculative. The 1531 draft does not work as part of the seamless garment of St. German's writings. Rockett and Bernard show how there may be no connection between St. German's writings and the policy to procure a divorce. Even if the writings of St. German were part of the king's strategy to procure a divorce through parliament,[81] More was removed "sone after" becoming chancellor from work on the king's "great mater" because in "conscience" he could not do so.[82] In this case, if the 1531 draft were a matter for the chancellor normally, it would not be so in More's case because the suggested law, contrary to Rockett and Bernard, pursues the king's divorce. Either scenario allows for More never to have read St. German's parliamentary draft.

In regard to the very great cunning man as a respectful epitaph for St. German, More does identify a group who was "very wrothe" with his *Apology*, a group that was rumored to brim with "diverse very great cunnyng men" out of which emerged a "greate cunnynge man" to reply to More. "But in good fayth," More adds, "I coulde but laugh at that" (4/11–32). The tone here is not one of respect for the man of great intellect whom More knew, but of slight regard— the term "cunning" is used ironically. More goes on to qualify such cunning, writing of the Pacifier's dialogue that "hys answeres were euyn very dull and dede" (6/20–21). Rather than cunning, the Pacifier represents to More an anticlerical propagandist with a limited understanding of canon law, an ignorant yet efficacious pen.

St. German is often designated as an anticlerical conservative, a proponent of curbing Church powers, yet a believer in orthodox doctrine. Such a characterization, though it may have applied to the king, More would question in any other person or propagandist who attacks the Church.[83] Because the Pacifier's conception of equity represents less of a philosophical inquiry and more of an attack

---

81. *New Additions*, according to Guy, *Chancery and Statute*, 25, first attracted the government's attention, but: "St. German's usefulness to the government rested expressly on this theory of statute in the immediate context of current plans for the royal divorce. The presumption must be that St. German's star automatically waned when, early in 1532, the decision was taken not to seek an annulment of the king's marriage solely under the authority of an act of parliament. It is with this background in mind that we should examine St. German's parliamentary draft."

82. *Corr.*, 495–96.

83. More relates his dispute with St. German to the "whole clergy of chrystendome" and the "whole corps of chrystendome" in *CW* 9, 99/27–100/10 and to the survival of the "catholyque chrysten fayth" in *CW* 10, 229/27–230/16.

upon the clergy, More probably viewed St. German's work as a continuation of the kind of attacks begun by Simon Fish's "Supplication for the Beggars" (1529), a defamatory tract condemning the English clergy and the doctrine of purgatory.[84] For Fish, the tactic was using political questions about the poor in order to defame the clergy and, thereby, render heresy more acceptable to the populace—or so More thought.

In reply to Fish, More distinguishes two kinds of assault against the Church. Heretics may either "wryte agaynst the fayth and the sacramentys" in an open attack of doctrine or "labour agaynst the church alone / & get the clergye dystroyd." This latter approach may achieve the goals of the first. For with the clergy lost, "they [heretics] parceyue well that the fayth and sacramentes wold not fayle to decay" (*CW* 7, 161/17–24). More believes Fish's *Supplication* is part of the second kind of attack and the result of changing strategy:

But when they [heretics] haue perceuyd by experyence y^t good people abhorred theyr abomynable bokes: then they beyng therby lernyd y^t the furst way was not ye best for ye furtherance of theyr purpose / haue now determined them selfe to assay the secunde way / that ys to wytte y^t forberynge to wryte so openly and dyrectley agaynste all the fayth & the sacramentys as good crysten men coulde not abyde the redyng / they wolde /with lyttell towchyng of theyre other heresyes / make one boke specially against ye church & loke how that wold proue. (162/5–14)

The first attack directly addresses theology, but it fails because the people find heretical books an abomination. Anticlerical propaganda, then, emerges as a revised approach, which uses politics to mask heresy's advance. More believes heretics were changing to this second mode by 1529:

Whyche if yt succede after theyre appetytys that they myght with false crymes layd vnto some / or with the very fawtis of some / brynge the hole churche in hatered and haue the clergye dystroyed: then shuld they more

---

84. For historical context and critical discussion of Fish's *Supplication* and More's reply, see *CW* 7, lxv–cxvii. More's *Supplication* is cited internally from this edition as *CW* 7.

esely wynne theyre purpose that waye. For when the prechours of the fayth
and very gospell were dystroyed or farre owte of credence wyth ye people
/ then shulde they haue theyre awne false gospellys preched. (162/14–22)

Here, then, is how More sees heresy expanding, if it were to do so.
Where doctrinal attacks were unsuccessful, anticlerical ones could
be. Once the clergy were sufficiently defamed, they would be rendered impotent. A "public relations" tactic would succeed where
evangelization failed. In this way, St. German's interpretation of
failed equity due to poor judges fits with such anticlericalism.

Given More's line of reasoning from the *Supplication* as prelude
to the subsequent controversial writings, St. German would represent a strange case for More, a doctrinally orthodox proponent of
the spread of heresy. Though it was a risk for More in "retirement"
to write against St. German, we may surmise why he did so. Brendan Bradshaw suggests More organizes his *Apology* so as to advance
"the one charge to which Henry VIII might prove susceptible, that
the programme being urged upon him by the anti-clerical alliance
provided a means of access for heretics."[85] In a similar manner, because More considered the Pacifier as orthodox in doctrine, he may
have thought his opponent would reconsider the integrity of the ecclesiastical courts once "reform" of them was known to be a way of
spreading heresy.

Even so, the Pacifier's combination of doctrinal orthodoxy, anticlerical sentiment, and agenda to curtail the judicial prerogatives
of ecclesiastical courts could account for More sincerely finding
in St. German an *unwitting* proponent of the very heresies explicitly condemned in *Division* and in *Debellation*.[86] More explains that
wherever he writes the Pacifier "doth this or that, to this euyll purpose or that: yet I mene euer, the dede his, the malice of the purpose
some other wyly shrewys." The purpose belongs to those who are

85. Bradshaw, "Controversial," 555. Bradshaw, however, thinks the unnamed divorce dispute is motivating More's *Apologia* and St. German's *Division*.

86. St. German accepts prayers for the dead, pilgrimages, veneration of images, purgatory,
and indulgences in the *Division* in *CW* 9, 179, and the eucharist in *Salem* at *CW* 10, 379/24–35.

not "of so good catholyke mynde as I thynke all waye this man is hym self," and the reason for this distinction is because the Pacifier "openly dysprayseth these new broched heresyes, and with detestacyon of them reherseth them by name" (*CW* 10, 64/1–7). More separates the ramifications of or the malice behind the Pacifier's arguments from its author, a distinction that seems an unusual rhetorical strategy for More, especially given the way he treated previous opponents such as William Tyndale.

The reason for such distinctions between argument and intention need not produce a case for a hoax enacted by More. For the Pacifier appears unable to reason through to the consequences of his own position, just as he was unable to grasp *ex officio* proceedings or to address equity with any sort of philosophical rigor. "It may be," suggests Kelly, "that More's answers ... were sufficient to make St. German realize his mistake and to conclude that he was making a fool of himself by insisting upon reforms to a system that already contained the procedures and safeguards that he required." By the summer of 1534, Kelly notes, St. German did not return to the subject in his *Additions of Salem and Byzance*.[87] Whether or not More educated St. German so, More condemns some wily shrews for abusing the Pacifier's "playn simplyctye" and asks: "Was not that a synful wily way of them, to begyle a good simple soule so?" (64/13–14). More's question about those who beguiled the good yet simple Pacifier was sincere. At the end of *Debellation*, More writes of him: "I rather byleue though hym selfe therto saye naye, that in those thynges whyche he wryteth so perylouse and so noughte, some wyly shrewes begyle the good innocent man, than that hym self in hys own mynde, meane all that harme" (230/23–27).

87. Kelly, "Inquisitorial Due Process," 894.

CONCLUSION
Iconic Thomas Mores on Trial

From the moment of his imprisonment, More refused to judge any man. His controversial work was a thing of the past, and he was concerned only with his own conduct. This makes him the great example of all those who, rather than profess to believe what they do not believe, have given their lives cheerfully for any cause.

R. W. Chambers, *Thomas More*, 1935

Sir Thomas More died for conscience' sake, but not for freedom of conscience, freedom of thought, or tolerance in religion.... By conscience he meant a recognition of an established truth, and he argued that the truth was established by a greater consensus than available in one realm alone.

G. R. Elton, *Policy and Police*, 1972

Everyone who has seen the film of A Man for All Seasons *wants to know about More, but not to know too much. Their illusions might be shattered, their ideals infringed, their delight in a moral tale defaced. The world will need More as much as ever in the third millennium, but not in an historical guise.*

John Guy, *Thomas More*, 2000

A "man of singular virtue" and paragon of the "dignity of human conscience" are descriptions of Thomas More whose laudatory tone Robert Bolt captures in his famous play, *A Man for all Seasons*.[1] So, too, "poet without shame" or "plaster saint created by the worship-

---

1. Roper's *Life of Sir Thomas More*, in *TMSB*, 18; for More as an example of conscience, see Pope John Paul II, *Motu Proprio: Proclaiming Saint Thomas More as Patron of Statesman and Politicians*, Oct. 31, 2000, sec. 1.

pers" embody Hilary Mantel's already influential version of More in *Wolf Hall: A Novel*.[2] In other descriptions, William Roper praises More, but William Tyndale labels More a "poet," a deceiver who juggles words, a "natural son of the father of all lies."[3] With similar variance, Pope John Paul II's promulgation of a "patron of statesman" in 2000 names More an example of conscience, and G. R. Elton decries More as a "plaster saint." Bolt's and Mantel's iconic versions of Thomas More, in other words, stage the ongoing debate over whether or not to celebrate him.

Mantel's more recent work, too, charts the advance of the "two Mores" and "real More" theories discussed in my introduction. As John Guy puts the question: "Were there 'two' Thomas Mores? Was there a Utopian reformer of 1516 and a persecutor of heretics? A Soft Man and Hard Man?"[4] Guy believes such an inquiry, once removed from anachronism, "cuts to the quick," and he rightly notes competing discourse communities surrounding the iconic More.[5] Bolt's humane, learned, and honest More juxtaposes Elton's "real Thomas More," a figure full of early ambition and later intolerance. Similarly, Mantel's depiction of an arrogant More, a composite of revisionist scholarship, stands against scholars such as Louis Martz, who presents More's "inner man," a designation that emphasizes lifelong commitments to humanism and to prayer, a wedding of faith and liberal learning.[6]

Indeed, the question of an "inner man" or a "real Thomas More" pertains to what More meant by "conscience," a term that remains so vexed that Guy believes More's trial is "one of the most frequently cited, but least understood, events in English history."[7] As Guy explains, Bolt's naming More a "hero of selfhood" represents an exis-

---

2. "Poete with out shame" is from *An Answere Unto Mores*, 188/30. "Plaster saint" is from Elton, "Thomas More," 347.

3. Tyndale, *Answere*, 189/3.   4. Guy, *Thomas More*, 219.

5. Ibid., 222.

6. See Louis L. Martz, *Thomas More: The Search for the Inner Man* (New Haven, Conn.: Yale University Press, 1992).

7. Guy, *Thomas More*, 186.

tential description alien to More's own thoughts about conscience.[8] When Bolt's More tells Norfolk, "what matters to me is not whether it's true or not but that I believe it to be true, or rather not that I *believe* it, but that *I* believe it," Bolt emphasizes the self, not the Catholic Church for which More died.[9] Guy correctly assesses Bolt's play, but the same accusation of historical inaccuracy applies to *Wolf Hall*. In Mantel, Elton found a champion to match, even exaggerate, his controversial theses surrounding More's last days and personality, which in *Wolf Hall* become a tale of arrogant blunders, seizures of fear, and point of profound contrast to the heroic melancholy and toleration of Cromwell. In fact, the popularity of Mantel's novel and its difference from Bolt illustrates how far revisionist scholarship may undermine *A Man for All Seasons* in the imagination of a general readership.

Yet I believe the "real Thomas More" appears in his letters from 1534 onward, revealing an *ethos* that substantiates part of the celebration of and detraction from More. Revisiting the last letters will show how carefully yet clearly More defies the king's newest title, thereby qualifying Chambers's and Bolt's depiction of a man who dies for individual liberty while substantiating a fundamental claim of Elton. More's clarity about the importance of conscience is such that one major part of Elton's revision of More's final days must be true: More's silence means "total disapproval" of the king as supreme head of the Church, even though it makes for an effective legal defense.[10] Yet the same letters also reveal how Elton bends their purport, confuses their tone, and advocates a Cromwell of tolerance and sympathy who doesn't exist. By extension, Mantel's *Wolf Hall* emerges as something other than just historical fiction. In illustrating points of convergence and difference between Bolt and Mantel with the findings from my previous chapters, this conclusion will show an ironic and subversive *ethos* in More's last letters.

8. Bolt, *Man for All Seasons*, xiv.
9. Ibid., 91; cf. Ackroyd, *The Life of Thomas More*, 389.
10. Elton, *Policy and Police*, 416.

CONSCIENCE, CROMWELL, AND THE "LEWD" NUN

Thirteen of More's letters written between mid-April 1534 and July 1535 survive, including the narratives of his interrogations and his so-called Dialogue of Conscience, which features an August 1534 letter to Alice Alington that was written with the help of Margaret.[11] Even before his imprisonment, though, in a March 5 letter of 1534, More explains his position to Cromwell:

> And therefore sith all Christendom is one corps, I cannot perceive how any member thereof may without the common assent of the body depart from the common head. And then, if we may not lawfully leave it by ourself, I cannot perceive (but if the thing were a treating in a general council) what the question could avail whether the primacy were instituted by God or ordained by the Church.[12]

The importance of consensus that I reviewed in chapter 4 corresponds with the reference to the authoritative teaching of "Christendom" above and, more particularly, to More's ultimate opposition to the Supremacy Act. As in the antiheretical tracts, More believes in the "common senses" or consensus of Catholicism. Theological doctrine develops over time and in conjunction with the action of the Holy Spirit.[13] More ensconces that operative principle in the axiom that Christians believe truths because the Church proclaims them in the *Dialogue Concerning Heresies*: "An so byleue you the chyrche / not bycause it is trouth that ye chyrche telleth you / but ye belieue the trouth of the thynge bycause the chyrche telleth it" (*CW* 6.1, 251/11–13). Revealed truth as a function of the Church's promulgations contradicts Bolt's depiction of More, which presents authenticity as an architectonic value. Yet truth as a function of Church teach-

---

11. "A Dialogue of Conscience" is the title from *TMSB*, 316. On More's authorship, Louis L. Martz, *CW* 12, lxi, writes: "I think one ends up with very little doubt that this letter is primarily More's own composition. One can imagine More and Margaret planning it together and speaking much of it aloud in More's Tower room. But its art seems to be all More's."

12. Thomas More, *LL*, 54; hereafter cited internally.

13. See, for example, *CW* 8.1, 337/27–33.

ing, too, clarifies More's position on the role of councils and popes, a complex position, but not as difficult as Guy suggests.

To begin, More's emphasis upon "consensus" within the Church does not simply equate with what the term "conciliarism" by itself may imply.[14] More thinks Church councils could depose a pope for egregious and prolonged misconduct,[15] but councils and popes are interdependent sources of tradition through which the Holy Spirit may guide the Church.[16] When More writes to Cromwell that he never favored a pope over a general council (LL, 54–55), then, we should distinguish between the order of priority, wherein consensus best emerges in councils, and the order of practice, which made the pope de facto pastor of the Church because councils were not in session perpetually. If councils move to solidify papal hegemony, too, the logic of More's position would necessitate his acceptance of that teaching. More himself writes in this same letter: "if I should follow the other side and deny the primacy to be provided by God; which if we did, yet can I nothing ... perceive any commodity [advantage] that ever could come by that denial, for that primacy is at the leastwise instituted by the corps of Christendom and for a great urgent cause in avoiding of schisms and corroborate[d] by continual succession more than the space of a thousand year at the least" (54). Indeed, the inexorable historical drift of conciliar teaching pointed toward papal primacy.[17] As Guy speculates about More's time in the Tower: "More's commitment to the Pope probably hardened" and, "by extrapolation, we might affirm that he died for the Pope."[18] When More defies the king, he affirms the Catholic Church, but with the line of reasoning, if not the exact words, found in Roper's Life: "And therefore am I not bound ... to conform my conscience to

14. See Gogan, Common Corps, 341–70.
15. On deposing a pope, see CW 8.2, 590/13–15, and commentary on this passage in CW 8.3, 1615–16.
16. Gogan, Common Corps, 348, writes: "More evidently looked on pope and council as correlative and co-responsible organs of authority."
17. See De Silva's commentary in More, LL, 153–54.
18. Guy, Thomas More, 204.

the Council of one realm against the General Council of Christendom."[19] That "general council" indicates that "no temporal prince" may "presume by any law" what belongs to "the See of Rome," a preeminence granted to "St. Peter and his successors."[20] Roper's account of More's words, often disputed, follows like a conclusion from the position of More's own letter to Cromwell.

Yet this same 1534 letter clarifies the relationship between Cromwell and More as adversarial. To More's idea of conscience, Elton writes, Cromwell envisions "the conscience of the subject," who owes obedience to the "King-in-parliament." Thus More earns his "sainthood at the hands of the papacy," but Cromwell "might have been amused" by the idea that the "modern national state might find some way of canonising him."[21] In a sense, though, Elton attempts to "canonize" Cromwell in the name of the modern state instead of More, identifying Cromwell's role as central to Henrician reform and valorizing such efforts with a sympathetic portrayal of how the master secretary deals with objectors such as More.[22] For Elton, More's refusal represents a catastrophe for the government; Henry's speculation that More encourages others in obstinacy is fundamentally accurate. Hence the imperative to convert More rather than let him alone is real. Cromwell, then, finds himself in the most difficult position of sating the king's desire for approval of his new marriage and title and dealing with More's intractable and wily intransigence. Yet instead of despising More, Elton asserts, Cromwell sympathizes with him. For only More knows that he would never refuse the oath and thereby thwart Cromwell's attempts to save the former chancellor. Cromwell did not suspect More's adamantine resistance; thus, there is never any overarching, long-term conspiracy to destroy More.[23] "Cromwell," writes Elton, "does not seem to have wanted

19. Roper, *TMSB*, 61.   20. Ibid., 59–60.

21. Elton, *Policy and Police*, 418.

22. On Elton's elevation of Cromwell and attack upon More, see especially, Elton, "Thomas More and Thomas Cromwell," 144–60.

23. See Elton, *Policy and Police*, 383–425.

More's death at all." In fact, Cromwell maintains all "the courtesies" proper during interrogations and shows himself "well disposed" to More.[24] In Elton's version of events, the humane, tolerant man for all seasons in Bolt's drama would seem better applied to Cromwell's actions and notion of conscience.

So, too, in *Wolf Hall* the problem is not with Henry's caesaro-papism but with More's obstinacy, which is a symptom of intellectual pride and radically intolerant religion, or so Mantel's Cromwell thinks: "More is too proud to retreat from his position. He is afraid to lose his credibility with the scholars in Europe. We must find some way for him to do it, that doesn't depend on abjection."[25] Cromwell's eagerness to help More, a depiction in obvious agreement from Elton's assertion above, contrasts with the absolute intolerance More projects toward heretics. Thus, when Cromwell investigates More's relationship with Elizabeth Barton, a nun whose visions foresaw Henry in hell for marrying Anne Boleyn, Mantel makes the scene one in which Cromwell petitions More for the life of John Frith, a man condemned for heresy. In *Wolf Hall*, Cromwell rather casually pursues More's correspondence with Barton, using the occasion primarily for an opportunity to discuss Frith's fate. Cromwell asks More of Frith: "If his doctrine is false and yours is true you can talk him back to you, you are an eloquent man, you are the great persuader of our age, not me—talk him back to Rome, if you can. But if he dies you will never know, will you, if you could have won his soul?"[26] After Frith is put to death and More imprisoned, More's family members converse with Cromwell. Margaret confesses, "My father has spoken very warmly of you." Mantel's Roper offers Crom-

24. Ibid., 419. Elton adds of Cromwell's good disposition to More: "Only the prejudice which supposes Cromwell incapable of decent or genuine feelings can deny this."
25. Mantel, *Wolf Hall*, 421.
26. Ibid., 376. Cf. Ackroyd, *Life of Thomas More*, 325: More "knew that Frith was being held in loose confinement and that he was being actively courted by Cromwell and his agents as a possible supporter of the king's 'divorce'; More's attack was a way of exposing him.... It was a means of warning Cromwell not to go too far, and perhaps of reminding Henry himself of his spiritual duties."

well his hand and says, "We know you are not vengeful, sir. Though God knows, he [More] has never been a friend to your friends." Instead of aggressively investigating an innocent More on the count of colluding with Barton, Cromwell experiences sympathies for all.[27]

Yet there was no such meeting between More and Cromwell, and we know the details of this investigation primarily through More's own letters.[28] More writes to Cromwell in March of 1534 to explain his visit to the "lewd," or uneducated, nun and encloses his own letter to Barton (36). At approximately the same time, More writes to the king, protesting his innocence and worrying whether "sinister information"—a misleading or malicious accusation—should cause any more "distrust" of More's "truth" and "devotion" (46). More elaborates upon the "sinister" informant or accuser, referring explicitly to whoever names him in the bill of attainder against Barton and her party. So, too, More implores Henry to "to take occasion hereafter" against "changeable people" that would "slander" him as a disloyal subject (47).

Though Henry himself is indignant with More and, in expanding the Barton case to include his former chancellor, ultimately directs Cromwell, More's anxieties over sinister accusers are well founded.[29] Cromwell manipulated an intelligence report for the king the year before to exaggerate the dangers of a Catholic conspiracy, replacing the name of George Joye, a Protestant informer whose bias would be easily inferred, with that of "oon whoo."[30] Cromwell as "sinister accuser," too, seems confirmed by the coercive measures he employs against More during the latter's imprisonment. Cromwell grants Margaret a visit to More in order to persuade her father to take the oath, but the visit occurs on the same day that

27. Ibid., 472. Compare Mantel's general characterization with Guy's elaboration upon one of "Cromwell's ways of dividing the [More] family" in Guy, *A Daughter's Love*, 251–52.

28. See Ackroyd's narrative of the Barton episode in *Life of Thomas More*, 328–37.

29. On how Henry and Cromwell handle the Barton case, see Elton, *Policy and Police*, 274–75.

30. Fox and Guy, *Reassessing the Henrician Age*, 116.

the Carthusians, who also refused the oath, are strapped to hurdles beneath More's window and dragged five miles to Tyburn. Cromwell and Audley, too, attempt "to dupe" Fisher and More by interviewing them individually and acting as if the other had "given in."[31]

So even though More's name is eventually removed from the bill of attainder against the Nun of Kent, we find More speculating in his letter to Margaret from the Tower in 1534: "I thought and yet think, that it may be that I was shut up again upon some new causeless suspicion, grown peradventure upon some secret sinister information, whereby some folk haply thought that there should be found out against me some other greater things" (100).[32] The sinister accuser emerges again in More's letter of June 3, 1535, where More posits "one that had informed his Highness many evil things of me that were untrue" (119). Likewise, the Guildhall Report of More's trial marks him speculating about malicious slander, which was devised to instill hatred against him in the king.[33]

More's repeated assertion that he is a victim of slander does more than express anxiety; it represents a counterattack against courtiers he cannot name. For Chambers, More and Cromwell are mighty opposites, the one a "Utopian" and the other a "Machiavel."[34] In *Wolf Hall*, though, Cromwell becomes a modern paradigm of toleration anachronistically applied to the early sixteenth century. Mantel's Cromwell may be a fictional depiction, but she creates him, in part, from Elton's man of sympathy.

Though historical fiction ought to take poetic license, the record of events surrounding Barton is clear enough such that Cromwell, even in revisionist accounts, aggressively investigates More.[35] In fact,

31. Guy, *A Daughter's Love*, 247.

32. "In the end, More's name was removed from the [February 1534] bill, but only because he petitioned to be allowed to give evidence in the House of Lords" (Guy, *Thomas More*, 169).

33. See the Guildhall Report in *Thomas More's Trial by Jury*, ed. Henry Ansgar Kelly, Louis W. Karlin, and Gerard B. Wegemer (Woodbridge: Boydell Press, 2011), 186–94, especially 191.

34. Chambers, *Thomas More*, 291.

35. "Cromwell had gathered a great deal of evidence implicating More in the affair of the Nun" (Marius, *Thomas More*, 452); cf., Guy, *Thomas More*, 168–69.

More refuses to listen to any prophecies about the king: his letter to Barton admonishes her. As More explains his view upon Barton's claims: "I assure you she were likely to be very bad, if she seemed good, ere I should think her other, till she happed to be proved naught" (42). Such seeming circumlocution actually indicates well More's basic position, which is that untested visions should not be approved. More employs doublespeak because he could say nothing in favor of the alleged prophecies. As More tells Father Rich, a proponent of the holy or mad nun, the prophecies were "strange tales," which form "no part of the creed" (43); these are matters for the local ordinary to investigate, not for preachers to spread without sanction. More's letter indicates careful and successful defense against Cromwell, but Mantel suppresses this context. Instead of an overreaching and failed attempt to ensnare More, Cromwell recognizes in an instant More's innocence and uses the moment to appeal on behalf of Frith.

TONE AND *HONESTAS*

As Mantel misrepresents Cromwell's "courtesies," Elton distorts More's own narrative voice, failing to note More's irony. We have seen how the March 5, 1534, letter describes More's position before the Act of Succession is passed on the twenty-sixth of the same month.[36] Misprision of treason is the penalty for refusing an oath in support of the act. Given such background, when More is interrogated on April 13 as the only layman called to Lambeth Palace and the first one to refuse the oath, his interrogators say More's refusal will "cause the King's Highness to conceive" both "great suspicion" of More and "great indignation" against him (58). Elton believes More's subsequent imprisonment for refusing this oath was not the first move to destroy More, who "was being held rather than punished," but Elton appears to contradict his earlier analysis, which finds the "real purpose" of both Henry and Cromwell in "the country's sworn accep-

36. See "Chronology," in *Thomas More's Trial by Jury*.

tance," not necessarily in Anne's offspring, but in the "major policy" that the marriage represents—what Elton terms as "political revolution and the religious schism."[37] In these passages from the same book that exonerates and exalts Cromwell, Elton writes that "More was quite right in practice" in viewing the oath as an implicit renunciation of papal authority and jurisdiction.[38] More, at least, writes to Margaret, "I would not deny to swear to the succession, yet unto the oath that there was offered me I could not swear without jeoparding of my soul to perpetual damnation" (58).[39] If More rejects Cromwell's "political revolution," however, it seems plausible that Cromwell's interrogation of More is an attempt to crush his opposition. "Surely the King's Highness," Cromwell iterates to More, "would now conceive a great suspicion" against More and think that "the matter of the nun of Canterbury was all contrived" by More himself (61). By insinuating that Barton's prophecies were More's creations, Cromwell contextualizes the earlier references to the king's "suspicion" and "indignation," producing blatant threats.

So, too, the dialogue More records in this same letter aligns with his description of events to indicate how the interrogation is no mere polite discussion of a serious matter. After initially refusing the oath, More is directed to go down into the garden and wait, but he stays in the "burned chamber" instead and looks out, perhaps, speculates Richard Marius, because "the garden below swarmed with men who had sworn the oath, and More did not want to be in their company."[40] More describes the scene, showing Doctor Hugh Latimer, who preached for the king on Wednesdays during the Lenten season of 1534, parading through a garden in a "very merry"

37. Elton, *Policy and Police*, 401, 226.
38. Ibid., 227.
39. Peter Marshall writes that More's position was well known: "More would not swear because the preamble to the oath upheld the spiritual validity of the king's second marriage and implicitly rejected the authority of the pope. For him [More] to swear such an oath against his belief to the contrary would have been perjury, not just a legal transgression but a cause of eternal damnation. Everyone understood that this was the position" ("The Last Years," 122).
40. Marius, *Thomas More*, 462.

fashion. Latimer laughs and takes "one or twain about the neck so handsomely," More writes, "that if they had been women, I would have went [thought] he had been waxen wanton" (58). More also notes his friend Doctor Wilson, a former chaplain and confessor of Henry VIII, who was asked to study the matter of the divorce and concluded with the minority (176). Accordingly, Wilson now refuses the oath and "gentlemanly" is sent "straight unto the Tower" (58). Women or gentlemen, gardens or towers, contrast in what More calls a "pageant" (59). More's portrayal of events provides not a paradigm of equanimity or liberty of conscience for all, but a disjunctive in which those with courage refuse the oath in contradistinction to what More sees as the pusillanimity of others who swear.

In fact, Elizabeth McCutcheon calls the above scenes "reminiscent" of the *History of Richard III*, an important observation for how these letters ought to be read. For McCutcheon, the letters are "artful and devious in the extreme." The scenes More describes may be played or performed, hearkening back to the language of political theater More uses to narrate Richard's rise to power—and to undermine that protector's pretense. When More writes the word "pageant" to describe the king's advisors, McCutcheon rightly senses a similarity of craft between the *History* and the last letters. In other words, More attempts to undermine his interrogators in the letters just as his narrator in the *History* does with the charades of Richard.[41]

There may be a direct allusion in that word "pageant" too. In the *History*, More's commoners conclude of Richard's machinations: "that these matters bee Kinges games, as it were stage playes, and for the more part plaied vpon scafoldes. In which pore men be but ye lokers on. And thei y^t wise be, wil medle no farther. For they that sometyme step vp and playe w^t them, when they cannot play their partes, they disorder the play & do themself no good" (*CW* 2, 81/6–10). The idea of political life as a stage play, or a pageant, More en-

---

41. Elizabeth McCutcheon, "More's Three Prison Letters Reporting on His Interrogations," in *Thomas More's Trial by Jury*, 99.

countered earlier in his studies of Lucian. In translating *Menippus*, More would have found:

I suppose you have often seen these stage-folk who act in tragedies, and according to the demands of the plays become at one moment Creons, and again Priams or Agamemnons.... And when at length the play comes to an end, each of them strips off his gold-bespangled robe, lays aside his mask ... and goes about in poverty and humility, no longer styled Agamemnon, son of Atreus.... That is what human affairs are like, it seemed to me as I looked. (*CW* 3.1, 177)

In this passage human affairs are capricious. The same man reigning as Agamemnon could next play the role of Thersites. There remains an echo of this teaching, too, in More's reply to Norfolk's warning, *"indignatio principis mors est,"* that death awaits those who anger princes: "Is that all my lord? Then in good faith is there no more difference between your Grace and me, but that I shall die today and you tomorrow."[42] At least, in terms of the pageant of More's first interrogation, the fact of his own death and, later, Latimer's execution as a "heretic" during the reign of Queen Mary, More's point about the dangerous nature of failing to play the part assigned you would be confirmed by subsequent events.

For the author of the *History* and of *Utopia*, what should emerge from reflection upon such stage plays are realistic expectations for courtiers, who will seek an agenda to make matters, as *Morus* put it in *Utopia*, as "little bad" as possible (*CW* 4, 101/2). Yet for the author of the prison letters, the admonition from the *History* about performing in political theater—"thei y^t wise be, wil medle no farther"—becomes a rule for survival. Indeed, that word "meddle" resounds throughout More's last letters, which continually affirm how More will not "meddle against" the king's "pleasure" and how he plans "no more to meddle of the matter" of the marriage (*LL*, 93). More even defines himself as "not a man meet to take upon" or "to meddle" in the case of another's conscience (106), perhaps, because

42. Roper, *Life of More*, in *TMSB*, 50.

they that wise be will meddle no further than More had already done.

If More's letters return to the treatment of politics from the *History*, they revisit the importance of *honestas* and how Cardinal Morton practiced it as well, showing how More's "devious prose" functions. In chapter 2, following Cicero's teaching on *decorum*, I defined "honesty" not as straightforward speaking but as knowing what to say or withhold, given a particular audience and a speaker's purpose. Like Morton in the *History*, More under questioning withholds. After observing Latimer's levity, More is recalled by Cromwell, who asks him to state his reasons for refusing the oath. More refrains from doing so, but given his earlier letter to Cromwell, it is an opinion that the master secretary already knows. More doesn't pretend Cromwell believes otherwise. He replies: "And that if I should open and disclose the causes why, I should therewith but further exasperate his Highness, which I would in nowise do" (*LL*, 59). More's refusal to incriminate himself and Cromwell's knowledge of what More believes about the oath mean that both men realize the very request for More's opinion on this matter will result in evidence against More. As More records, his answer would put him "in the danger" of the statute (ibid.). "If it so be that in some things for which I refuse the oath," More elaborates, "I have (as I think I have) upon my part as great a council and greater too." Thus, More concludes: "I am not then bounden to change my conscience, and confirm it to the council of one realm, against the general council of Christendom" (60). More provides his earlier explanation to Cromwell, but in a conditional way, explaining his position by way of hypothetical statements in order to parry charges of malice. Yet Cromwell obviously recognizes what More means. The master secretary responds by swearing a "great oath" that he would rather "his own only son" had "lost his head" than More should refuse the oath (61). The withholding by More is not only honest but necessary.

More's tone also becomes a question in this exchange. Contrary to Elton's portrayal of Cromwell as a man of sympathy, the point is not that Cromwell loves More like a son, but that More will be killed for his refusal to accept the king's new title. "Cromwell's purpose in hinting at the prospect of possible consequences," Elton writes of similar threats by Cromwell against More, is "to move More to compliance, not to contemplate a certainty for which preparations were being made."[43] Yet describing Cromwell's words as a simple petition for compliance ignores the fact that noncompliance eventuates in death, or so Cromwell suggests. No one, not Cromwell's son or even an ex-chancellor, will fail to take the oath, if the king desires that person to do so. In More's letter, where Cromwell mentions his son in the threatening "great oath" above, More interposes, "which is of truth a goodly young gentleman, and shall I trust come to much worship" (61). By speaking of the "goodly young gentleman" More attempts to diffuse Cromwell's suggestions, ignoring the threat by praising the son of the very man who seeks his life. Instead of Elton's perceived "courtesies," More's grim irony, as in the *History*, emerges in instances such as these. Thus, More writes, Cromwell is "he that tenderly favoreth me" (ibid.). So, too, Cromwell's talk of "heinous pains" causes More to name Cromwell as his "special tender friend" (100). Thomas Wilson's *The Art of Rhetoric* (1560) would later record that More was famous for his ironical mocking, specifically, undermining a person with false praise, a practice for which "Socrates" and "Sir Thomas More with us here in England" deserve admiration.[44] The practice of praising the unworthy abounds in More's *History*, from the account lauding the "trusting" Hastings, a man who dies, though, for "trusting too much," or in Doctor Shaa's encomium of Richard, which praises the hunchbacked tyrant as "the special pattern of knightly prowess."[45] More's words about a "special tender friend" who threatens him continue the practice.

For McCutcheon, More's voice in the letters combines both "ob-

43. Elton, *Policy and Police*, 405.   44. Wilson, *The Art of Rhetoric* (1560), 175.
45. See CW 2, 52/22, 67/28.

server" and "performer," showing how such a narrative position requires "tremendous control." Because More is now involved in the events he describes, his tonal mixture of irony, bravado, sarcasm, and caution requires self-command.[46] Yet the same ironic tone functions in the *History*. Like Tacitus, in the *History* More's narrative voice is that of an "ironic historian" who contrasts "the smooth surface of events and the ruinous moral vacuum that lies beneath them."[47] So, too, More's last letters expose Cromwell's "courtesies" in terms of the master secretary's "sinister" purpose. Elton's own lament that the *History* "has not attracted as much study as one might hope" becomes instructive for his own reading of More's letters.[48] The similarity in tone between the *History* and the last letters indicates how More thought of himself and his accusers right from the start of his interrogations. More saw himself involved in king's games that would be played out upon the scaffold.

Even so, More's "subversive prose" shows how Elton rightly maintains that More's silence was a "major embarrassment" to Henry's policy. Contrary to Chambers's biography or the impression left by Bolt's later drama, during the years before trial and execution, More's position is not neutral or essentially in favor of individual liberty. As in the case of Cromwell's ostensible sympathy for More, the keys to understanding More's statements of neutrality are in analysis of tone and in awareness of Morton's *honestas*. More ends his explanation why he will refuse the oath in the letter above: "as touching the whole oath, I never withdrew any man from it, nor never advised any to refuse, nor never put, nor will, any scruple in any man's head, but leave every man to his own conscience. And methinketh in good faith that so were it good reason that every man should leave me to mine" (61). Compared with More's argument after he receives sentence of death—that the common corps of Chris-

46. McCutcheon, "Thomas More's Three Prison Letters Reporting on His Interrogation," 99.
47. Sylvester, *CW* 2, xcvii.
48. Elton, "Humanism in England," 213.

tendom takes priority over a regional council—the point here about leaving "every man to his conscience" emerges as a technical, legal defense, an apologia More uses often.

That same kind of neutrality, for example, More employs for defense and as cover for his own attack in his conversation with Margaret. Recorded in the August 1534 letter of Margaret Roper to Alice Alington, More claims not to dispute or judge "any other man's conscience" because it "lieth in their own heart" (84). Yet in the same letter, More not only repeats the arguments above about how a general council takes priority over a local one, but also employs language that should be read as attacking those who reject the authority of the Catholic Church. "Now if it so hap," More argues, "that in any particular part of Christendom, there be a law made, that be such as for some part thereof some men think that the law of God cannot bear it, and some other think yes, the thing being in such manner in question ... in this case he that thinketh against the law, neither may swear that law lawfully made, standing his own conscience to the contrary, nor is bounden upon pain of God's displeasure to change his own conscience therein." For if "any particular law made anywhere, other than by the general council or by a general faith grown by the working of God universally through all Christian nations," More posits, "I can see none that lawfully may command and compel any man to change his opinion, and to translate [transfer] his own conscience from the one side to the other" (83). By extrapolation to More's own case, without consensus within the Church as a whole, England cannot compel him to swear. There is a corollary to this position. Those who defy the consensus of the Church with contrary belief are compelled to change their position. "But Mary," More adds, "if on the other side a man would in a matter take a way by himself upon his own mind alone, or with some few, or with never so many, against an evident truth appearing by the common faith of Christendom, this conscience is very damnable" (84). Though spoken hypothetically here and not in direct reference to any of the king's statutes, the inference seems clear enough: The king's claims are not in accord with consensus; those who swear, ipso facto, fall into schism.[49] After reasoning to the conclusion of "damnable conscience" More continues, "for what causes I refuse the oath, the thing (as I have often told you) I will never shew you, neither you nor nobody else" (84). Yet More just indicated why he refuses to swear. In this particular case, because More does not specifically reference the oath, he cannot be accused for condemning it. As Morton speaks suggestively in the *History*, so does More. Like Morton's "stops," or suggestive silences, More's silence about the oath says something.

In the same letter, More indirectly addresses the king's propaganda and legislation in favor of supremacy claims. More tells Margaret, "I never intend (God being my good lord) to pin my soul at another man's back, not even the best man that I know this day living; for I know not whither he may hap to carry it" (79). As Marc'hadour explains these lines, the parenthetical phrase acknowledges "that divine grace is needed for total fidelity to conscience" and "to pin" may paraphrase "to peg" or "to glue" or "other words expressing dependence."[50] The allusiveness, though, constitutes its true power. More's refusal "to pin" his soul "at another man's back" contrasts with Christopher St. German's statement in the *New Additions* that "the hyghe soueraygne ouer the people ... hath not onely charge on the bodies, but also on the soules of his subiectes."[51] Likewise, Henry's 1531 Pardon of the Clergy originally included not only the "supreme head" claim *(supremum caput)* but also the assertion that the king had the "cure" or "care" of his subjects' souls *(curae animarum)*.[52]

49. Cf. More's argument to Margaret here with his later statement at trial: "I say further that your Statute is ill made, because you have sworn never to do anything against the Church, which through all Christendom is one and undivided, and you have no authority, without the common consent of all Christians, to make a law or Act of Parliament or Council against the union of Christendom" (*TMSB*, 354).

50. Germain Marc'hadour, "Saint Thomas More and Conscience (Remembering Australia and New Zealand)," *Moreana* 30, no. 113 (1993): 57.

51. See *New Additions* in St. German, *Doctor and Student*, 327.

52. J. Scarisbrick, "The Pardon of the Clergy, 1531," *Cambridge Historical Journal* 12, no. 1 (1956): 34.

The statement that "even the best man" cannot be responsible for More's own soul contradicts the propaganda surrounding the king's claim of responsibility for his subjects' souls, further indicating how More expressed his opinion through "silence." More's language of nonjudgmental neutrality shows that he never argues specifically against the oath of succession, even if he remains clear about the overall question of the king's claim to rule the Church of England. More's own *honestas* requires an economics of sincerity that would convey his opinion without falling victim to the statuary penalties.

INTEGRITY, LIES, AND SELFHOOD

More's careful defiance shows how the significance of his last days has become obscured. We have seen how for Bolt and others More's words are the apologetics of selfhood. As André Prévost writes, for More "conscience is a self-sufficient absolute, which each individual can rest upon."[53] Chambers, too, refers to More's conscience as a "great plea for the liberty of silence," suggesting individual liberty as an ideology for viewing More's death.[54] Revisionists such as Stephen Greenblatt provide the opposite opinion. Rather than Bolt's individuality, More intends solidarity with the Church, an erasure of selfhood rather than its distinctive statement. So Greenblatt claims More's last letters show a desire to lose the "intimate sense of himself" in the "communal solidarity" of Christendom.[55]

Yet Greenblatt reproduces the two Mores thesis in terms of "selfhood," a lexicon of analysis similar to that of Bolt's play. In Greenblatt's view, More represents a rhetorical, performative self, which enabled a "life lived as histrionic improvisation," an identity that accompanies the "real self" of "scholar." Though Greenblatt places the term "real" in quotation marks, the designation implies the im-

---

53. André Prévost, "Conscience the Ultimate Court of Appeal" in *EA*, 566.
54. Chambers, *Thomas More,*336–37.
55. Greenblatt, *Renaissance Self-Fashioning*, 69–70.

portance of authenticity, a premise shared by Bolt. For Greenblatt, however, this "real self" of More dreams of "a cancellation of identity itself," which would provide "an end to all improvisation, an escape from narrative."[56] In this line of argument, the prison letters would show a wish for self-cancellation as the "ironic, complex sense of self" gives way to a scaffold, which becomes a place not just for those who played king's games but also where identity becomes drowned in the sea of Catholic tradition.[57]

Greenblatt's theory of self-erasure parallels Alistair Fox's psychological assessment of More as one possessed by a death wish. "The significance of his death," writes Fox of More, "cannot be objectively grasped without knowledge of the personal philosophy that eventually led him to it."[58] Fox, in the words of Elton, posits that More finds "human history" a "sequence of temptations to desert an all-demanding God."[59] And Fox himself writes of More that "from the beginning, the *modus vivendi* he chose for himself implied an incipient *modus moriendi*." More's "deeply sprung recoil from the world's frustrations, mutability, injustice, tribulation, and its even more satanic allurements" creates an imperative to leave the world. "Perhaps," Fox speculates, "More found it psychologically necessary to die."[60] Though Fox and Greenblatt employ very different approaches, both find More searching out death for reasons that seem imprecisely located within the rhetoric of the letters.

A second position related to that of Greenblatt and Fox is Guy's insinuation that More's motivation is love of fame because More desires and achieves individual distinction precisely by dying for the "communal solidarity" with Christendom. Of the letter to Alice Alington, Guy believes that More intends to shape "an interpretation of Catholic 'conscience,'" which would become "a perpetual memorial." "It is impossible at this distance," Guy writes, "to judge the

---

56. Ibid., 31–32.   57. Ibid., 72–73.
58. Fox, *History and Providence*, 254.
59. The description of Fox's project comes from Elton, "Humanism in England," 225.
60. Fox, *History and Providence*, 254.

extent to which More's Tower letters are designed to bolster an image and to what extent they can be read literally."[61] Memorial building, then, means erecting a monument to one's own conscience, an aspiration that suggests More as a myth-maker, a poet of his own individuality as well as for the teachings of Catholicism. Instead of Greenblatt's version in which More's self-fashioning terminates because of a turn to religion in the Tower, More's last letters show the ongoing cultivation of personal reputation through rhetoric.

Mantel's depiction of events mirrors these descriptions especially. "More says he loves England, and he fears all England will be damned," Cromwell thinks. So More must be "offering some kind of bargain to his God, his God who loves slaughter."[62] A god who "loves slaughter" resonates with the "all demanding God" cited above, but now such a description of More's religious belief dovetails with More's putative arts of self-aggrandizement. After an interrogation of More, in Mantel's version, Cromwell, Cranmer, and Audley converse about how More publishes all his letters. More publishes even those that attack him in order to make "a fine show of his humility." Yet this self-fashioning poses a problem because Audley believes More will write of his interrogation. "Depend upon it," he says to Cromwell, "in the eyes of Europe we will be the fools and the oppressors, and he will be the poor victim with the better turn of phrase."[63] From the historical record of More's own defense to Cromwell's threats, Mantel provides a revised More, a self-fashioning interloper upon practical and fair men who serve on the king's council.

The notion of self-fashioning, finally, suggests the accusation of More's mendacity, a charge I reviewed in my introduction and one that many detach from the Ciceronian context of *honestas*. Instead of a man of integrity and conscience, More appears as a typical courtier, in fact, a liar. When Elton discusses More's opposition to

61. Guy, *Thomas More*, 177.   62. Mantel, *Wolf Hall*, 512.
63. Ibid., 465.

Henry on the matter of divorcing Catherine, he shows More as a behind-the-scenes operator, no different from any other politician of intrigue, a characterization that recent scholarship rebuts.[64] Greenblatt, too, addresses More's presentation of Henry's case against Catherine to both Houses of Parliament on March 30, 1531, as evidence of duplicity. More's words on this occasion are "a command performance," but a performance nevertheless. Greenblatt writes: "This extreme theatrical improvisation at the very center of power, this tense, cunning suppression of his true beliefs could not long be sustained, either at the level of politics or at the level of More's own soul."[65] Greenblatt explains More's presentation of Henry's case as an example of *Morus's* teaching on the *obliquus ductus,* or "indirect approach."[66] As Elton argued that More lied to Erasmus about entering Henry's service, Greenblatt reads the speech of *Morus* as a general license for prevarication, a teaching More put into practice before parliament.[67]

We have seen there is no general approval of mendacity in More's writings, even if special exceptions may exist. Morton, I suggested in chapter 2, goes beyond withholding, manipulating Buckingham, because tyrannical regimes create special circumstances that intervene upon normative ethics. In tyrannical regimes, the imperative to withhold truth may extend to other actions required to remove such rulers from power, including the practice of deceit. Following Cicero in the figure of Morton, More explores fissures between what *honestas* and *utilitas* require, paradoxically, in the name of noble action. Greenblatt's "theatrical improvisation" and "cunning suppression," then, appear as elaborations that ignore crucial Ciceronian contexts.

64. G.R.Elton, "Sir Thomas More and the Opposition to Henry VIII," in *EA,* 79–91. Cf. Marshall, "The Last Years," 117.

65. Greenblatt, *Self-Fashioning,* 67.

66. Ibid.

67. For Roper's version of More's address to Commons, see his *Life of Sir Thomas More,* in *TMSB,* 40–41.

More never follows the example of Morton's stratagems for Richard III and manipulation of Duke Buckingham, but he recognizes how *necessitas* along with *honestas* may form the horizon of accommodation. In the case of More appearing before parliament, the "necessity" is that, as chancellor, More *should* introduce the opinions in favor of the king's divorce. Even so, the degree to which More behaved disingenuously remains a question. Rather than recapitulate the scholarship in his own voice, More makes a brief speech, and the king's opinions are read aloud by the clerk. As Elton writes of More's presentation: "But his omissions must surely have been noted: not a word from him to suggest that the opinions to be read out were in fact the truth."[68] There are reasons to believe, too, that even at this late hour More believes Henry might change his mind, and so More's appearance before parliament would allow him to keep his role of opposition alive from within the Privy Council.[69]

Despite More's views about the adaptability of political discourse, his own version of *honestas* isolates the speech involved in oath-taking because perjury constitutes a mortal sin; acts of perjury call God to witness to a lie. Revisionists rightfully note how More occasionally uses something other than candor, but critics such as Greenblatt diminish the special role of what oaths signify for More. So, too, Bolt translates the idea of perjury by removing its theological implication. More tells Margaret: "When a man takes an oath, Meg, he's holding his own self in his own hands. Like water. (He cups his hands) And if he opens his fingers *then*—he needn't hope to find himself again. Some men aren't capable of this, but I'd be loathe to think your father one of them."[70] Bolt's version of self-possession as integrity misreads More's refusal to swear. More specifically addresses perjury in the *Dialogue Concerning Heresy*, writing that "I holde this ones for a sure [once and for certain] & an infallyble conclusion / y^t a man may neuer lawfully be forsworne (*CW* 6.1, 281/19–21). Six or seven years later,

---

68. Elton, "Opposition to Henry VIII," 84.   69. See Guy, *Thomas More*, 155–57.
70. Bolt, *Man for All Seasons*, 140.

More writes what Richard Sylvester calls a "Tower memorandum," a brief statement on perjury, which declares that "every (act of) perjury is … a mortal sin without any exception whatsoever" *(omne periuri-um est … mortale peccatum citra vllam exceptionem prorsus)*.[71] More's position on perjury, whether in defending the practice of inquisition in the *Dialogue* or his own later refusal to swear, appears consistent. In short, More's refusal to take the oath involves neither self-affirmation nor self-fashioning.

Sylvester finds More's note on perjury "to have been composed by More as a brief note to himself during his incarceration in the tower" (*CW* 6.2, 768). Here More discusses Augustine's and Jerome's dispute about the *mendacium officiosum*, or "officious" lie (*CW* 6.2, 764/29), what More calls a "harmlesse lye devisid to do good withall" in *A Dialogue of Comfort against Tribulation* (*CW* 12, 132/18). The context of the latter proves enlightening because it provides an example of the adaptability of speech that remains outside formal, legal contexts. More addresses the case of a man who plans to commit suicide because he believes it would be "godes pleasure" to do so (131/15). What counsel should be given to someone delusional? The question of counsel here is exceptional but not entirely removed from the contexts of counsel and where and how it should be given, if at all, from *Utopia*. Here More's "Anthony" answers that any advice "must be done vnder such swete plesaunt maner, as the man shuld not abhorre to here it" (*CW* 12, 131/28–132/1). As Greenblatt rightly notes, *Morus* from *Utopia*, too, warns against ruining the drama of politics, proposing counsel as a play, a performance in which tragic lines of truth ought not to be blurted out in the comedy of human affairs (see *CW* 4, 99). Yet More's Anthony goes beyond discreet silence, suggesting a speaker should contrive some "plesaunt spech" to entice the suicidal man. "Yf he be proud ye shall

71. Both More's text and Sylvester's commentary and translation are from *CW* 6.2, 763–69. For the Latin, see ibid., 764/1–4. Sylvester, "More's Discussion of Perjury," *Moreana*, no. 55 (1977): 73–77 is an earlier, slightly different version of the same.

mich better please hym with a commendacion than with a dirige,"
More writes (CW 12, 132/9–11). Untrue compliments may be necessary to deal with the proud just as *Morus* believes the court requires
decorous language. Such harmless lies, in the *Dialogue,* will worry
only a "very greate scrupulouse conscience," and, according to some
Church Fathers, may not be sinful (132/17–24).[72] The approach here
corresponds to how Cardinal Morton first addresses though not ultimately treats Buckingham, using the language of flattery that Erasmus condemns but that More shows as useful. Even ingratiating
speech should serve noble ends, from opposing tyranny to saving a
man's life. Apart from speech under oath, then, these cases suggest
how More may persuade through oblique or flattering speech or refuse to engage by withholding. What is often exaggerated as an irreconcilable division between honesty and lying fails to note More's
treatment of *honestas* and a difference in types of discourse. More's
integrity would be compromised in swearing an oath he found false,
but other forums for speech, especially in politics, appear less strict,
providing maneuverability not for acquiring power but for making
matters as "little bad" *(minime malum)* as possible (CW 4, 100/1–2).

Rather than an ethical contradiction, the moral imperative to
speak truly combines with the teaching on adaptable speech in the
ironic and defiant *ethos* of More's letters. From the Tower, More conveys the nonjudgmental rhetoric of refusing to "meddle" in his letter to Wilson, the same friend who initially refused the oath but who
will be freed for changing his mind. More begins by suggesting that
Wilson cannot find comfort from More for his anguish in refusing
the oath because, as More writes, "it lieth not in me to give you such
kind of comfort" (LL, 91). More repeats what the king told him and
what More intends to follow: that he should "look first unto God"
and "after God" to the king (92). In the first statement, the "kind
of comfort" Wilson requires provokes a question. In the anecdote

---

72. On officious lies, see the commentary to CW 12, 132/17–21, 388.

about the king's words, an answer is proposed. Wilson should look to God, a point More emphasizes in his *Dialogue of Comfort*.[73] The alternative to God's comfort in tribulation would be relief from the fear of punishment, but this relief would be occasioned by taking the oath, swearing to something known to be false.

More next reminds Wilson of how long and in what depth they already discussed the question of the king's marriage (92); More, then, rehearses all those authorities they had reviewed, including Augustine, Jerome, Gregory, and Chrysostom (93). Yet More will not "meddle" in the matter now, he writes, "for I neither understand the doctors of the law nor well can turn [ponder] their books" (94). More's statement that he cannot "turn," or "ponder," the books of "the doctors of the law" represents self-deprecation rather than the truth, a statement that Wilson would recognize as a gentle, if crafty, admonition.[74] More approaches Wilson according to Anthony's advice. In the same manner, More explains that the "King's noble heart" will be favorable to them both because "like flowing water is the heart of the king in the hand of God, who turns it where he pleases."[75] That last line is quoted from Proverbs 21:1, but the following one, not quoted by More but one he could have expected Wilson to know, reads: "Everyman is right in his own eyes, but the Lord weighs the heart."[76] And the heart of Wilson, as More reminds him at length in the same letter, was settled through long hours of study *against* taking the oath. Indeed, because of people like Wilson, More tells Margaret about those hearts "far out" of his "sight," persons More will not judge, adding, however, that he never heard "the cause" why they changed their minds (84). He will not judge the motivations or reasons which "might hap make some men either

---

73. See *CW* 12, 293–94.

74. On More's irony in dealing with Wilson, see Martz, *Inner Man*, 56.

75. *Sicut diuisiones aquarum, ita cor regis in manu Domini, quocunque voluerit, inclinabit illud* (*Corr.*, 537/166–67). For the translation cited, *LL*, 181.

76. Proverbs 21: 2 in *The Holy Bible*, Revised Standard Version, Catholic Edition (Princeton, N.J.: Scepter, 1952).

swear otherwise than they think, or frame their conscience afresh to think otherwise than they [once] thought" (85). Though More claims not to meddle with another man's conscience, he challenges those who disagree with him.

More's rhetoric in passages such as these is not neutral or self-memorializing but artful defiance. Wilson is told to do as he will even as he is reminded of the arguments against the oath, and Margaret is playfully called "mistress Eve," offering apples to her father (73). What strikes Prévost as an anticipation of transcendent self-hood is actually an indirect way of encouraging others to stand fast for a moral, legal, and political principle: the rights and privileges of the Church. Likewise, Greenblatt and Guy's speculation—about either self-erasure or self-memorializing—distort More's rhetoric. The letters of More to Margaret and Wilson show that conscience includes the legality of the oath and an individual obligation to seek and find right judgment through study, as More reminds Wilson, providing a parallel to what More argued a study of law and the liberal arts would do in his *Letter to Oxford.*

More's own sense of political prudence may be noted in the compromise he makes in deciding to present the case for Henry's divorce to parliament and especially in the careful way he deals with the controversy surrounding Barton. More is obviously discreet, calculating the political effects and costs of his words and action, yet that hardly means More is a man of contradiction. For the same prudential judgment that guides his political choices also informs his conscience where there can be no compromise, as in the case where More parts ways with his good friend, Dr. Wilson, or with his own daughter, Margaret. Instead of a contradiction between conscience and political realism, More distinguishes between accommodation and resistance because the same judgment that guides his indirect argument also teaches him where he must resist without compromise.

BIBLIOGRAPHY

Ackroyd, Peter. *The Life of Thomas More*. London: Chatto & Windus, 1998.

Adams, Robert P. *The Better Part of Valor: More, Erasmus, Colet, and Vives on Humanism, War, and Peace, 1496–1535*. Seattle: University of Washington Press, 1962.

Adams, Simon. "The Eltonian Legacy: Politics." *Transactions of the Royal Historical Society*, 6th ser., 7 (1997): 247–66.

Allen, Peter R. "*Utopia* and European Humanism: The Function of the Prefatory Letters and Verses." *Studies in the Renaissance* 10 (1963): 91–107.

Aquinas, Thomas. *The Summa Theologica*. 2nd ed. Translated by the Fathers of the English Dominican Province. *http://www.newadvent.org/summa/*.

Aristotle. *Nichomachean Ethics*. Translated by Hippocrates G. Apostle. Grinnell, Iowa: Peripatetic Press, 1984.

———. *Rhetoric and Poetics*. Translated by W. Rhys Roberts. New York: Modern Library, 1954.

Armstrong, W. A. "The Elizabethan Conception of the Tyrant." *Review of English Studies* 22, no. 87 (1946): 161–81.

Augustine. *City of God*. Translated by Henry Bettenson. London: Penguin Books, 1984.

———. *On Christian Teaching*. Translated by R. P. H. Green. Oxford: Oxford University Press, 1997.

Baker, J. H. *An Introduction to English Legal History*. 4th ed. London: Butterworths Tolley, 2002.

Basil. *Address to Young Men on the Right Use of Greek Literature*. *http://www.terullian.org/fathers/basil_litterature01.htm*.

Baumann, Ewe. "Thomas More and the Classical Tyrant." *Moreana* 86 (1985): 108–27.

Benfey, Christopher. "Renaissance Men." *New York Times*, November 1, 2009.

Bernard, G. W. "Review." *Historical Journal* 31, no. 1 (1988): 159–82.

Bolt, Robert. *A Man for All Seasons*. New York: Vintage Books, 1990.

Boyce, Benjamin. *The Theophrastan Character in England to 1642*. Cambridge, Mass.: Harvard University Press, 1947.

Bradshaw, Brendan. "The Christian Humanism of Erasmus." *Journal of Theological Studies* 32, no. 2 (1982): 411–47.

———. "The Controversial Thomas More." *Journal of Ecclesiastical History* 36, no. 4 (1985): 535–69.

———. "More on Utopia." *Historical Journal* 24, no. 1 (1981): 1–27.

———. "The Tudor Commonwealth: Reform and Revision." *Historical Journal* 22, no. 2 (1979): 455–76.

Branham, R. Bracht. "Utopian Laughter: Lucian and Thomas More." *Moreana* 86 (1985): 23–43.

Carey, John. "Sixteenth and Seventeenth Century Prose." In *English Poetry and Prose, 1540–1674*, edited by Christopher Ricks, 339–432. London: Barrie & Jenkins, 1970.

Chambers, R. W. *Thomas More*. Ann Arbor: University of Michigan Press, 1958. Original edition 1935.

Chuilleanáin, Eiléan Ní. "Motives of Translation: Reading Thomas More's Translation of Pico della Mirandola's Life and Works." In *Italian Culture: Interactions, Transpositions, Translations*, edited by Cormac Ó Cuilleanáin, Corinna Salvadori, John Scattergood, 105–20. Portland, Ore.: Four Courts Press, 2006.

Cicero, Marcus Tullius. *De Officiis*. Translated by Walter Miller. Cambridge, Mass.: Harvard University Press, 1975.

———. *De Oratore*. Translated by E. W. Sutton and H. Rackham. Cambridge, Mass.: Harvard University Press, 1949.

———. *De Partitione Oratoria*. Translated and edited by H. Rackham. Cambridge, Mass.: Harvard University Press, 1942.

———. *Orator*. Translated by H. M. Hubbell. Cambridge, Mass.: Harvard University Press, 1952.

Colet, John. *Joannis Coleti Opuscula quaedam theologica*. Translated and edited by J. H. Lupton. London: George Bell and Sons, 1876.

———. *John Colet's Commentary on First Corinthians*. Translated by Bernard O'Kelly and Catherine A. L. Jarrott. Binghamton, N.Y.: Medieval & Renaissance Texts & Studies, 1985.

———. *A Life of John Colet*. Translated and edited by J. H. Lupton. Eugene, Ore.: Wipf & Stock, 2004.

Colish, Marcia. "Cicero's *De Officiis* and Machiavelli's *Prince*." *Sixteenth Century Journal* 9, no. 4 (1978): 81–93.

Croft, Pauline. "The Eltonian Legacy: The Parliament of England." *Transactions of the Royal Historical Society*, 6th ser., 7 (1997): 217–34.

Curtis, Cathy. "'The Best State of the Commonwealth': Thomas More and Quentin Skinner." In *Rethinking the Foundations of Modern Political Thought*, edited by Annabel Brett and James Tully, 93–112. Cambridge: Cambridge University Press, 2006.

Curtright, Travis. "Humanist Lawyer, Public Career: Thomas More and Conscience." *Moreana* 46, no.176 (2009): 77–96.

———. "A 'Pre-Machiavellian Moment': Thomas More's Poetry and the *History of Richard III*." *Ben Jonson Journal* 13 (2006): 63–82.

Daniell, David. *The Bible in English: Its History and Influence*. New Haven, Conn.: Yale University Press, 2003.

———. *William Tyndale: A Biography*. New Haven, Conn.: Yale University Press, 2001.

Davies, C. S. L. "Bishop John Morton, the Holy See, and the Accession of Henry VII." *English Historical Review* 102, no. 402 (1987): 2–30.

———. "The Eltonian Legacy: The Cromwellian Decade: Authority and Consent." *Transactions of the Royal Historical Society*, 6th ser., 7 (1997): 177–96.

Dean, Leanord F. "Literary Problems in More's *Richard III*." *PMLA* 58, no. 1 (1943): 22–41.

Derrett, J. Duncan M. "Neglected Versions of the Contemporary Account of the Trial of Sir Thomas More." *Bulletin of the Institute of Historical Research* 33 (1960): 214–23.

Dick, John A. R. "Review: *William Tyndale: A Biography*." *Renaissance Quarterly* 50, no. 2 (1997): 596–97.

Dickens, A. G. "The Shape of Anticlericalism and the English Reformation." In *Politics and Society in Reformation Europe*, edited by E. I. Kouri and T. Scott, 379–410. London: Palgrave Macmillan, 1987.

Donno, Elizabeth Story. "Thomas More and *Richard III*." *Renaissance Quarterly* 35, no. 3 (1982): 401–47.

Dorsh, T. S. "Sir Thomas and Lucian: An Interpretation of *Utopia*." *Archiv für das Studium der Neueren Sprachen und Literaturen* 203 (1967): 345–63.

Duffy, Eamon. "'The comen knowen multytude of crysten men': A Dialogue Concerning Heresies and the Defence of Christendom." In *The Cambridge Companion to Thomas More*, edited by George M. Logan, 191–215. Cambridge: Cambridge University Press, 2011.

Elton, G. R. "The Actor Saint." *New York Review of Books*, January 31, 1985.

———. "Humanism in England." In *Studies in Tudor and Stuart Politics and Government*. Vol. 4: *Papers and Reviews 1982–1990*, 209–29. Cambridge: Cambridge University Press, 1992.

———. *Policy and Police: The Enforcement of the Reformation in the Age of Thomas Cromwell*. Cambridge: Cambridge University Press, 1985.

———. "The Political Creed of Thomas Cromwell." *Transactions of the Royal Historical Society*, 5th ser., 6 (1956): 69–92.

———. *Return to Essentials: Some Reflections on the Present State of Historical Study*. Cambridge: Cambridge University Press, 1991.

———. "Review of *The Complete Works of St. Thomas More, Volumes 12–14.*" *English Historical Review* 93 (1978): 399–404.

———. "Sir Thomas More and the Opposition to Henry VIII." In *Essential Articles for the Study of Thomas More*, edited by Richard Standish Sylvester and Germain Marc'hadour, 79–91. Hamden, Conn.: Archon Books, 1977.

———. "Thomas More." In *Studies in Tudor and Stuart Politics and Government.* Vol. 3: *Papers and Reviews 1973–1981*, 344–55. Cambridge: Cambridge University Press, 2002. Essay originally published 1980.

———. "Thomas More and Thomas Cromwell." In *Studies in Tudor and Stuart Politics and Government*. Vol. 4: *Papers and Reviews 1982–1990*, 144–60. Cambridge: Cambridge University Press, 1992.

———. "Thomas More, Councillor." In *St. Thomas More: Action and Contemplation*, edited by Richard S. Sylvester, 85–122. New Haven, Conn.: Yale University Press, 1972.

Erasmus, Desiderius. *Antibarbarorum liber*. Translated by Margaret Mann Phillips. In *The Erasmus Reader*, edited by Erika Rummel, 51–64. Toronto: University of Toronto Press, 1990.

———. "De libero arbitrio." In *Luther and Erasmus: Free Will and Salvation*. Edited and translated by E. Gordon Rupp and A. N. Marlow. Library of Christian Classics 17. London: SCM Press, 1969.

———. *The Education of a Christian Prince*. Translated and edited by Lisa Jardine. Cambridge: Cambridge University Press, 2003.

———. "Enchiridion." In *Collected Works of Erasmus*, vol. 66, *Spiritualia*, edited by John W. O'Malley, 79–84. Toronto: University of Toronto Press, 1988.

———. "Julius Excluded from Heaven: A Dialogue." In *Collected Works of Erasmus*. Volume 27. Translated by Michael J. Heath. Toronto: University of Toronto Press, 1986. 155–197.

———. *Letters 842–992: 1518–1519*. Translated by R. A. B. Mynors and D. F. S. Thomson. Annotated by Peter G. Bietenholz, Wallace K. Ferguson, and James K. McConica. Vol. 6 of *The Collected Works of Erasmus*. Toronto: University of Toronto Press, 1974.

———. *Literary and Educational Writings*. Edited by Craig R. Thompson. Vol. 23 of *The Collected Works of Erasmus*. Toronto: University of Toronto Press, 1978.

———. *The Praise of Folly*. Translated by Clarence Miller. New Haven, Conn.: Yale University Press, 1979.

Falco, Raphael. *Charismatic Authority in Early Modern English Tragedy.* Baltimore: Johns Hopkins University Press, 2000.

Fox, Alistair. "Archetype and Antitype: The History of King Richard III, The Four Last Things." In *Thomas More: History and Providence,* 75–107. New Haven, Conn.: Yale University Press, 1985.

———. "Review of *Debellation.*" *Catholic Historical Review* 75, no. 4 (1990): 848–50.

———. *Thomas More: History and Providence.* New Haven, Conn.: Yale University Press, 1985.

Fox, Alistair, and John Guy. *Reassessing the Henrician Age: Humanism, Politics and Reform, 1500–1550.* New York: Basil Blackwell, 1986.

Gabrieli, Vittorio. "Giovanni Pico and Thomas More." *Moreana* 15–16 (1967): 43–57.

Gilmore, Myron. "More's Translation of Gianfranceso Pico's Biography." In *L'Opera e il Pensiero di Giovanni Pico della Mirandola nella Storia dell'Umanismo,* 2:301–4. Florence: Instituto Nanzionale di Studi sul Rinascimento, 1965.

Gogan, Brian. *The Common Corps of Christendom: Ecclesiological Themes in the Writings of Sir Thomas More.* Leiden: Brill, 1982.

Goodrich, Peter. "We Orators: Review Article of Brian Vickers' *In Defense of Rhetoric.*" *Modern Law Review* 53, no. 4 (1990): 546–63.

Greenblatt, Stephen. *Hamlet in Purgatory.* Princeton, N.J.: Princeton University Press, 2001.

———. *Renaissance Self-Fashioning.* Chicago: University of Chicago Press, 1980.

Gregg, Samuel. "Legal Revolution: St. Thomas More, Christopher St. German, and the Schism of King Henry VIII." *Ave Maria Law Review* 5, no. 1 (2007): 173–205.

Gueguen, John. "Review of *The Public Career of Sir Thomas More.*" *Sixteenth Century Journal* 14, no. 2 (1983): 248–49.

Guy, John. *The Cardinal's Court: The Impact of Thomas Wolsey in Star Chamber.* Totowa, N.J.: Rowman and Littlefield, 1977.

———. *Christopher St. German on Chancery and Statute.* London: Seldon Society, 1985.

———. *A Daughter's Love: Thomas More and His Dearest Meg.* London: Fourth Estate, 2008.

———. "The Henrican Age." In *The Varieties of British Political Thought, 1500–1800,* edited by J.G.A. Pocock, Gordon J. Schochet, and Lois G. Schwoerer, 13–22. Cambridge: Cambridge University Press, 1996.

———. "Law, Equity, and Conscience." In *Reassessing the Henrician Age: Humanism, Politics and Reform 1500–1550.* Oxford: Blackwell Publishers, 1986.

————. *The Public Career of Sir Thomas More*. New Haven, Conn.: Yale University Press, 1980.

————. *Thomas More*. London: Arnold, 2000.

————. "Thomas More and Christopher St. German: The Battle of the Books." In *Reassessing the Henrician Age: Humanism, Politics and Reform 1500–1550*. Oxford: Blackwell Publishers, 1986.

Haigh, Christopher. *English Reformations: Religion, Politics and Society under the Tudors*. Oxford: Oxford University Press, 1993.

————. "The Recent Historiography of the English Reformation." *Historical Journal* 25, no. 4 (1982): 995–1007.

————. "Religion." *Transactions of the Royal Historical Society*, 6th ser., 7 (1997): 281–300.

Hanham, Allison. "The Texts of More's *History of King Richard III*." In *Richard III and His Early Historians, 1483–1535*, 206–13. Oxford: Oxford University Press, 1975.

Harpsfield, Nicholas. *The Life and Death of Sir Thomas Moore, Knight*. Edited by E. V. Hitchcock. London: Humphrey Milford, 1963.

Harpsfield, Nicholas, and William Roper. *Lives of Saint Thomas More*. Edited by E. E. Reynolds. New York: Everyman's Library, 1963.

Hastings, Margaret. "Sir Thomas More: Maker of English Law?" In *Essential Articles for the Study of Thomas More*, edited by Richard Standish Sylvester and Germain Marc'hadour, 104–18. Hamden, Conn.: Archon Books, 1977.

Headley, John M. "The Problem of Counsel Revisited: More, Castiglione and the Resignation of Office in the Sixteenth Century." *Moreana* 40, nos. 153–54 (2003): 99–119.

Hexter, J. H. *More's Utopia: The Biography of an Idea*. Westport, Conn.: Greenwood Press, 1976.

————. "Thomas More and the Problem of Counsel." In *Quincentennial Essays on St. Thomas More*, edited by Michael J. Moore, 55–66. Albany, N.Y.: Appalachian State University, 1978.

Hicks, Michael. "The Making of a Monster." In *Richard III: The Man behind the Myth*, 142–60. London: Collins and Brown, 1991.

Hilton, Walter. *Mixed Life*. Translated by Rosemary Dorward. Oxford: SLG Press, 2001.

————. *The Scale of Perfection*. Translated, with introduction and notes, by John P. H. Clark and Rosemary Dorward. New York: Paulist Press, 1991.

Hitchcock, James. "Review: *William Tyndale: A Biography*." *American Historical Review* 101, no. 2 (1996): 478.

Hoffmann, Manfred. "Faith and Piety in Erasmus's Thought." *Sixteenth Century Journal* 20, no. 2 (1989). 241–58.

Holmes, Clive. "The Eltonian Legacy: G. R. Elton as a Legal Historian." *Transactions of the Royal Historical Society*, 6th ser., 7 (1997): 267–80.

The Holy Bible. Revised Standard Version, Catholic Edition. Princeton, N.J.: Scepter, 1952.

Hoyle, R. W. "The Eltonian Legacy: Place and Public Finance." *Transactions of the Royal Historical Society*, 6th ser., 7 (1997): 197–216.

Hutson, Lorna, and Victoria Kahn, eds. *Rhetoric and Law in Early Modern Europe*. New Haven, Conn.: Yale University Press, 2001.

Ives, E. W. *The Common Lawyers of Pre-Reformation England: Thomas Kebell, A Case Study*. Cambridge: Cambridge University Press, 1983.

Jardine, Lisa, ed. *Erasmus: The Education of a Christian Prince with the Panegyric for Archduke Philip of Austria*. Cambridge: Cambridge University Press, 1997.

Jayne, Sears Reynolds. *John Colet and Marsilio Ficino*. London: Oxford University Press, 1963.

Jenkins, Rev. Claude. "Cardinal Morton's Register." In *Tudor Studies*, edited by R. W. Seton-Watson, 26–74. Freeport, N.Y.: Books for Libraries Press, 1969.

John Paul II. *The Apostolic Letter Issued Motu Proprio Proclaiming Saint Thomas More Patron of Statesmen and Politicians*. http://www.vatican.va/holy_father/john_paul_ii/motu_proprio/documents/hf_jp-ii_motu-proprio_20001031_thomas-more_en.html.

———. *Christifideles Laici*. http://www.vatican.va/holy_father/john_paul_ii/apost_exhortations/documents/hf_jp-ii_exh_30121988_christifideles-laici_en.html, sec. 17.

Joseph, Miriam. *Shakespeare's Use of the Arts of Language*. New York: Hafner Publishing, 1966.

Kantorowicz, Ernst Hartwig. *The King's Two Bodies*. Princeton, N.J.: Princeton University Press, 1997.

Kaufman, Peter Iver. *Augustinian Piety and Catholic Reform*. Macon, Ga.: Mercer University Press, 1982.

———. "Henry VII and Sanctuary." *Church History* 53, no. 4 (1984): 465–76.

———. *Incorrectly Political: Augustine and Thomas More*. Notre Dame: University of Notre Dame Press, 2007.

Kelley, Donald R. "History, English Law and the Renaissance: A Rejoinder." *Past and Present* 72 (1976): 143–46.

———. "Law." In *The Cambridge History of Political Thought: 1450–1700*, edited by J. H. Burns, 66–94. Cambridge: Cambridge University Press, 1991.

Kelly, Henry Ansgar. "Inquisition and the Prosecution of Heresy: Misconceptions and Abuses." *Church History* 58, no. 4 (1989): 439–51.

———. *Inquisitions and Other Trial Procedures in the Medieval West*. Aldershot: Ashgate, 2001.

———. "The Right to Remain Silent: Before and after Joan of Arc." *Speculum* 68, no. 4 (1993): 992–1026.

———. "Thomas More on Inquisitorial Due Process." *English Historical Review* 123, no. 503 (2008): 847–94.

Kelly, Henry Ansgar, Louis W. Karlin, and Gerard B. Wegemer, eds. *Thomas More's Trial by Jury*. Woodbridge, UK: Boydell Press, 2011.

Kincaid, Arthur Noel. "The Dramatic Structure of Sir Thomas More's *History of Richard III*." *Studies in English Literature* 12, no. 1 (1972): 223–42.

Kisch, Guido. "Humanistic Jurisprudence." *Studies in the Renaissance* 8 (1961): 71–87.

Kristeller, Paul Oskar. "Thomas More as a Renaissance Humanist." *Moreana* 65 (1980): 5–22.

Lehmberg, Stanford E. "Sir Thomas More's Life of Pico della Mirandola." *Studies in the Renaissance* 3 (1956): 61–74.

Leon, Alberti. *I Libri Della Famiglia*. Translated by Renee Neu Watkins. Long Grove, Ill.: Waveland Press, 2004.

Lewis, C. S. "Thomas More." In *Essential Articles for the Study of Thomas More*, edited by Richard Standish Sylvester and Germain Marc'hadour, 388–401. Hamden, Conn.: Archon Books, 1977.

Logan, George M., ed. *The Cambridge Companion to Thomas More*. Cambridge: Cambridge University Press, 2011.

———. "Interpreting *Utopia*: Ten Recent Studies and the Modern Critical Traditions." *Moreana* 31 (1984): 203–58.

———. *The Meaning of More's Utopia*. Princeton, N.J.: Princeton University Press, 1983.

———. "More on Tyranny: *The History of King Richard the Third*." In *The Cambridge Companion to Thomas More*, edited by George M. Logan, 168–90. Cambridge: Cambridge University Press, 2011.

———. "*Utopia* and Deliberative Rhetoric." *Moreana* 31, nos. 118–19 (1994): 103–20.

MacDonald, Alasdair A., R. W. M. von Martels Zweder, and Jan R. Veenstra, eds. *Christian Humanism: Essays in Honour of Arjo Vanderjagt*. Leiden: Brill, 2009.

Machiavelli, Niccolo. *Discourses on Livy*. Translated by Harvey C. Mansfield and Nathan Tarcov. Chicago: University of Chicago Press, 1998.

———. *The Prince*. Translated by Leo Paul de Alvarez. Long Grove, Ill.: Waveland Press, 1980.

Mack, Peter. *Elizabethan Rhetoric*. Cambridge: Cambridge University Press, 2002.

Maclean, Ian. *Interpretation and Meaning in the Renaissance: The Case of Law*. Cambridge: Cambridge University Press, 1992.

Macnair, Mike. "Equity and Conscience." *Oxford Journal of Legal Studies* 27, no. 4 (2007): 659–81.

Maitland, F. W. "English Law and the Renaissance." In *Selected Historical Essays of F. W. Maitland*, 135–51. Boston: Beacon Press, 1962.

Majeske, Andrew J. *Equity in English Renaissance Literature: Thomas More and Edmund Spenser*. New York: Routledge, 2006.

Mantel, Hilary. *Wolf Hall: A Novel*. New York: Henry Holt, 2009.

Marc'hadour, Germain. "Basil the Great and Thomas More." *Moreana* 29, nos. 111–12 (1992): 43–54.

———. "Saint Thomas More and Conscience (Remembering Australia and New Zealand)." *Moreana* 30, no. 1 (1993): 55–64.

Marius, Richard. *Thomas More: A Biography*. New York: Vintage Books, 1985.

Marotti, Arthur F. "'Love Is Not Love': Elizabethan Sonnet Sequences and the Social Order." *ELH* 49 (1989): 396–428.

Marsh, David. *Lucian and the Latins: Humor and Humanism in the Early Renaissance*. Ann Arbor: University of Michigan Press, 1999.

Marshall, Peter. "The Last Years." In *The Cambridge Companion to Thomas More*, edited by George M. Logan, 116–38. Cambridge: Cambridge University Press, 2011.

Martz, Louis L. *Thomas More: The Search for the Inner Man*. New Haven, Conn.: Yale University Press, 1992.

McConica, James K. "The Recusant Reputation of Thomas More." In *Essential Articles for the Study of Thomas More*, edited by Richard Standish Sylvester and Germain Marc'hadour, 136–49. Hamden, Conn.: Archon Books, 1977.

McCutcheon, Elizabeth. "More's Three Prison Letters Reporting on His Interrogations." In *Thomas More's Trial by Jury*, ed. Henry Ansgar Kelly, Louis W. Karlin, and Gerard B. Wegemer, 94–110. Woodbridge, UK: Boydell Press, 2011.

Melanchthon, Philip. *The Praise of Eloquence*. In *Renaissance Debates on Rhetoric*, edited and translated by Wayne A. Rebhorn, 97–110. Ithaca, N.Y.: Cornell University Press, 2000.

Mermel, Jerry. "Preparations for a Political Life: Sir Thomas More's Entry into the King's Service." *Journal of Medieval and Renaissance Studies* 7 (1977): 53–66.

Monti, James. *The King's Good Servant but God's First: The Life and Writings of Saint Thomas More*. San Francisco: Ignatius Press, 1997.

More, Thomas. *The Correspondence of Sir Thomas More*. Edited by Elizabeth Frances Rogers. Princeton, N.J.: Princeton University Press, 1947.

———. *The History of King Richard III: A Reading Edition*. Edited by George M. Logan. Bloomington: Indiana University Press, 2005.

———. *The Last Letters of Thomas More*. Annotated ed. Edited by Alvaro De Silva. Grand Rapids, Mich.: Wm. B. Eerdmans, 2001.

———. *Selected Letters*. Edited by Elizabeth Frances Rogers. New Haven, Conn.: Yale University Press, 1961.

———. *Utopia*. Edited by George M. Logan and Robert M. Adams. Cambridge: Cambridge University Press, 1996.

———. *The Yale Edition of the Complete Works of Thomas More*. Vol. 1: *English Poems, Life of Pico, The Last Things*. Edited by Anthony S. G. Edwards, Katherine Gardiner Rodgers, and Clarence Miller. New Haven, Conn.: Yale University Press, 1997.

———. *The Yale Edition of the Complete Works of Thomas More*. Vol. 2: *The History of King Richard III*. Edited by Richard S. Sylvester. New Haven, Conn.: Yale University Press, 1963.

———. *The Yale Edition of the Complete Works of Thomas More*. Vol. 3, pt. 1: *Translations of Lucian*. Edited by Craig R. Thompson. New Haven, Conn.: Yale University Press, 1974.

———. *The Yale Edition of the Complete Works of Thomas More*. Vol. 3, pt. 2: *The Latin Poems*. Edited by Clarence H. Miller, Leicester Bradner, Charles A. Lynch, and Revilo P. Oliver. New Haven, Conn.: Yale University Press, 1984.

———. *The Yale Edition of the Complete Works of Thomas More*. Vol. 4: *Utopia*. Edited by Edward Surtz and J.H. Hexter. New Haven, Conn.: Yale University Press, 1965.

———. *The Yale Edition of the Complete Works of Thomas More*. Vol. 5: *Responsio ad Lutherum*. Edited by J.M Headley. New Haven, Conn.: Yale University Press, 1969.

———. *The Yale Edition of the Complete Works of Thomas More*. Vol. 6, pt. 1: *A Dialogue Concerning Heresies*. Edited by Thomas Lawler, Germain Marc'hadour, and Richard Marius. New Haven, Conn.: Yale University Press, 1981.

———. *The Yale Edition of the Complete Works of Thomas More*. Vol. 6, pt. 2: *A Dialogue Concerning Heresies*. Edited by Thomas Lawler, Germain Marc'hadour, and Richard Marius. New Haven, Conn.: Yale University Press, 1981.

———. *The Yale Edition of the Complete Works of Thomas More*. Vol. 7: *Letter to Bugenhagen, Supplication of Souls, Letter against Frith*. Edited by Frank Manley, Germain Marc'hadour, Richard Marius, and Clarence H. Miller. New Haven, Conn.: Yale University Press, 1990.

———. *The Yale Edition of the Complete Works of Thomas More*. Vol. 8, pt. 1: *The Confutation of Tyndale's Answer*. Edited by Louis A. Schuster, Richard

C. Marius, James P. Lusardi and Richard J. Schoeck. New Haven, Conn.: Yale University Press, 1973.

———. *The Yale Edition of the Complete Works of Thomas More.* Vol. 8, pt. 2: *The Confutation of Tyndale's Answer.* Edited by Louis A. Schuster, Richard C. Marius, James P. Lusardi, and Richard J. Schoeck. New Haven, Conn.: Yale University Press, 1973.

———. *The Yale Edition of the Complete Works of Thomas More.* Vol. 8, pt. 3: *The Confutation of Tyndale's Answer.* Edited by Louis A. Schuster, Richard C. Marius, James P. Lusardi, and Richard J. Schoeck. New Haven, Conn.: Yale University Press, 1973.

———. *The Yale Edition of the Complete Works of Thomas More.* Vol. 9: *The Apology.* Edited by J. B. Trapp. New Haven, Conn.: Yale University Press, 1979.

———. *The Yale Edition of the Complete Works of Thomas More.* Vol. 10: *The Debellation of Salem and Bizance.* Edited by John Guy, Ralph Keen, Clarence H. Miller, and Ruth McGugan. New Haven, Conn.: Yale University Press, 1987.

———. *The Yale Edition of the Complete Works of Thomas More.* Vol. 12: *A Dialogue of Comfort against Tribulation.* Edited by Louis L. Martz and Frank Manley. New Haven: Yale University Press, 1976.

———. *The Yale Edition of the Complete Works of Thomas More.* Vol. 13: *Treatise on the Passion, Treatise on the Blessed Body, Instructions and Prayers.* Edited by Garry E. Haupt. New Haven, Conn.: Yale University Press, 1976.

———. *The Yale Edition of the Complete Works of Thomas More.* Vol. 15: *In Defense of Humanism.* Edited by Daniel Kinney. New Haven, Conn.: Yale University Press, 1986.

Moynahan, Brian. *God's Bestseller: William Tyndale, Thomas More, and the Writing of the English Bible—A Story of Martyrdom and Betrayal.* New York: St. Martin's Press, 2003.

Murphy, Clare. "Humanist Values in Thomas More's Life of Giovanni Pico della Mirandola." In *Acta Conventus Neo-Latini Cantabrigiensis,* edited by Jean-Louis Charlet and Rhoda Schnur, 419–25. Tempe: Arizona Center for Medieval and Renaissance Studies, 2003.

Nelson, William. "Thomas More, Grammarian and Orator." In *Essential Articles for the Study of Thomas More,* edited by Richard Standish Sylvester and Germain Marc'hadour, 150–60. Hamden, Conn.: Archon Books, 1977.

O'Donnell, Anne M. "Agapē and Synonyms in New Testament Translations of St. Thomas More." *Moreana* 45, no. 175 (2008). 121–46.

O'Kelly, Bernard, and Catherine A. L. Jarrott, eds. *John Colet's Commentary on First Corinthians.* Binghamton, N.Y.: Medieval and Renaissance Texts and Studies, 1985.

Osgood, Russell K. "Law in Sir Thomas More's *Utopia* as Compared to His Lord Chancellorship." *Thomas More Studies* 1 (2006): 183. http://www.thomas-morestudies.org.

Pace, Richard. *De Fructu Qui Ex Doctrina Percipitur.* Edited and translated by Frank Manley and Richard Sylvester. New York: Renaissance Society of America, 1967.

Parks, George B. "Pico Della Mirandola in Tudor Translation." In *Philosophy and Humanism: Essays in Honor of Paul Oskar Kristeller*, edited by Edward P. Mahoney, 352–69. Leiden: Brill, 1976.

Peltonen, Markku. *Classical Humanism and Republicanism in English Political Thought: 1570–1640.* Cambridge: Cambridge University Press, 1995.

Peters, John G. "Sanctuary in More's *The History of Richard III.*" *Moreana* 34, nos. 131–32 (1997): 25–36.

Pincombe, Mike. *Elizabethan Humanism: Literature and Learning in the Later Sixteenth Century.* London: Longman, 2001.

Pineas, Rainer. "A Response to Alistair Fox's Treatment of Thomas More as a Religious Polemicist." *Moreana* 21, no. 82 (1984): 119–25.

Pius II. *Pius II: Commentaries.* Vol. 1. Edited by Margaret Meserve and Marcello Simonetta. Cambridge, Mass.: Harvard University Press, 2003.

Plato. *The Republic of Plato.* Translated by Allan Bloom. New York: Basic Books, 1968.

Plett, Heinrich R. *Rhetoric and Renaissance Culture.* Berlin: Walter de Gruyter, 2005.

Poliziano, Angelo. *Letters.* Vol. 1. Edited and translated by Shane Butler. Cambridge, Mass.: Harvard University Press, 2006.

Pollard, A. F. "The Making of Sir Thomas More's Richard III." In *Essential Articles for the Study of Thomas More*, edited by Richard Standish Sylvester and Germain Marc'hadour, 421–31. Hamden, Conn.: Archon Books, 1977.

Prall, Stuart E. "The Development of Equity in Tudor England." *American Journal of Legal History* 8, no. 1 (1964): 1–19.

Prevost, Andre. "Conscience the Ultimate Court of Appeal." In *Essential Articles for the Study of Thomas More*, edited by Richard Standish Sylvester and Germain Marc'hadour, 563–68. Hamden, Conn.: Archon Books, 1977.

Puttenham, George. *The Art of English Poesy: A Critical Edition.* Edited by Frank Whigham and Wayne A. Rebhorn. Ithaca, N.Y.: Cornell University Press, 2007.

Quintillian. *Institutio Oratoria.* Translated by H. E. Butler. Loeb Classical Library. Cambridge, Mass.: Harvard University Press, 1922, 1968.

———. *The Orator's Education.* Vol. 1, bks. 1 and 2. Edited and translated by Donald A. Russell. Cambridge, Mass.: Harvard University Press, 2001.

Rabelais, François. *Gargantua and Pantagruel.* Translated by Burton Raffell. In *The Norton Anthology of World Masterpieces,* vol. 1. 7th ed. New York: W. W. Norton, 1999.

Rex, Richard. "Thomas More and the Heretics: Statesman or Fanatic?" In *The Cambridge Companion to Thomas More,* edited by George M. Logan, 93–115. Cambridge: Cambridge University Press, 2011.

Richards, Jennifer. *Rhetoric and Courtliness in Early Modern Literature.* Cambridge: Cambridge University Press, 2003.

Ridley, Jasper. *Statesman and Saint.* New York: Viking Press, 1982.

Rigg, J. M. "Introduction." In *Giovanni Pico della Mirandola: His Life by His Nephew Giovanni Francesco Pico,* iii–xiv. London: D. Nutt, 1890.

Rockett, William. "More and St. German: Ex Officio and Lay-Clerical Division." *Moreana* 34, no. 129 (1997): 21–43.

———. "Temporal and Spiritual: Prolegomenon to the More–St. German Controversy." *Moreana* 37 (2000): 5–36.

Rogers, William J. "Thomas More's Polemical Poetics." *English Literary Renaissance* 38, no. 3 (2008): 387–408.

Roper, William. *Life of Sir Thomas More.* In *A Thomas More Source Book,* edited by Gerard B. Wegemer and Stephen W. Smith, 16–65. Washington, D.C.: The Catholic University of America Press, 2004.

Ross, Charles. *Richard III.* Berkeley: University of California Press, 1981.

Russell, Conrad. "The Eltonian Legacy: Thomas Cromwell's Doctrine of Parliamentary Strategy." *Transactions of the Royal Historical Society,* 6th ser., 7 (1997): 235–46.

Scarisbrick, J. "The Pardon of the Clergy, 1531." *Cambridge Historical Journal* 12, no. 1 (1956): 22–39.

Schoeck, R. J. "Lawyers and Rhetoric in Sixteenth-Century England." In *Renaissance Eloquence: Studies in the Theory and Practice of Renaissance Rhetoric,* edited by James J. Murphy, 274–91. Berkeley: University of California Press, 1983.

———. "Thomas More and the Italian Heritage of Early Tudor Humanism." In *Arts Liberaux et Philosophie au Moyen Age,* 1191–97. Montreal: Institute d'etudes medievales, 1969.

———. "Thomas More, Humanist and Lawyer." In *Essential Articles for the Study of Thomas More,* edited by Richard Standish Sylvester and Germain Marc'hadour, 569–79. Hamden, Conn.: Archon Books, 1977.

Screech, M. A. *Rabelais.* Ithaca, N.Y.: Cornell University Press, 1979.

Shagan, Ethan H. "Anticlericalism, Popular Politics and the Henrican Reformation." In *Popular Politics and the English Reformation,* 131–61. Cambridge: Cambridge University Press, 2003.

Shanske, Darien. "Four Theses: Preliminary to an Appeal to Equity." *Stanford Law Review* 57, no. 6 (2005): 2053–86.

Shaw, William Hudson. *Introductory Lectures on the Oxford Reformers: Colet, Erasmus, and More.* Philadelphia: American Society for the Extension of University Teaching, 1893.

Simpson, James. *Burning to Read: English Fundamentalism and Its Reformation Opponents.* Cambridge, Mass.: Belknap Press of Harvard University Press, 2007.

Skinner, Quentin. "The Eltonian Legacy: Sir Geoffrey Elton and the Practice of History." *Transactions of the Royal Historical Society*, 6th ser., 7 (1997): 301–16.

———. *The Foundations of Modern Political Thought.* Vol. 1: *The Renaissance.* Cambridge: Cambridge University Press, 1978.

———. *Reason and Rhetoric in the Philosophy of Thomas Hobbes.* Cambridge: Cambridge University Press, 1996.

———. "Republican Virtues in an Age of Princes." In *Visions of Politics,* vol. 2: *Renaissance Virtues,* 118–59. Cambridge: Cambridge University Press, 2007.

———. "Thomas More's *Utopia* and the Virtue of True Nobility." In *Visions of Politics,* vol. 2: *Renaissance Virtues,* 213–44. Cambridge: Cambridge University Press, 2007.

Stapleton, Thomas. *The Life and Illustrious Martyrdom of Sir Thomas More.* Translated by Philip E. Hallett. New York: Benziger Brothers, 1928.

St. German, Christopher. *Doctor and Student.* Edited by T. F. T. Plucknett and J. L. Barton. London: Seldon Society, 1974.

Strohm, Paul. *Politique: Languages of Statecraft between Chaucer and Shakespeare.* Notre Dame: University of Notre Dame Press, 2005.

Suzuki, Yoshinori. "Thomas More's View of Politics as a Profession." *Moreana* 24, no. 93 (1987): 29–40.

Sylvester, Richard [Standish]. "'Si Hythlodaeo Credimus': Vision and Revision in Thomas More's *Utopia.*" In *Essential Articles for the Study of Thomas More,* edited by Richard Standish Sylvester and Germain Marc'hadour, 290–301. Hamden, Conn.: Archon Books, 1977.

———. "Thomas More: Humanist in Action." In *Essential Articles for the Study of Thomas More,* edited by Richard Standish Sylvester and Germain Marc'hadour, 462–69. Hamden, Conn.: Archon Books, 1977.

Sylvester, Richard Standish, and Germain Marc'hadour, eds. *Essential Articles for the Study of Thomas More.* Hamden, Conn.: Archon Books, 1977.

Tacitus, Cornelius. *The Annals.* Translated by A. J. Woodman. Indianapolis: Hackett Publishing, 2004.

Tayler, Christopher. "Henry's Fighting Dog." *Guardian*, May 2, 2009.

Thecla, M. "S. Thomas More and the Catena Aurea." *Modern Language Notes* 61, no. 8 (Dec. 1946): 523–29.

Thompson, Craig R. "The Humanism of More Reappraised." *Thought* 52, no. 206 (September 1977): 231–48.

Thornley, Isobel. "The Destruction of Sanctuary." In *Tudor Studies*, edited by R. W. Seton-Watson, 198–207. Freeport, N.Y.: Books for Libraries Press, 1969.

Trapp, J. B. *Erasmus, Colet and More: The Early Tudor Humanists and Their Books.* London: British Library, 1991.

Tucker, P. "The Early History of the Court of Chancery: A Comparative Study." *English Historical Review* 115 (2000): 791–811.

Tyndale, William. *An Answere unto Sir Thomas Mores Dialoge.* Edited by Anne M. O'Donnell and Jared Wicks. Washington, D.C.: The Catholic University of America Press, 2000.

———, trans. *The New Testament: The Text of the Worms Edition of 1526 in Original Spelling.* Edited by W. R. Cooper. London: British Library, 2000.

———. *Tyndale's Answer to Sir Thomas More's Dialogue.* Edited by Henry Walter. Cambridge: Cambridge University Press, 1850.

Walpole, Horace. "Historic Doubts on the Life and Reign of King Richard III." In *Richard III: The Great Debate*, edited by Paul Kendall. 159–239. London: Folio Society, 1965.

Wegemer, Gerard B. "Ciceronian Humanism in More's *Utopia.*" *Moreana* 27, no. 104 (1990): 5–26.

———. "The Civic Humanism of Thomas More: Why Law Has Prominence over Rhetoric." *Ben Jonson Journal* 7 (2000): 186–98.

———. *Thomas More on Statesmanship.* Washington, D.C.: The Catholic University of America Press, 1996.

———. "The Utopia of Thomas More: A Contemporary Battleground." *Modern Age* 37, no. 2 (Winter 1995): 135–41.

Wegemer, Gerard B., and Stephen W. Smith, eds. *A Thomas More Source Book.* Washington, D.C.: The Catholic University of America Press, 2004.

Weiss, Roberto. *Humanism in England during the Fifteenth Century.* Oxford: B. Blackwell, 1943.

Wells, Robin Headlam. *Shakespeare's Humanism.* Cambridge: Cambridge University Press, 2005.

White, R. S. *Natural Law in English Renaissance Literature.* Cambridge: Cambridge University Press, 1996.

Willow, Mary Edith. *An Analysis of the English Poems of St. Thomas More.* Nieuwkoop: Hes & De Graaf, 1974.

Wilson, Thomas. *The Art of Rhetoric* (1560). Edited by Peter E. Medine. University Park: Pennsylvania State University Press, 1994.

Wormald, Patrick, John Gillingham, and Colin Richmond. "Elton on *The English:* A Discussion." *Transactions of the Royal Historical Society,* 6th ser., 7 (1997): 317–36.

Ziskind, Martha A. "John Selden: Criticism and Affirmation of the Common Law Tradition." *American Journal of Legal History* 19, no. 1 (1975): 22–39.

INDEX

Act for Punishment of Heresy (1534), 145
action: contemplation and, 7, 11–12, 15, 21–
27, 108; dialogue of counsel and, 77–78;
faith and, 7; *Life of Pico* and, 11–12; love
and, 39–40; *otium* and *negotium*, 76, 77,
80–81, 85; politics and, 33; sanctification
and, 39; *vita activa* and *contemplativa*, 11
Act of Succession, 183
Act of Supremacy, 106, 141, 152, 177, 191
Additions of Salem and Byzance (St. German), 173
Address to Young Men on . . . Greek Literature
(Basil), 22
Admonition (Colet), 39
agape, 124
Ajax, 131
Alberti, Leon, 24
Alington, Alice, 176, 190, 193
allegory, 133
allusion, 25, 98, 109, 157
amor. See love
amor Dei in nobis, 17, 86
anachronism, 8, 175, 182
Annals (Tacitus), 43
Annotationes in XXIV libros Pandectarum
(Budé), 90
Anthony, 197–98, 199
Antibarbari (Erasmus), 20, 21, 29, 113
anticlericalism, 14, 140, 152, 160, 163,
170–72. *See also* clergy
Apology of Sir Thomas More, Knight (More),
140, 142, 170, 172

aposiopesis, 63
apostasy, 148
apostles, 91, 133
Aquinas, St. Thomas, 83n49, 150; conscience and, 156; law and equity and,
155; praise of, 28–29, 111; reason and,
156; St. German and, 152–53, 159
arbitration, 99–100, 101
aristocracy, 52, 53, 54, 61
Aristotle, 76, 92; Aquinas and, 29; equity
and, 93, 97–98, 100, 148, 153, 156; tyranny and, 78
The Art of Poesy (Puttenham), 94
The Art of Rhetoric (Wilson), 94, 188
asceticism, 15n1, 19
Assertio (Henry VIII), 133
Atreus, 186
Audley, Thomas, 182, 194
Augustine, St., 26, 199; honor and, 23, 24,
41; humanism and learning and, 109;
human nature and, 7; love and, 36, 39;
lying and, 197; mixed life and, 34, 80;
philosophy and theology and, 22; Pico
and, 30; signs and, 121
authenticity, 176, 193
authority, 88; Church and, 108, 190; faith
and reason and, 118–19; heresy and,
114; liberal arts and, 117; More and St.
German and, 14; papal, 184; Parliament
and, 152; reason and, 123; tradition and,
125, 127

Bainham, James, 169
baptism, 122
Barton, Elizabeth, 180–83, 200
Barton, J. L., 156, 157–58
Basil, St., 18, 22
Batt, 21
Bayfield, Richard, 169
Bernard, G. W., 152, 169, 170
best way of life, 34, 38, 132, 134
Bible, 6n18, 29, 109, 125
Bilney, Thomas, 30, 116–17, 136, 169
Boleyn, Anne, 180, 184
Bolt, Robert, 8, 9, 14, 174, 175–76, 180, 189, 192–93, 196
Boyce, Benjamin, 114
Bradner, Leicester, 47
Bradshaw, Brendan, 10, 75, 76–77, 85–86, 88, 102–3, 172
bragging, 18, 115
Branham, R. Bracht, 19
Buckingham, Duke of, 50–51, 55, 56, 57, 59, 61–65, 67, 71, 82, 195, 198; Cardinal Morton and, 83
Budé, Guillaume, 90–92

Cabalism, 29
caesaropapism, 180
Cambridge Companion to Thomas More Studies, 9, 10
Cambridge University, 110
canon law, 13, 141–44, 146, 148, 169
Canzone dello Amore Celeste e Divino (Pico), 29
The Cardinal's Court (Guy), 147, 148
Carey, John, 138
Carthusians, 16, 34, 182
Catherine of Aragon, 195
Catholic Church. See Church
cavillation (cavillatio), 57
Cestius, Gaius, 57
Chambers, R. W., 1, 2, 3, 9, 106, 174, 176, 182, 189, 192
Chancery courts, 75, 89, 99, 101, 151
charism, 49
charity, 25, 125; action and contemplation and, 34–35; Church and, 132; community and, 86; faith and, 132; God and, 80;

piety and, 21; profit and, 35; truth and, 161; in Tyndale's translation, 124
Charterhouse monastery, 19
Chaucer, Geoffrey, 93
Christ, 21, 33, 97; commandments of, 91; communion with God in, 7; crucifixion of, 112; kingship and, 50; mystical body of, 49; Scripture and, 133; as Word, 126
Christendom: authoritative teaching of, 176; common corps of, 13, 14, 121, 176, 189–90; common senses and, 128; communal solidarity of, 192, 193; General Council of, 179
Christian humanism. See humanism
Christianity: humanism and, 11; human nature and, 112; paganism, pagans and, 16, 17–18, 21–22; skepticism about, 6n18; theocentric, 123
Christifideles laici, 7
Chrysostom, St. John, 199
Church, 7; allegory of, 133; authority and, 108; authority of, 190; charisms within, 49; charity and, 132; Christ, mystical body of, and, 49; common sense and, 135, 176; community and, 13, 50, 132, 133–34; consensus and, 106, 123, 190–91; doctrine and, 13; faction in, 115; heresy and, 13, 171; laity and, 140; learning and, 26, 110; More's defense of, 10, 14, 106, 140; piety and, 110; power of, 162, 170; profitable learning and, 23, 24, 26, 27, 33; Scripture and, 13, 125, 133; signs in, 108, 120–23; state and, 162; tradition and, 108, 127; trust in, 122–23, 139; truth and, 176–77; in Tyndale's translation, 124; universal, 133
Church Fathers, 114, 126, 128, 135, 198
Church of England, 192
Cicero, 90; decorum and, 64, 97, 187; De Officiis, 25, 64, 66, 77, 79, 81, 82, 99, 130; Dialogue Concerning Heresies and, 131; honesty and, 64–67, 81–82, 84, 187, 194; honor and, 41; justice and, 83; law and, 93; Life of Pico and, 25; Morton and, 195; negotium and otium, 76, 77; Plato and, 77, 79; theology and, 29; wit and the arts and, 130

Circe, 37

citizens, 76, 79, 80, 84, 154, 155

City of God (Augustine), 23

Civil Code, 90

civilis sapientia, 90

civil law, 90

clementia, 81, 83

clergy: character of, 140, 168; Ecclesia Anglicana and, 14, 140; equity and, 159–66, 170–71; grace and, 7; justice and, 162; laity and, 140, 168; political action and, 61; poor conduct of, 162; powers of, 152; sacraments and, 125

clericalism, 7

Colet, John, 12, 17, 20, 29, 30, 38, 39–40

Colt, Jane, 16

common good, 34, 60n40, 81n35, 83n49, 87, 153, 154

common law, 56, 57, 58, 59, 75, 88, 91, 98–99, 102, 147, 149–50, 156–57, 158

common sense (sensus communis), 120–23, 128, 134; Church and, 135, 176; community and, 129–36; humanism and, 139; poetry and, 132; rhetoric and, 132; theology and, 132; wit and, 131

communal deliberation, 61, 71

communitas, 13, 134, 139

community: Catholic Church and, 13; charity and, 86; Church and, 50, 132, 133–34; common senses and, 129–36; of consensus, 129; humanism and, 129–36; of love, 49, 50; love and, 86; reformers and, 136. See also communitas

conciliarism, 178

Confutation of Tyndale's Answer (More), 121, 127, 128

congregation: in Tyndale's translation, 124

conscience, 75, 98; as absolute, 192; common law and, 158; definition of, 148, 158; dignity of, 174; divorce of Henry VIII and, 169–70; equity and, 99, 159; fidelity to, 191; freedom of, 174, 185; hierarchy of, 157; human law and, 156; importance of, 176; judges and, 165; judgment and, 156; law and, 159; meddling in another's, 186–87, 200; memorial building and, 194;

More and, 3, 10, 174, 175, 176, 179; neutrality and, 189–90; positive human law and, 148–49; positive law and, 158; reason and, 157; St. German and, 143; synderesis and, 155–56. See also equity

consensus, 177–78; Church and, 190; community of, 129; ecclesial, 106, 123; importance of, 176; translating Scripture and, 125, 126; traditional, 135, 139

consent: consilium, 61; kingship as fatherhood and, 71; of the governed, 44; of the people, 59–60

conspiracy, 52, 63, 66, 82, 108, 154, 179, 181

contemplation: action and, 7, 11–12, 15, 21–27, 108; "dialogue of counsel" and, 77; freedom and, 33; learning and, 34; liberal arts and, 136; Life of Pico and, 11–12; love and, 39

Cooper, Thomas, 131–32

Corinthians, 21, 49, 133

Corneo, Andrea. See Corneus

Corneus, 31–34, 36, 79, 109

corruption, 115, 164

councils, 56–58, 60, 61–62, 65, 73, 76, 97, 147, 152, 169, 177, 178–79, 187, 190, 194, 196

counsel (advice): consilium, 61; dialogue of, 12, 72–104; faith and, 86; good, 76; problem of, 61, 78, 86, 197; state and, 88; Utopia and, 61

courts: Chancery, 75, 89, 99, 151; equity and, 13; Star Chamber, 75, 89, 99, 102, 103, 147–48. See also ex officio proceedings

Coventry, 115

Cranmer, Thomas, 194

Cromwell, Thomas, 141, 176, 178, 194; Barton and More and, 180–83; conscience and, 179, 180; heroism of, 9; letters of More and, 187–89; More's refusal to take oath, 187–88; oath of succession and, 183–84; political influence of, 4, 184; trial of More and, 177–83

Crucifixion, 112

culture, 11, 30, 93, 137

cunning, 23, 24, 25, 26, 27
Curtis, Cathy, 48
Cynic, 20
cynicism, 18–19
Cynicus (Lucian), 16, 19

Daniell, David, 105, 124, 127–28
A Daughter's Love (Guy), 102
death, 1, 4, 5, 7, 48, 67, 68, 69, 87
"Death Unassisted Kills Tyrants" (More), 67
The Debellacyon of Salem and Byzance (More), 140, 160, 167, 172
deception, 66, 172; princes and, 59; rhetoric and, 66; tyrannicide and, 44, 46, 66, 82. *See also* Machiavelli; rhetoric
decorum, 64, 97, 187. *See also* Cicero; rhetoric
Decree and Order Book, 100
De Doctrina (Augustine), 109, 121
De Ente et Uno (Pico), 29
defamation, 164
De Heretico Comburendo (1401), 106
De legibus (Cicero), 90
deliberation, 58, 61, 71, 98
De libero arbitrio (Erasmus), 64
Democritus, 18
De modo cacandi (Tartaretus), 112–13
De Officiis (Cicero), 25, 64, 66, 77, 79, 81, 82, 99, 130
De Oratore (Cicero), 65
De Partitione Oratoria (Cicero), 81
despotism, 82
detachment, 19, 41
devil, 23, 24
devotion, 11, 113
Dialogue Concerning Heresies (More), 107, 134, 138, 139, 176, 196–97; common sense and, 120–23; epistemological trust and translating Scripture, 123; faith and reason and, 136; liberal arts and, 95, 111–13, 117–19, 130; reason and authority in, 117–20; Scholasticism and, 113
Dialogue of Comfort (More), 111n19
A Dialogue of Comfort against Tribulation (More), 197, 199
Dialogue of Conscience, 176

dialogue of counsel, 12–13, 72–104; action and contemplation and, 77; equity and, 75, 89–98; More as judge and, 98–101; More's humanism and, 77; More's political philosophy and, 72–73; multiple Mores and, 76–88; *otium* and *negotium*, 75, 76, 77, 80–81; reform and, 72, 101–4; rhetoric and, 78
Dighton, John, 68
dignity of man, 37–38
diplomacy, 137
dissimulation, 5, 8, 65–66, 82
divine law, 158
divorce, 152, 169, 195, 200
Doctor and Student (St. German), 143, 148, 149, 150, 151, 152, 154, 156–57, 158–59, 166
doctrine, 13–14, 25, 125; orthodoxy and, 172; truth and, 114, 123
Dominicans, 33
Duffy, Eamon, 9, 107

Ecclesia Anglicana, 14, 140
ecclesial consensus, 106, 123
education. *See* learning; liberal arts
Education of a Christian Prince (Erasmus), 83, 159
Edward IV, 50n24; imprudence of, 51, 53; love and, 52–53; paternal models of kingship and, 46–50, 53–54; sensuality of, 51–53; tyranny and, 51
Edwards, A. G., 39
egalitarianism, 103
Egypt, 109
Egyptians, 109
ekklesia, 124
elder: in Tyndale's translation, 125
Elton, G. R., 1, 3–8, 9, 14, 74, 77, 138, 141, 142, 165, 166, 174–76, 179, 183–84, 188, 193, 194–95, 196
Enchiridion (Erasmus), 77
Enlightenment, 103
epigrams, 19, 20, 44, 47–48, 60, 61, 87
epikekia, 92, 148, 153. *See also* equity
epistemological trust, 123, 139
Epistle on the Mixed Life (Hilton), 34
equity: arbitration and, 99–100; Aristo-

tle and, 153, 156; clergy and, 159–66; common law and, 88, 91, 147, 149–50; conscience and, 99, 159; courts and, 13; decorum and, 98; dialogue of counsel and, 75; humanism and, 89–98; inquisitorial courts and, 143, 147–51; judges and, 159–66; jurisdiction and, 75, 148, 160–61; justice and, 150; law and, 13, 99, 103, 152–59; liberal arts and, 104; prudence and, 13, 75; rhetoric and, 75, 92–93, 93–94, 97; theft and, 92; virtue and, 153. *See also* conscience

equivocation, 109

Erasmus, 17, 19, 77, 83, 90, 113, 128, 133, 159; action and contemplation and, 78; Aquinas and, 29; despotism and, 82; dialogue of counsel and, 73; expediency and, 45, 64; flattery and, 65; holiness and, 54; humanism and piety and, 109; Julius II and, 59; Latin translations of, 1; learning and, 20–22, 41, 110; *Letter to a Monk* and, 27; Lucian translations by, 18; More's entry into royal service and, 4, 74, 195; More's epigrams and, 20; politics and utility and, 44–45; removal of tyranny and, 83; Scholasticism and humanism and, 113; translating Scripture and, 126, 128–29; *viva sapientia* and, 39

eternal law, 155, 159

Ethics (Aristotle), 93

ethos, 14, 143–44, 164. *See also* rhetoric

ex officio proceedings, 140–44; anonymity and, 144, 146, 167; common law and, 150; equity and, 143–44, 147–51, 159–66; witnesses and, 144–47, 160, 163–64, 167–68

expediency, 64, 65, 81; Erasmus and, 45; honesty and, 46, 84; justice and, 67; Machiavelli and, 45; Morton and, 62; *necessitas* and, 46; philosophy and, 85; politics and, 86; prudence and, 85

experience, 6n18, 19

fables, 42, 114, 123

faith: action and, 7; authority and, 118; charity and, 132; counsel and, 86; cul-

ture of public, 136; learning and, 108, 175; liberal arts and, 107, 112, 117, 118, 138; reason and, 6n18, 112, 118–20, 123, 136; role of, 10; Scripture and, 132; theology and, 137

Fallen man. *See* human nature

fama publica, 145–46

fame, 23, 24, 25, 26, 193

fatherhood: kingship as, 44, 46–48, 50, 71

Fathers of the Church, 114, 126, 128, 135, 198

fideism, 6n18, 119

fides, 81, 83

fides et ratio, 111

figures of speech: allusion, 25, 98, 109, 157; *aposiopesis*, 63; irony, 183, 188, 189; metaphor, 24, 25, 32, 52, 68, 86, 98, 115; *paradiastole*, 164; paradox, 8, 48, 64, 95, 114, 185; puns, 26, 32, 48, 54; stop, 63; understatement, 158

Fish, Simon, 171

flattery, 46, 65, 198

Florentine histories, 70

force: fraud vs., 81, 81n38

Forest, Miles, 68

fortune: history and, 71; human nature and, 70; justice and, 68, 71; poetry and, 67–68, 69; providence and, 68, 70; prudence and, 70

Fox, Alistair, 6, 9, 19, 21, 36, 41, 50, 68, 106, 107, 193

Francis, 40–41

fraud, 58, 81, 81n38, 100

freedom: of conscience, 174, 185; contemplation and, 33; intellectual, 27; tyranny and, 67; virtue and, 33. *See also* liberty

Frith, John, 180

Gabrieli, Vittorio, 38

Gamaliel, 21

Gargantua, 112

Gargantua and Pantagruel (Rabelais), 113

Gerson, Jean, 150, 153

Giles, Peter, 90

Gilmore, Myron, 28, 29–30

glory, 23, 24, 25, 83, 103

God, 6n18, 33, 68, 120, 162, 194; agency
in human affairs of, 68; charity and,
80; communion with, 7; the Father,
112; glory of, 24; governance of, 48, 52;
honor of, 121; immediacy of, 41; law
of, 190; love of, 16, 17, 26, 27, 39–40;
providence of, 63, 68; vocation and, 7,
16, 33; will of, 7
Gonell, William, 24, 26, 27, 30, 37, 39
governance, 12; divine, 50; of God, 48, 52;
good, 48; household, 35–36, 80; human,
50; kingship as fatherhood and, 71
Gower, John, 93
grace, 38; clergy and, 7; salvation and, 10;
sanctification and, 10, 85
grammar, 2
greed, 20
Greek, 1, 93, 128, 194
Greeks, 3, 11, 103, 108–11
Greenblatt, Stephen, 4, 192, 195, 196, 197,
200
Gregory of Nazianzus, St., 126, 199
Grey, Elizabeth, 50n24
Grocin, William, 30, 93
Gueguen, John, 102–3
Guildhall Report, 182
Guy, John, 1, 2, 4–5, 7–9, 36, 75, 99, 102–3,
106–7, 141, 142, 147–48, 149, 152, 153,
155, 158–59, 174, 175, 178, 193–94, 200

Haigh, Christopher, 166
Harpsfield, Nicholas, 9
Hastings, Margaret, 69–70, 100–101
Headley, John M., 133
Hebrews, 133
Henry Tudor, 62
Henry VIII, 133, 172; caesaropapism and,
180; divorce of, 152, 169–70, 195, 200;
liberal learning and, 110; marriage of,
199; More's service to, 4, 73–76, 105,
106; More's defiance of, 178; oath of
succession and, 181–85; reform and,
179; schism and, 141; supremacy and,
176, 191
Heptaplus (Pico), 29
heresy, heretics: authority and, 114; canon
law and, 13; Church and, 13, 171; De

Heretico Comburendo and, 106; Dialogue
Concerning Heresies and, 111–17; ex officio
proceedings and, 140–73; humanism
and, 13; ignorance and, 115; law and, 161,
163; Letter to Oxford and, 108–11; Luther,
6, 6n18, 28, 29n42, 107, 108, 110, 111,
122, 133, 136, 137; Lutheranism, 107,
109, 115; More's treatment of, 3, 105–39,
144; orthodoxy and, 13; Pico and, 28,
29–30, 117; politics and, 171–72; politics
of, 4; preaching, 113–14; pride and,
113–14, 115–17; punishment of, 165–66;
reformers and, 117; Scholasticism and,
117; Scripture and, 113–14; trials for, 117;
Trojans, Greeks, and, 108–11; Tyndale,
6n18, 28, 29n42, 105–6, 110, 111, 115,
121–22, 124–28, 133, 136, 173
heroism, 2, 7, 9
Hesketh, Thomas, 101
Hexter, J. H., 72, 73
Hilton, Walter, 34–35, 39, 80
history, 2, 42, 43, 71, 83, 96, 130, 131, 137,
193
The History of Richard III (More), 75;
consent of the governed and, 44; conspiracy and, 63; Edward IV and, 46–54;
expediency and, 64, 65; honesty in, 187;
law as sanctuary and, 54–62; letters
of More and, 185; More's intellectual
development and, 46; Morton and,
62–70, 187; motive of conception, 42,
71; paternal models of kingship, 44,
46–48; poetry and, 71; political limitations of, 72; political philosophy and, 12;
political reform and, 12–13; politics and
utility and, 187; tone of, 188–89; Utopia
and, 13, 46
Hitton, Thomas, 169
holiness, 28, 29n42, 54, 115
Holy Spirit, 127, 133, 176, 178
honesty (honestas), 77; decency and, 64;
decorum and, 64, 97; definition of, 187;
expediency and, 46, 84; importance of,
187; lying and, 198; moderation and, 64;
neutrality and, 189; prudence and, 65;
rhetoric and, 66; service and, 80; tone
and, 183–92; utility and, 43, 81–82

honor: of God, 121; profit and, 22–27; virtue and, 22–23, 24, 25–26, 28
household governance, 35–36
humanae gloriae, 23, 24
human fulfillment, 10
humanism: Christianity and, 11; civic, 80; common sense and, 132, 139; community and, 13, 129–36; definition of, 10, 11, 103, 107; equity and, 89–98; heresy, heretics and, 13; *humanitas* and, 10, 95, 131–32, 135; *humaniter* and, 7; human nature and, 137; humanocentric, 123; *imago Dei* and, 10; immediacy of God and, 41; Italian, 11, 23, 24, 30, 43; justice and, 100; law and, 88, 89–90; learning and, 30; legal reform and, 92; letters of More and, 108; of More, 2, 4, 5–6, 10–13, 17, 30, 41, 43, 76, 77, 80, 103, 105, 108, 132, 136, 165, 175; Northern, 11, 43; orthodoxy and, 110; philosophy and, 36; piety and, 16, 109; polemical theology and, 17; public life and, 11; religion and, 107; Renaissance, 3; rhetoric and, 2; Scholasticism and, 27, 112, 113; secular, 84; social justice and, 92; *studia humanitatis*, 2, 90, 132; theology and, 109; vocation and, 10; writings of More and, 107
humanitas, 10, 95, 131–32, 135, 136
human law, 155, 156, 157, 159, 166
human nature, 6–7; Christian understanding of, 112; humanism and, 137; knowledge of, 132; liberal arts and, 112, 130; Lucian and, 18; reason and, 130; teleology of, 10; universal laws of, 131
Hume, Richard, 136
humility, 23, 25, 26, 194
humor, 2, 114
hypocrisy, 66
Hythloday, Raphael, 33, 61, 72–74, 78, 79, 84–88, 91, 98

ignorance, 21, 108, 115
I Libri Della Famiglia (Alberti), 24
images, religious, 117, 121
imago Dei, 10, 37–41, 136
impiety, 28, 33

incontinence, 20
Inghirami, Thomas, 44–45
inheritance, 91
Innocent VIII, 56
Inns of Court, 93
inquisitorial courts. *See ex officio* proceedings
integrity, 8, 10, 12, 14, 65, 192, 194, 196, 198
intolerance, 4, 5, 136, 180
irony, 183, 188, 189

Jerome, St., 126, 197, 199
John, Gospel of, 126
John Chrysostom, St., 19
John Paul II, 5, 7, 175
Joye, Gregory, 181
judgment: common sense and, 156; conscience and, 156; *humanitas* and, 135; law and, 60, 95, 96, 99; learning and, 109, 200; prudential, 63, 96, 95, 97, 98; reason and, 156; ripe, 95
Julius exclusus, 44
Julius II, 44–45, 54, 59
jurisdiction: equity and, 75, 148, 160–61; papacy and, 184; positive human law and, 150
jurisprudence. *See* law
justice, 24, 34, 45, 165; clergy and, 162; equity and, 150; ethics and, 81; expediency and, 67; force and, 81; fortune and, 68, 71; fraud and, 81; humanism and, 100; law and, 61, 154; learning and, 26; love and, 39; miscarriage of, 165; social, 91, 92; strict, 91
Justinian, 90

Kaufman, Peter Iver, 55–56
Kelly, Henry Ansgar, 142, 143, 144, 146, 147–51, 166, 167, 173
King James Bible, 124
kingship, 44, 46–48, 53–54, 71, 72, 87
Kinney, Daniel, 113, 129–30
Kisch, Guido, 91–92
knowledge: common sense and, 121; of human nature, 132; liberal, 132; science and, 156; self-fashioning, 131
Kristeller, Paul, 2–3, 11

Labeo, Quintus Fabius, 100
Laelius, Gaius, 130–31
laity, 37; Church and, 140; clergy and, 140; 168; mission of, 7; sanctuary and, 55; silencing of, 162; unity of life of, 7; vocation and, 7, 35
Lambeth Palace, 183
Latimer, Hugh, 184–85, 186, 187
Latin, 1, 11, 15, 20, 49, 111, 128
Latinity, 3
law: canon, 13, 141, 142, 143, 144, 146, 148, 169; civil, 90; common, 56, 57, 58, 59, 75, 88, 91, 98, 102, 149, 156–57; conscience and, 159; divine, 158; enforcement of, 148; equity and, 13, 99, 103, 152–59; eternal, 155, 159; feudal, 90; of God, 190; of guardianship, 58–59; heresy, 161, 163; hierarchy of, 155, 158; The History of Richard III and, 54–62; human, 155, 156, 157, 159, 166; humanism and, 3, 88, 89–90; justice and, 61, 154; kingship and, 48; knowledge of, 88; legal reform, 88, 92, 101–4; liberal arts and, 104; More as judge, 98–101; natural, 56, 59, 131, 155, 158, 159; natural law, 57; philosophy and, 76; positive, 91, 148–49, 157–58; property, 157; Protestant Reformation and, 137; reason and, 155, 157, 158; rhetoric and, 94–96, 103–4; right of wreck and, 158, 166; Roman, 89–90; as sanctuary, 54–62; tyranny and, 48, 56; universal, 98
Laws (Plato), 93
lawyers: common, 94, 148, 149; humanist, 93, 96, 103; judges, 149; More as, 75, 103
laziness, 108
Lear, King, 52
learning, 16; abuse of, 25; action and, 31; Church and, 26, 110; contemplation and, 31, 34; faith and, 108, 175; fame and, 26; Greek, 108–11; humanism and, 30; justice and, 26; liberal arts and, 108; mixed life and, 109; modesty and, 21; moral nature of, 16; new, 30; paganism and, 17–18, 21, 109; philosophy and, 28; piety and, 17, 20–21, 26, 33, 107, 108,

109–11; praise and, 30; preaching and, 33; pride and, 20–21, 30; profit and, 16, 31, 33; Protestant Reformation and, 137; reason and, 136; rhetoric and, 93; salvation and, 111; secular, 111; soul and, 111; theology and, 111; virtue and, 17, 20, 24, 27, 30, 41, 109, 111. See also liberal arts
Lee, Joyce, 16, 38
legal positivism, 91
Lehmberg, Stanley, 27, 29, 38
leisure, 34
letters of Thomas More: to Alice Alington, 176, 193; Dialogue of Conscience and, 176; The History of Richard III and, 185; to Margaret Roper, 1–2, 182, 184, 199, 200; Margaret Roper and, 176; More's humanism and, 108; politics and utility and, 187; real Thomas More and, 176; to Thomas Cromwell, 179, 181, 187–89; to Thomas Ruthall, 16, 17, 20, 21; to Thomas Wilson, 198–99, 200; to William Gonel, 24, 26, 27, 30, 37, 39. See also writings of Thomas More; and individual titles
Letter to a Monk (More), 108, 115, 126, 127
Letter to Dorp (More), 108, 120, 129, 130, 132, 133, 134–35, 136, 138
Letter to Oxford (More), 107, 108–11, 112, 113, 123, 131, 136, 200
Lewis, C. S., 2
liberal arts, 16, 96; authority and, 117; contemplation and, 136; Dialogue Concerning Heresies and, 111–13, 117–19, 130; equity and, 104; faith and, 107, 112, 117, 118, 136, 138; history and, 130; human nature and, 112, 130; judgment and, 109; law and, 104; learning and, 108; Letter to Oxford and, 108–11; mixed life and, 109; moral development and, 18; oratory and, 130; orthodoxy and, 28–30, 111; philosophy and, 109; piety and, 17, 108, 109–11, 136; poetry and, 130; prudence and, 104, 109; reason and, 112, 136; faith and, 136; Scholasticism and, 117; Scripture and, 125n47; soul and, 136; study of, 10; theology and, 109; virtue and, 136. See also learning

liberality, 36
liberty: importance of, 26; individual, 176, 192; intellectual freedom and, 27. *See also* freedom
Life of Pico (More), 11, 75, 139; action and contemplation and, 11–12, 15, 21–27, 79–80; Aquinas and, 28–29; faith and learning and, 107; honor and profit in, 22–27; *imago Dei* and piety, 37–41; learning and piety, 110; mixed life and, 16, 32, 34, 79–80; More's humanism and, 12, 108; orthodoxy and the liberal arts and, 28–30; paternal models of kingship, 48; philosophy and, 12; piety and, 16; polemical theology in, 13; Scholasticism and, 111; spiritual idealism in, 12; *Utopia* and, 13; virtue and, 12; vocation and, 33. *See also* Pico della Mirandola, Giovanni
Life of Sir Thomas More (Roper), 8n29, 178–79
Linacre, Thomas, 30, 93
Lincoln's Inn, 93
literature: Greek, 11, 22; history and, 109; Latin, 11; pagan, 18, 109; secular and, 109
Logan, George, 3, 43–44, 74, 75, 77–79, 84–85, 91
logic, 112, 120, 132, 138
Louvain, University of, 90
love, 124; action and, 39–40; communal, 46–47; community and, 49, 50, 86; contemplation and, 39; of fame, 193; of God, 16, 17, 26, 27, 39–40; justice and, 39; of neighbor, 158; piety and, 39; of truth, 34; virtue and, 46; wisdom and, 39
Lucian, 16, 41, 107, 186; cynicism and, 18–19; heresy and, 115, 117; human nature and, 18; morality and, 114; moral philosophy and, 18; More's translation of, 17–22; polytheism of, 21; theology and, 22; value of, 18
Luther, Martin, 6, 6n18, 7, 28, 107, 108, 110, 111, 133, 136, 137
Lutheranism, Lutherans, 107, 109, 114
luxury (*luxuria*), 19, 20, 87
Lycinus, 20

lying, 114, 115, 198
Lynch, Charles A., 47

Machiavelli, Niccolo, 45, 56, 59, 65, 81, 83, 141, 159, 182
Macnair, Mike, 89, 98, 99, 100, 101, 151
magister, 26
Maitland, F. W., 89
Majeske, Andrew J., 93, 97
malice, 58, 129, 172, 173, 187
A Man for All Seasons (Bolt), 8, 14, 174, 176, 192
Mantel, Hilary, 8, 14, 175, 180, 194
Marc'hadour, Germain, 96, 120, 191
Marius, Richard, 4, 6, 9, 106, 116, 141–42, 184
Marotti, Arthur F., 52
marriage, 15–16, 40, 50–51, 199
Marsh, David, 18
Martha, 35, 80
martyrdom, martyrs, 2, 106
Mary, Blessed Virgin, 35, 80, 115, 190
Mary, Queen, 186
McCutcheon, Elizabeth, 185, 188–89
Melanchthon, Philip, 96
memorial building, 194
mendacity, 194, 195
Menippus (Lucian), 19, 186
mercenary philosophy, 31, 32
messenger, 111–13, 117–18, 119–20, 136
metaphors, 24, 25, 32, 52, 68, 86, 98, 115
miracles, 114, 119
mixed life, 16, 32, 34, 37, 79–80, 109
moderation, 19, 36, 64
modesty, 20, 21, 25
monarchy, 45
morality: Lucian and, 114; necessity and, 82; reason and, 39; religion and, 85
morality plays, 42
moral philosophy, 2, 11, 18, 22
moral wisdom, 18, 41
More, Thomas: authority and tradition and, 108, 117–20, 125, 127; as chancellor, 98, 100, 165, 170; conscience, 3, 10, 148, 174, 175, 176, 179; consensus and, 177–78; contemplation and action, 7; controversies and, 2, 3, 5–6, 105, 107, 114;

More, Thomas: *(cont.)*
  correspondence of, 1–2, 14, 16, 17–18,
  19, 20, 21, 24, 26, 27, 30, 37, 39; as
  councilor and chancellor, 3, 4–5, 77, 96;
  Cromwell and, 176, 177–83; defense of
  Church, 10, 14, 106, 140; devotion of, 2,
  11; as diplomat, 4–5; dissimulation and,
  5, 8; divorce of Henry VIII and, 170;
  educational ideas of, 16, 18; entry into
  king's service, 4–5, 73–76, 195; equity
  and, 147–51, 159; execution of, 1, 4, 5, 7,
  176, 186, 188, 189, 192, 193; Henry VIII
  and, 4, 195; heresy and, 3, 6, 13, 105–39,
  144; heroism of, 2, 7; historical accounts
  of, 1, 10; humanism of, 2–3, 4, 5–6, 7,
  10–13, 17, 30, 41, 42, 43, 76, 77, 80, 103,
  105, 108, 132, 136, 165, 175; humor of, 2,
  114; iconic, 175; imprisonment of, 1–2, 5,
  14, 174, 176, 178, 181, 183, 197; integrity
  of, 2, 106; intellectual biography of,
  2, 106; interrogations of, 176, 183, 186,
  194; as judge, 98–101; last days of, 192;
  as lawyer, 75, 103; Lucian translations
  by, 16, 17–22; marriage and, 15; as martyr, 2; multiple Mores, 2, 76–88; neutrality and, 189, 192; oath of succession
  and, 2, 179, 181–85, 187–89, 191–92,
  196–200; oath of supremacy and, 176;
  obstinacy of, 180; one Thomas More, 14,
  73, 138–39; orthodoxy and, 13, 28–30; as
  persecutor of Protestants, 1; polemical
  theology of, 12, 13, 28–29, 106–8, 123,
  141; political philosophy and, 3, 4, 46,
  72–73, 75, 83; politics and, 8, 11; real
  Thomas More, 5, 6, 123, 144, 175, 176;
  religion and, 4, 5, 6, 12, 96, 136, 194;
  as saint, 2, 7, 175, 179; St. German and,
  1, 14, 140–73; as scholar, 2, 6, 6n19,
  12; self-fashioning, 5; silence of, 176,
  191–92; as statesman, 2, 10, 103; tone
  of, 14, 39, 183–92; traditional portrait of,
  4, 9, 14; trial of, 5, 8–9, 175, 177–83, 189;
  truth and, 4, 9; two Mores theory, 3,
  5–6, 103, 106, 107, 123, 127, 175, 192–93;
  vocation and, 1, 15–16, 36, 85; wit of, 130
mortal sin, 196, 197
Morton, Cardinal, 82, 83, 87–88; Buckingham's manipulation by, 62–65, 195–96,
  198; Cicero and, 195; decorum and honesty and, 97; eulogy of, 88; expediency
  and, 46, 62; fortune and, 62–70; Henry
  Tudor and, 62; honesty and, 187, 189; as
  manipulator, 62–63; More's refusal of
  oath and, 191; prudence and, 88; sanctuary and, 56; utility and, 45
Morus, 12, 73, 74, 103, 186, 195, 197–98
Moynahan, Brian, 105, 123, 127
Murphy, Clare, 26

natural law, 56, 57, 59, 131, 155, 156, 158, 159
natural philosophy, 22
nature. *See* human nature
necessity *(necessitas),* 12, 45, 46, 81, 82
negotium, 75, 76, 77, 80–81
Neoplatonism, 29
Netherlands, 73
neutrality, 189–90
New Learning, 30
New Testament, 124–28
Ní Chuilleanáin, Eiléan, 26
Nicomachean Ethics (Aristotle), 98
Norfolk, Duke of, 176, 186
Nun of Kent, 180–83

Oath of Succession, 2, 179, 181–85, 187–89,
  191–92, 196–200
Oath of Supremacy, 106, 141, 152, 176
obedience, 163, 179
oligarchy, 78
On Christian Doctrine (Augustine), 22
one Thomas More, 138–39
On Reading Pagan Literature (Basil), 18
"On the Good King and His People"
  (More), 49
"On the Lust for Power" (More), 54
Oration on the Dignity of Man (Pico), 38
oratory, 130
orthodoxy, 13, 41, 89; doctrine and, 172;
  heresy, heretics and, 13; humanism and,
  110; liberal arts and, 28–30, 111; St. German and, 170
otium, 75, 76, 77, 80–81
Oxford University, 107, 108–11, 112, 113, 123

Pace, Richard, 18, 110
Pacifier, 163, 166, 167, 168, 170–71, 172, 173. *See also* St. German
Padua, 18
paganism, pagans: asceticism of, 19; Christian revelation and, 16; Christian teaching and, 17–18, 21–22; learning and, 109; theology and, 109
Palmer, Sir Thomas, 9
papacy, 54, 177; authority of, 184; hegemony of, 178; jurisdiction and, 184; More's sainthood and, 179. *See also individual popes by name*
paradiastole, 164
paradox, 8, 48, 64, 95, 114, 185
Pardon of the Clergy (*1531*), 191
Paris, University of, 113
Parliament, 55, 106, 107, 152, 169, 170, 179, 195, 196, 200
Parnell, John, 9
Paul, St., 20, 21, 23, 24, 39, 49–50, 64
perjury, 8, 8n29, 196–97
persona pietatis, 115
persuasion, 61, 96
pessimism, 6
Peter, St., 112, 134, 178–79
Peters, John G., 55
Petrarch, 11, 40, 41
philosophy, 25; action and contemplation and, 31–32; Enlightenment and, 103; expediency and, 85; humanism and, 36; *imago Dei* and, 41; isolation and, 12; Italian, 11; law and, 76; liberal arts and, 109; mercenary, 31, 32; moral, 2, 11, 18, 22; natural, 22; piety and, 33; political, 3, 12, 46, 72–73, 75, 78, 103; politics and, 79; pride and, 32; profitable learning and, 28; profit and, 31–32; public life and, 36; reason and faith and, 136; religion and, 27; theology and, 109, 112; wisdom and, 39
Pico della Mirandola, Gianfrancesco, 16, 25, 28, 30, 31, 33, 36, 38, 41
Pico della Mirandola, Giovanni: abuse of learning and, 25; action and contemplation and, 33, 79–80; Augustine and, 30; as Christian paradigm, 15; fame of, 24,

25; heresy and, 28, 29–30, 117; household governance and, 35–36, 80; humanism and, 12; impiety of, 33; learning of, 24, 26, 30; letter to Corneus, 31–34, 36, 79, 109; letter to Francis, 40–41; mixed life and, 32, 34, 37; philosophy and, 31, 33; Scripture and, 28; syncretism of, 29; twelve rules of, 23; vocation and, 16, 33, 41, 80. *See also Life of Pico*
piety (*pietas*), 25, 71, 123; charity and, 21; Church and, 110; faith and, 107; humanism and, 16, 109; *imago Dei* and, 37–41; intelligence and, 23; learning and, 17, 20–21, 26, 33, 107, 108, 109–11; liberal arts and, 17, 28–30, 108, 109–11, 136; love and, 39; mixed life and, 109; orthodoxy and, 28–30; paganism and, 17; *persona*, 115; philosophy and, 33; virtue and, 54
pilgrimages, 113, 117, 121
Plato, 3, 29, 51, 76, 77, 79, 86, 93
poetry, poets, 2, 17, 20, 44, 67; common sense and, 132; *The History of Richard III* and, 71; humanism and, 2; liberal arts and, 130; *Life of Pico* and, 16–17; piety and, 37–39; politics and, 47, 52, 53, 56, 60–61, 67, 71, 94; rhetoric and, 94; tyranny and, 69
polemical theology, 12, 17, 29, 106, 107, 123, 141
policy. *See* public policy
Policy and Police (Elton), 174
political philosophy, 3, 46, 75; Greek, 78, 103; *The History of Richard III* and, 12, 72–73
politics: accommodating approach to, 12, 13, 88; action and, 33; classical-Christian approach to, 12; expediency and, 86; of heresy, 4; heresy and, 171–72; *The History of Richard III* and, 12, 44; More and, 8, 11; More's poetry and, 44n7; philosophy and, 79; power and, 45; prudence and, 84; tyranny and Church, 45; utility and, 44–45; vice and, 33; virtue and, 12
Politics (Aristotle), 78, 93
Poliziano, Angelo, 38
Pollard, A. F., 42, 71

polytheism, 21
Poor Clare Convent, 16
positive law, 91, 148–49, 150, 157–58
positivism, 91
power, 71; absolute, 82; desire for, 54; king-
    ship and, 72, 87; politics and, 45
prayer, 40–41, 48, 175
preaching, 33; heretical, 113–14; learning
    and, 33; people and, 114, 115
prebuteros: in Tyndale's translation, 124
prejudice, 128
Prévost, André, 192, 200
pride, 23, 24, 108; faction in the Church,
    115; heresy and, 113–14, 115–17; intel-
    lectual, 180; learning and, 20–21, 30;
    philosophy and, 32; singularity and, 136;
    sin of, 36, 37
priest: in Tyndale's translation, 124
priesthood. See clergy
primitivism, 137
The Prince (Machiavelli), 69, 81, 159
privacy, 11
profit: action and contemplation and, 31;
    charity and, 35; honor and, 22–27; learn-
    ing and, 16, 31, 33; philosophy and, 31–32
progressivism, 103
property law, 157
property rights, 91, 150, 158
Protestantism, Protestants, 137; communi-
    tas and, 139; More as persecutor of, 1, 3,
    17. See also heresy, heretics
Protestant Reformation, 6, 6n18, 13, 17,
    107, 115
providence, 63, 68, 70
prudence, 61, 65, 88, 98; equity and, 75;
    expediency and, 85; liberal arts and,
    104, 109; political, 200; politics and, 84;
    rhetoric and, 96
prudential calculation, 13
The Public Career of Thomas More (Gueg-
    uen), 102
public policy, 4, 81
puns, 26, 32, 48, 54
purgatory, 33, 36, 80, 171
purging, 122
Puttenham, George, 63
Pythagoreanism, 29

Questions (Aquinas), 29
Quintillian, 21, 130

Rabelais, François, 112–13
realism, 59
real Thomas More, 5–6, 144, 175, 176
reason, 38; authority and, 117–20, 123;
    conscience and, 157; cultivating life of,
    85; faith and, 6n18, 112, 118–20, 123,
    136–37; human development and, 10;
    human nature and, 130; judgment and,
    156; law and, 155, 157, 158; learning and,
    136; liberal arts and, 112; morality and,
    39; role of, 10; theology and, 137
reform, reformers, 30, 86, 129; authority
    and reason and, 123; community and,
    136; Elton, 165; faith and reason and,
    123; heresy and, 117; The History of
    Richard III and, 12–13; ideology of, 103;
    legal, 88, 92, 101–4, 160; Marius, 106;
    moral imperative of, 13; More's entry
    into king's service and, 105; political,
    12–13; Scripture and, 135; social, 72;
    utopian, 12–13, 101–4
Reformation. See Protestant Reformation
religion, 96, 194; humanism and, 107;
    morality and, 85; More and, 12, 136;
    old, 6; philosophy and, 27; scholarship
    and, 11; writings of More and, 107
religious images, 117, 121
religious intolerance, 4, 5, 136, 180
religious signs, 108, 123
Renaissance, 3, 6, 42, 57
Replication (St. German), 148
Republic (Plato), 78, 93
Responsio ad Lutherum (More), 106
revelation, 16, 33, 119, 123
revisionists, 144, 192; Barton and More
    and, 182–83; Elton, 3–8, 9, 14, 74, 77,
    138, 141, 142, 166, 183–84, 196; faith
    and reason and, 123; Fox, 6, 9, 19, 36,
    41, 50, 68; Greenblatt, 4, 5, 192; Guy,
    1, 2, 4, 7–9, 36, 99, 102–3, 106, 141,
    142, 147, 149, 158; Marius, 5, 9, 106,
    116, 141–42, 184; More and, 3, 5–6, 7, 8,
    9; paganism and, 16; St. German and,
    14, 147

Rex, Richard, 10, 137, 144
rhetoric: common sense and, 132; deception and, 66; "dialogue of counsel" and, 78; English Renaissance and, 42; equity and, 75, 92–93, 93–94, 97; honesty and, 66; humanism and, 2, 3; law and, 94–96, 103–4; learning and, 93; personal reputation and, 194; poetry and, 94; prudence and, 96; self-fashioning, 5, 164, 194
Rhetoric (Aristotle), 93, 100
Rich, Richard, 8–9, 8n29, 183
Richard III: leadership and, 62; model for, 43–44; monarchy of, 45; Morton and fortune, 62; rise to power, 42, 185; tyranny of, 46
Richards, Jennifer, 64
Ridley, Jasper, 105
Rigg, J. M., 29
right of wreck, 158, 166
robbery, 35, 36
Rockett, William, 152, 169, 170
Romans, 3, 66, 83, 89–90
Roper, Margaret, 1–2, 176, 180–82, 184, 190, 191, 199, 200
Roper, William, 8, 8n29, 9, 98, 175, 178–79
Ruthall, Thomas, 16, 17, 19, 20, 21

sacraments, 121–22, 125, 151, 171
St. German, Christopher, 1, 14, 191; anticlericalism and, 142, 150, 160, 163, 170–72; Aquinas and, 152–53, 159; battle of the books and, 140–73; canon law and, 141, 142, 143, 144, 146, 148, 169; clergy and, 159–66, 170–71; conscience and, 143, 154–59; divorce of Henry VIII and, 152; equity and, 142, 143, 147–51, 152–59, 170–72; law and, 152–59; orthodoxy and, 170; Parliament's authority and, 152
sainthood, saints, 28, 121, 175; More and, 2, 7, 179
Salem and Bizance (St. German), 140, 143, 144
salvation, 10, 111
sanctification: action and, 39; baptism and, 122; in everyday life, 7; grace and, 10, 85

sanctity, 109
sanctuary, 54–62
Savonarola, 33
scaffolds, 1, 189, 193
Scala perfectionis (Hilton), 34
schism, 141, 191
Schoeck, R. J., 30, 92
Scholasticism, 10, 27, 28, 93, 111, 123, 129, 135; common sense and, 120; *Dialogue Concerning Heresies* and, 113; heresy and, 117; humanism and, 112, 113; liberal arts and, 117; logic and, 132; *persona* piety and, 115; reason and faith and, 118
science, 156
scientia, 20, 21, 71
Scipio, 130–31
Scripture, 28, 108; Christ and, 133; Church and, 13, 125, 133; faith and, 132; heresy and, 113–14; interpretation of, 117; liberal arts and, 125n47; meaning of, 132; reformers and, 135; study of, 111; translating, 52, 117, 123–26, 128–29; trust and, 123
sedition, 114
self-fashioning, 194, 197
selfhood, 175–76, 192–93, 200
Seneca, 29, 79
senior: in Tyndale's translation, 124, 125
separation, principle of, 150
Shakespeare, William, 52, 94
ship of state metaphor, 86
signs, 108, 120–23, 124, 134
Simpson, James, 117, 129
sin: mortal, 196, 197; occasions of, 35–36; perjury and, 196–97; of pride, 36, 37
skepticism, 2, 3, 6n18, 8
Skinner, Quentin, 3, 22–23, 46, 70, 74, 75, 77, 78, 79, 81, 83, 89–90
Smith, Thomas, 90, 94
social justice, 3, 91, 92
social reform, 72, 73
Socrates, 1, 2, 36, 131
solidarity, 192, 193
solifideism, 7
Solon, 131
sophistry, sophists, 61, 86, 112
Sorbonne, 112

soul, 122; learning and, 111; liberal arts and, 136
Stapleton, Thomas, 9
state: Church and, 162; counsel and, 88
studia humanitatis, 2, 90, 132
Suetonius, 43
Summa Rosella (Trovomara), 163, 168
"Supplication for the Beggars" (Fish), 171
The Supplication of Souls (More), 172
Sylvester, Richard, 57, 59, 130, 131, 132, 134, 197
syncretism, 29

Tacitus, 43, 57, 189
Talmud, 29n42
Tartaretus, Peter, 112
temptation, 137, 193
Terrence, 1
Tewkesbury, John, 169
theft, 35, 36, 91, 92
Themistocles, 131
theology, 3; common sense and, 132; faith and reason and, 137; humanism and, 109; learning and, 111; liberal arts and, 107–8, 109; logic and, 112; Lucian and, 22; More's focus on, 106; paganism and, 109; philosophy and, 109, 112; polemical, 12, 13, 17, 29, 106, 107, 123; Reformation, 13
Theophrastus, 115
Thersites, 186
Thomas More (Chambers), 174
"Thomas More" (Elton), 1, 4
Thomas More (Guy), 1, 102, 174
Thomas More and Providence (Fox), 6
Thomas More's Public Career (Guy), 148, 149
Thompson, Craig R., 3, 11
Thornley, Isobel, 55–56
Tiberius, 43
tolerance, 174
toleration, 165, 182
tone, 14, 183–92
Tower of London, 1, 178, 185, 198
tradition: authority and, 125, 127; Church and, 122, 123, 127–28; consensus of, 30,

125, 135, 139; intellectual, 46; rhetoric and, 93; Scripture and, 124–25
treason, 69, 183
A Treatise Concernynge . . . Spirytualitie and Temporaltie (St. German), 140, 144, 145, 151, 160, 161, 162, 168, 172
Trinity, 29
Trojans, 108–11, 114, 117
Trovomara, Baptista, 163
trust: in Church, 122–23, 139; epistemological, 123, 139; Scripture and, 123
truth, 4, 9, 19, 22, 77; charity and, 161; Church and, 176–77; doctrine and, 114, 123; leisure and, 34; love of, 27, 34
The Tudors (TV show), 106
"The Twelve Weapons of Spiritual Battle" (More), 37–38
two Mores theory, 3, 5–6, 103, 107, 123, 127, 138, 175, 192–93
Tyndale, William, 6n18, 28, 29n42, 105–6, 110, 111, 115, 121–22, 124–28, 133, 136, 173, 175
Tyrannicida (More), 69
tyranny, tyrants, 50n24, 64; Aristotle and, 78; character of, 43; Church politics and, 45; death and, 67; deception and, 44; freedom from, 67; kingship and, 48; law and, 56; removal of, 46, 65–66; tyrannicide and, 46, 65–66, 82, 83

Ulysses, 131
unity of life, 7
utilitas publica, 45
utility (utilitas), 45, 71; honesty and, 43, 81–82; politics and, 44–45; prudence and, 65; tyrannicide and, 46
Utopia (More), 1, 6, 33, 159, 186, 197; counsel, problem of and, 61; dialogue of counsel in, 12–13, 72–104; equity and, 76; equity and humanism and, 89–98; The History of Richard III and, 13, 46; Life of Pico and, 13; More's humanism and, 3, 12, 105; More's political philosophy and, 83; political reform and, 12–13; prejudice and, 128; publication of, 90, 107
Utopians, 73

vainglory, 23, 51, 114, 162
vice, 21, 24, 26, 33, 115, 153
virtue, 76, 88; action and contemplation and, 36–37; *amor Dei in nobis* and, 17; appetite for, 20; aspirations for, 12; equity and, 153; false, 36; fame and, 25; freedom and, 33; glory and, 24; honor and, 22–23, 24, 25–26, 28; ideals of, 12; *imago Dei* and, 37; learning and, 17, 20, 24, 27, 30, 41, 109, 111; liberal arts and, 136; love and, 46; mixed life and, 109; piety and, 17, 54; politics and, 12; reason and faith and, 118; universal, 36; utility and, 25
virtus, 17
vita activa, 11
vita contemplativa, 11
Vita Pici. See Life of Pico
viva sapientia, 39, 86
vocation, 1, 93; as call to perfection, 10, 85; crisis of, 15–16; God and, 16, 33; *humanitas* and, 10; *imago Dei* and, 10; laity and, 7, 35; More and, 36, 85; Pico and, 15–16, 80; refusal of, 36–37, 41, 80

way of life, 34, 38, 134, 138
Wegemer, Gerard, 130, 137
Wells, Robin Headlam, 137
Westminster Abbey, 55
White, R. S., 93, 156

Willow, Mary Edith, 16
Wilson, Thomas, 63, 94, 188, 198–99, 200
wisdom, 11; abusive, 64, 66; Christian rewards of, 25; love and, 39; moral, 18, 41; philosophy and, 39; revelation and, 119
wit, 18, 26, 130, 131
witnesses, 144–47
Wolf Hall (Mantel), 8, 9, 10, 14, 175, 176, 180, 182
Wolsey, Cardinal, 90, 102–3, 104, 110, 147–48
Woodville, Elizabeth, 54, 58–60
writings of Thomas More: analysis of, 10; correspondence, 1–2, 14, 16, 17–18, 19; devotional, 2; division of, 2, 106, 107, 138; epigrams, 20, 47, 59–60, 87; heresy and, 6; humanism and, 107; organization of, 2; personality of More and, 6; poetry, 17, 20, 37, 44, 47, 49, 50, 54, 59–60, 67, 69, 71; psychological reading of, 9; religion and, 107; two Mores theory, 138. *See also* letters of Thomas More; *and individual titles*

Year Book Reports, 151
young people: honor and, 24; virtue and, 24

Zasius, Ulrich, 90

The One Thomas More was designed and typeset in Scala by Kachergis Book Design of Pittsboro, North Carolina. It was printed on 55-pound Natures B19 Cream, and bound by Maple Press of York, Pennsylvania.